READING THE PLAYS OF

Wendy Wasserstein

READING THE PLAYS OF
Wendy Wasserstein

Jan Balakian

APPLAUSE
THEATRE & CINEMA BOOKS
AN IMPRINT OF
HAL•LEONARD®
New York

Published in 2010 by Applause Theatre & Cinema Books
An Imprint of Hal Leonard Corporation
7777 West Bluemound Road
Milwaukee, WI 53213

Trade Book Division Editorial Offices
19 West 21st Street, New York, NY 10010

Printed in the United States of America

Book design by Bob Antler, Antler Designworks

Library of Congress Cataloging-in-Publication Data

Balakian, Jan.
  Reading the plays of Wendy Wasserstein / Jan Balakian.
    p. cm.
  Includes bibliographical references and index.
  ISBN 978-1-55783-725-7
  1. Wasserstein, Wendy--Criticism and interpretation. I. Title.
  PS3573.A798Z35 2010
  812'.54--dc22

                              2009048311

www.applausepub.com

For my parents

Contents

Acknowledgments

I would like to thank the following people: Wendy Wasserstein for giving me so much time when she was so busy. As I look back at the interviews, I appreciate how candid she was. Gary Bonasorte and Terrence McNally, who enabled my meeting with Wendy. Christopher Durang for his thoughtful and generous conversations and e-mails about American culture and Wendy's work; Jeffery Eric Jenkins, who connected me with Dan Sullivan, who led me to insights about the plays that he directed and was so generous with his time; Mary Jane Patrone for providing me with the Mount Holyoke details; Alma Cuervo for providing essential information about *Uncommon Women and Others*; the people at the Mount Holyoke archives—including Jennifer Gunter King, Patricia Albright, Nora Mariano—for their assistance with their extensive collection of Wasserstein manuscripts; Emily Mann, who enlightened me about the women's movement and the arts in the seventies and eighties; Brenda Murphy for inviting me to write the Wasserstein chapter for the *Cambridge Companion to American Women Playwrights*; Steve Centola for long ago prompting me to start the book; Judith Barlow for editing *Plays by American Women*, published by Applause, which gave me the idea to contact them. Michael Messina for enthusiastically signing me on to Applause, and the team at Applause—John Cerullo, Carol Flannery, Clare Cerullo, Marybeth Keating, Jessica Burr, and Sarah Gallogly; Jackson R. Bryer for his fastidious eye, guidance, and passion for American drama; and Pam Wasserstein for her support and graciousness.

Without a sabbatical from Kean University, I could not have possibly completed this book. I also want to thank the talented faculty at Kean

University and my students, who inspire and teach me; my capable student Leonard Lopez for his assistance; star student Erica Holan for typing the index; Ed Weil for his flow of clippings that he sent to me on campus when he was dean; and the nameless library workers at Kean University who bound all of those back issues of magazines and journals so that I could pore over real pages late into the night.

Many thanks to my long line of outstanding teachers, from Joel Flegler at Stillman to Jack Wheatcroft at Bucknell. At Cornell: Ellen Gainor, who exposed me to American women playwrights, Anthony Caputi for steeping me in the male dramatic tradition, Bruce Levitt for the independent study in American drama, and Joel Porte for teaching me about the American literary tradition.

Jonathan Schwartz's American Oldies became my soundtrack as I wrote, and Joe's Grill fueled me as I worked. Thanks to Bob Gruen for his generous photo of John Lennon; Bob McNeely for his generous photo of Wendy with the Clintons at the White House; Thomas Giroux for the Air-Port and iTunes; Michael Petronko for wise counsel; and Phil Birsh for the generous Playbills.

Thanks to my family for their encouragement, above all, the matriarch; Lu, who clipped everything related to women; and the grandmothers and aunts on both the Balakian and Aroosian sides. To my most loyal friend, Renaissance Woman, Debby Harwick, for her steadfast encouragement, and to my other Superwomen friends, Christine Enger and Jeanne Athos, for inspiring me always. To Sophia—future anthropologist—who encouraged me at critical moments, and to the future generation, Ally, Katherine, Nicky, and Jamie—yes, you can!

The 2008 election, the Olympics, and the U.S. Open provided me with special inspiration—possibilities come from perseverance.

READING THE PLAYS OF

Wendy Wasserstein

Science Fairs
Who? Cathy
                Johnathen
Jews. Who gets the Highest College
Boards.
            Cathy
who
Cathy Jews, Who are the richest bankers
I don't   in the world? The Rothchilds.
know   Cathy
         Well, maybe I'm not smart enough
to be a Jew.
           Johnathen
Patience, my friend, patience
Should I take my pipe or my cigarettes
        Cathy
Cigarettes
           Johnathen
You sure? The pipe is a Dunhill
          Cathy
I'm sure. the pipe makes you look like
Dr. Shaman in pictured fairy tales.
           Johnathen
O.K. Marlboros, wallet, matches,
key to the room. You'll watch Mitch
Miller with mother
          Cathy
I'll watch Mitch Miller with mother
        Johnathen
Shit.

Notebook page showing Wasserstein's early focus on Jewish Americans in
her musical *Miami*. (Courtesy of the Wendy Wasserstein estate)

Introduction

Wendy Wasserstein is a comedic, social, and historical playwright whose central concerns are gender, class, and ethnicity in America from the fifties through 2005. While her major focus is the situation of educated American women, social class and Jewish-American identity also fascinate her. When giving lectures, she would jokingly ask, "Am I here to discuss being a playwright, being a woman, or being Jewish?" An observer of American culture at a transitional time for women, she told me, "People are products of the time in which they came of age. I know that to be true. In my plays these women are very much of their times."

Accordingly, I have let the plays and my interviews with the playwright lead me to the historical events, ideas, trends, music, movies, books, and journalism that shaped them. My study of Arthur Miller's plays also taught me that you cannot understand anything without understanding its context. To understand a literary work or anything else you have to reach beyond its edges and study the world that shaped it. For social playwrights who observe the way a society shapes a character, plays are like fossils of their time. There are few writers who require footnotes for Fluffernutter and Weejuns on the one hand, and Emma Goldman and Henry Clay Frick on the other. I was chasing news stories about Zoe Baird and Lani Guinier and listening to Leonard Cohen's "Suzanne," reading *The Feminine Mystique* and learning about "mixers" and "Gracious Living," reminding myself of when John Lennon was shot and when George H. W. was inaugurated, reviewing *The Greening of America* and brushing up on Ulysses S. Grant, researching the 1968 Eugene McCarthy Rally and the 1969 protest against the Miss America

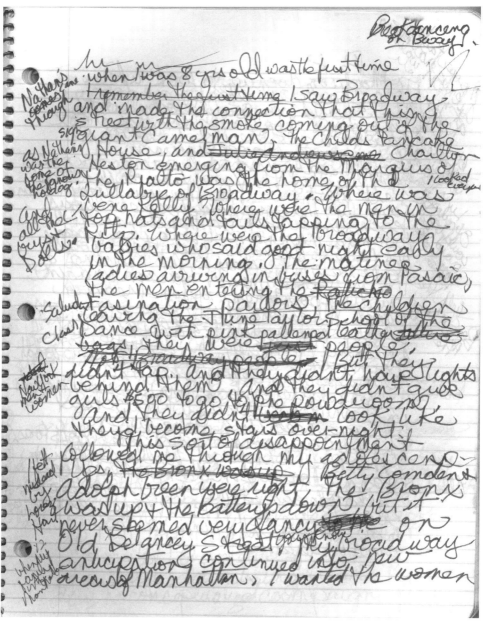

Page from unlabled Wasserstein notebook with writing on the influence of Broadway, with reference to *On the Town*. (Courtesy of the Wendy Wasserstein estate)

Pageant, the Gilded Age and consciousness-raising groups. High and low culture sit comfortably together in Wasserstein's plays, as they should in plays intended for commercial Broadway audiences. Growing up on Broadway musicals, Wasserstein adopted them as one of her models: "You laugh, you cry, stars, beautiful set, a fulfilling afternoon. And then you go to Schrafft's."

Although Wasserstein wrote about the women's movement in a historical way, many feminist literary critics felt her plays, like Beth Henley's and Marsha Norman's, did not challenge patriarchal culture, either thematically or dramaturgically. Yet Wasserstein was writing in the tradition of earlier American women playrights Zona Gale, Rachel Crothers, and Marion Craig Wentworth. As Patricia Schroeder notes, these playwrights wrote in the style of realism "to promote positive social change for women" in the early twentieth century. However, some feminist literary critics in the seventies were arguing that realism's linear form reflected male experience exclusively. More recently, critics have claimed that realism "normalizes the traditionally unequal power relations between genders and classes." I have never been convinced that realism is male.

Wasserstein was never interested in experimental theatrical forms like those of the Living Theatre and the Open Theatre in the sixties. Her writing stands in contrast to the plays of Maria Irene Fornes, Judy Grahn, and Megan Terry, who were part of the sixties' avant-garde theater movement. Nor was she interested, as Tina Howe is, in the absurdists, like Beckett and Ionesco. Her plays feel more like what Alfred Kazin, speaking of the American literature of the thirties, called a "documentary literature of social investigation and national self-discovery." Like Susan Glaspell and the Provincetown Players in the early twentieth century, Wasserstein was also committed to "the premise that art and life were inextricably linked," though she was never interested in modernism's experimental forms as Glaspell was.

Wasserstein says that she studied no female playwrights at the Yale School of Drama, where she became determined to write a play with an all-female curtain call. She does mention the influence of the social comedies of S. N. Behrman, Philip Barry, Moss Hart, Noel Coward, and George S. Kaufman, which I discuss in my chapter on *The Sisters Rosensweig*. Howard Stein, dean of the Yale School of Drama when Wasserstein was a student, aptly compares Wasserstein's wit to that of Dorothy Parker, the American writer known for her wisecracks about twentieth-century urban foibles.

As a writer of comedy, Wasserstein must have read comedies by early American women later in her career: Mercy Otis Warren (b. 1728), Susan Haswell Rowson (1762–1828), Judith Sargent Murray (1751–1820), Mary Carr Clarke (1815–1838), and Sara Pogson (1807–18). These writers adapted English forms of sentimental comedy, social comedy, comic opera, and satire "to represent American identities, experiences, and perspectives." As Amelia Howe Kritzer notes, American women playwrights defined the United States in terms of the idea of the American woman—in terms of the "unparalleled freedom it offered women, despite the fact that it denied them the political rights it established for men." Their plays represented women with "energy, intelligence, and responsibility."

As in Wasserstein's plays, the pursuit of happiness emerged as the central concern in comedies by early American women. While plays like Rowson's *Slaves in Algiers* (1794) insisted that happiness could only come with freedom of choice, Wasserstein's plays convey that with greater freedom came more confusion. But there was also the twentieth-century fact that greater equality for women still did not mean complete equality. Wasserstein adamantly told me, "I do know the issues of women would not be taken care of unless women take care of them. Given a male world, gay or straight."

Wasserstein never wanted to be called a feminist playwright, because she insisted that good playwriting is about character, rather than about a political philosophy. Similarly, literary critic Elaine Showalter says, "Women writers should not be studied as a distinct group on the assumption that they write alike, or even display stylistic resemblances distinctively feminine," even though they have a different relationship to the literary marketplace. Both resisted "ghettoizing" feminism or anything else. Placing formidable female characters on stage was itself a political act, and the commercial quality of the plays reached more audiences than did more radical feminist playwrights.

As Matthew Roudane clarifies, Wasserstein is part of the women's tradition of playwriting that dramatizes "the female hero." This female heroism defines itself through the perspective, values, and nuances of female identity and experience. This shift in American drama reflects the emergence of the women's movement, which enabled women to become creators of their destinies. As Marsha Norman put it, "Women have become central characters in their own lives." The plays of Wendy Wasserstein represent the historical, social, and sexual forces that have shaped female identity.

Academics have read Wasserstein's plays in a variety of ways: Miriam M. Chirico uses the ideas of Susanne Langer and Northrop Frye to discuss Wasserstein's comedy; Gail Ciociola examines the plays as examples of "Fem-en(act)ment"; Helene Keyssar reads the plays within a Bakhtinian framework. Deborah Anderson writes from the perspective of an actor and director, using Uta Hagen's theories. Gaylord Brewer examines the impact of Chekhov on Wasserstein's work; Robert F. Gross traces Wasserstein's protagonists back to Ibsen's, concluding that Wasserstein's represent "the consequences of liberal individualist drama at an extreme." Stephanie Hammer calls Wasserstein a "female schlemiel," focusing on Wasserstein's essays to discuss her plays. William Boles compares Wasserstein's plays with those of Caryl Churchill and Charlotte Keatley. Glenda Frank examines the Jewish stereotypes in Wasserstein's plays and also finds parallels between *An American Daughter and Everyman.* All make valuable contributions to the academic conversation about Wasserstein's plays, but they do not locate the plays in their cultural and historical context for general readers as Bette Mandl begins to do in her essay "Women's Movement: The Personal as Political." This is my project. Wasserstein, after all, wrote for mainstream audiences.

Rather than working from theoretical frameworks, I read from the inside out, taking my cues from the plays themselves. I quote extensively from them, because everything begins and ends with the playwright's words. In libraries around the world, Wasserstein wrote by hand in spiral notebooks. Those words became characters first, plots later, and finally productions that lit theaters around the world. I wanted to give readers a sense of her creative process by reproducing pages from the notebooks piled high in Mount Holyoke's archives.

As I leafed through yellowed copies of *Ms., New York*, the *New York Times* and its Style section, the *Paris Review,* the *Nation, the Journal of Marriage and the Family, Time,* and *Newsweek* in the Kean University library, I found that the plays were indeed cultural artifacts reflecting their time. My trips to the Mount Holyoke archives and conversations with Wasserstein's classmates confirmed that Wasserstein is a social chronicler; the Mount Holyoke bulletins, handbooks, classmates, and rituals all made their way into her first play, *Uncommon Women and Others* (1975). I concluded that the plays are time capsules. Like an anthropologist, Wasserstein was documenting the conflicts and concerns of educated women.

Educated at the Calhoun School, a private girls' school on the Upper West Side of Manhattan, from 1964 to 1967, and then at Mount Holyoke College from 1967 to 1971, Wasserstein was always surrounded by accomplished women. Mount Holyoke's mission statement includes "fostering the alliance of liberal arts education with purposeful engagement in the world," and it encourages female leadership: Mary Lyon founded Mount Holyoke, and women's rights activist Lucy Stone (1839), poet Emily Dickinson (1849), secretary of labor Frances Perkins (1902), and physician Virginia Apgar (1929) all emerged from Holyoke. As a history major, Wasserstein took the history of women as her natural subject and her way of engaging with the world.

Wasserstein entered college at a transitional moment for women that defined her literary career. Freshman year, students were hoping to be pinned and then "to marry Harvard," or they were "saving themselves for Yale." An "MRS" would accompany a BA or a BS. Suburban housewives of that time were sending away for *How to Develop Poise and Self-Confidence and How to Be a More Interesting Woman* from Amy Vanderbilt's Success Program for Women. Wasserstein grew up with those traditional values. Moreover, her mother sent her to the Helena Rubinstein Charm School and to the June Taylor School of Dance. She recalled, "Smith is to bed and Holyoke is to wed, so my mother sent me to Holyoke." She explained to me: "Women who graduated in '64 and '65, right before feminism . . . a lot of them are angry. They're the ones who got married at twenty-two, had the kids right away."

By 1969, however, the Junior Class Show at Mount Holyoke ended with students shouting "Suburbia Screw!" The class of '69, Wasserstein recalls, "had no intention of waking up from a marriage at forty-five abandoned in a Scarsdale kitchen, with the kids in college and a vague interest in Bernini." By 1970 students were carrying copies of Betty Friedan's *The Feminine Mystique*, Simone de Beauvoir's *The Second Sex*, and Germaine Greer's *The Female Eunuch*. Wasserstein wrote in the *New York Times* in 1981, "They changed the rules in the middle of the game, and what you get is both confusion and liberation."

The confusion interested her more than the liberation: "I can't help feeling that some members of that 1969 junior class now secretly believe they were screwed too." She observed the self-recrimination women were feeling for not having become a certain kind of woman because they pursued independent lives. Eventually that "'have-it-all' optimism imploded"; women began judging themselves harshly if they did not

Wendy Wasserstein at the White House in 1999 shaking Hillary Clinton's hand, with Forrest Sawyer and Bill Clinton in the background. (Bob McNeely)

have a family and a wonderful job by the time they were forty. Wasserstein saw feminism backfiring. Each play grapples with the tug of war between the feminine mystique and feminism.

Hillary Rodham exemplified this transitional moment for Wasserstein. "Suddenly women had the same career opportunities as the men they were supposed to wed." "Marriage would be for love or companionship," but no longer a substitute "for individual destiny." At the same time, Wasserstein saw a disconnect between women's colleges instructing students how to fold napkins in hostess gowns for high tea on the one hand, and the competitive workplace they would enter on the other. *Uncommon Women* responded to this gap and documents the beginning of the end of the feminine mystique.

The cultural distance between then and now is so great that CNN journalist Campbell Brown asked Hillary Rodham during the 2008 presidential campaign what she meant by "the old boys' network." Shocked, Hillary responded, "C'mon, Campbell. There have been certain impediments." In conversation Wasserstein told me, "If Hillary Clinton had graduated a few years later, she might not have thought she had to marry the guy who was going to become the president. She could have said, 'I want to be a senator.'" Her words were prophetic, and she would be marveling that Hillary is now secretary of state.

The women's movement gave women new opportunities and also new frustrations. While women were beginning to enter the gates of a male professional world, they found that they had not achieved equality in rank or salary. Or they were overwhelmed by options. Wasserstein, for instance, applied simultaneously to graduate school in law, business, and creative writing, not knowing which direction she would take. Moreover, many women felt their personal lives were suffering. Every play registers this fact. Like the first 1971 cover of *Ms.* magazine—a woman multitasking with eight arms and tears rolling down her cheeks—many American women felt pulled in too many directions.

Wasserstein recollected a feeling of solidarity that accompanied her coming of age in the sixties, "a sense of we were going to change things. The whole sense of the women's movement was that it [would] change women's expectations of themselves, both externally and internally." The lyrics of John Lennon's "Imagine" and Aretha Franklin's "Respect" carry the ideal of social justice for which Wasserstein longed, while her other soundtracks reflect the hangover of the feminine mystique: Judy Collins, the Dixie Cups, Sam Cooke, Janis Joplin, Mary Wells, Betty Everett, the Beach Boys, and Sinatra. Still others convey the counterculture of the sixties, like Jefferson Airplane's "White Rabbit" or the time in general: James Taylor and Bob Dylan. As I read, my iPod expanded. Wasserstein's protagonists want both "[Their] Guy" and "Respect."

The Kennedy years represented hope, and Wasserstein recalled fondly that Jacqueline Onassis attended her first, unsuccessful musical, *Miami*, about the Maidman family vacationing on Miami Beach in 1959, which contained the seeds of feminism and of *The Heidi Chronicles*. The unpublished manuscript reads: "Things change. People move on. That's progress. If you're smart, you take a leap and go first. . . . You need a strategy. Especially now. It's a new decade. There'll be rockets to the moon, a new president; Castro will rebuild Cuba." Wasserstein really wanted a new social structure that would provide true equality for women, and her plays reflect that America had not yet found a strategy for achieving that goal. The story of the collapse of the feminist movement in *The Heidi Chronicles* resonated with many women's experiences: Helen Gurley Brown, Nora Ephron, Gloria Steinem, Judy Blume, Susan Isaacs, and Marlo Thomas flocked to the early run of the play.

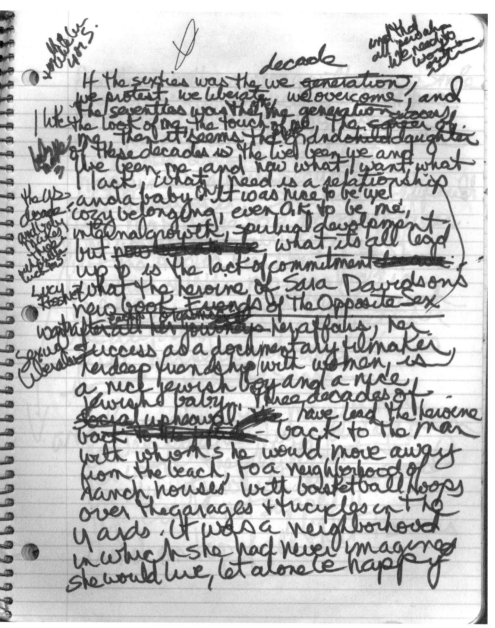

If the sixties was the we generation, we protest, we liberate, we overcome, and ~~like~~ the seventies ~~I like the look of me, the touch of me, the~~ then it seems the ~~heir~~ daughter of these decades is the *we been me and I've been me* and now what I want, what I lack, what I need is a relationship and a baby. It was nice to be me, cozy belonging, even ok to be me, internal growth, spiritual development, but ~~~~ what it's all lead up to is the lack of commitment ~~~~ Lucy ~~~~ what the heroine of Sara Davidson's new ~~book~~ Friends of the Opposite Sex ~~~~ want after all her ~~journeys~~ her affairs, her ~~~~ success as a documentary filmmaker, her deep friendship with women, is a nice jewish boy and a nice jewish baby. Three decades of ~~social upheaval~~ have lead the heroine ~~back~~ — back to the man with whom she would move away from the beach, to a neighborhood of ranch houses with basketball hoops over the garages + tricycles in the yards. It was a neighborhood in which she had never imagined she would live, let alone be happy

Page from unlabeled notebook about the contrast between liberal and traditional values. (Courtesy of the Wendy Wasserstein estate)

There seems to be a connection between Wasserstein's nostalgia for liberal ideals, her feminism, and her Jewish background. In "Nice J ewish Girls," Carole Bell Ford explains, "'Tikn olam,' the repair or improvement of the world, meant social work. 'Tsedakah' meant responsibility for the welfare of the community, but not only through charity—through other types of service." Because of traditional female roles in the fifties, however, the opportunity to serve became the domain of men and boys. Boys were pushed to succeed by these values, but the girls had to struggle against being limited to "marriage, home, children, family," Ford recollects.

Yet patriarchy is certainly not unique to Judaism. Wasserstein was simply writing about the tradition she knew. The joke about the Jewish mother who frantically yells into a dark theater, "Is there a doctor in the house? My daughter is in the audience!" conveys the values on which Wasserstein was raised. Good Jewish girls should marry nice Jewish doctors. Security and prestige came with the husband's professional status. When I asked Wasserstein whether she found Judaism to be more patriarchal than other religions, she responded, "No. In the books it's patriarchal. It's all mixed messages, because it's run by the mother. . . . Girls were brought up to be good girls in my house. It's always, my brother was a 'genius,' and we were 'very smart.'"

In addition to the connection between gender roles and being Jewish, Wasserstein also writes about Jewish-American assimilation, about feeling an outsider in an Anglo culture, and about Jewish humor:

> I think in many ways my idea of show business comes both from temple, not that I really practice, but that sense of community and melancholy, and spirituality is there. My folks used to travel every year to Miami, twice a year, Christmas and New Year's, and to San Juan, and the entertainment that I knew was those Jewish comics.

Moving from a Jewish neighborhood in Flatbush, Brooklyn to the Upper East Side of Manhattan when Wasserstein was twelve meant moving from middle to upper class and to a more ethnically diverse population. As a result, almost every play grapples with the tension between being Jewish and "American," being an insider and an outsider, and, later, between old and new money. For the daughter of the inventor of velveteen, and the sister of a high-risk arbitrageur and a vice-president of Citicorp, business was part of the family conversation. Moreover, she felt that as an American playwright, she needed to understand how social class shaped our culture, and so she wrote *Old Money* (2000).

In the end, democracy, not gender or class in particular, interested Wasserstein. In *Third* (2005), a woman professor unjustly accuses a male student of plagiarism, nearly destroying his academic career. Similarly, *An American Daughter* examines a collapsing liberalism by exposing the way the media destroys the first female nominee for surgeon general.

Wasserstein always had her eye not just on the headlines, but also on the invisible forces beneath the news. There she found double standards for women, a collapsing feminist movement, and contradictions within the liberal and conservative establishments. As a result, her comedy has a dark edge; like the plays of Chekhov that she so admired, her drama combines melancholy and humor. Like Chekhov's sisters, too, her characters seek a utopia that is forever out of reach. Each play reflects the yawning gap between the ideal of social justice and the reality of inequality. From that tension comes the possibility of transforming our social structure, which is the ultimate goal of drama.

Dating

During the week the Mount Holyoke world is books and classes, coffee at the C.I., bridge when you should be studying, and staying up all night talking to the girl down the hall. It's a girl's world where no one really cares if you don't have time to set your hair. Come Friday, however, it's a different scene. The social whirl begins as suitcases are snapped shut and girls take off for Amherst, Williams, Wesleyan, Yale, Dartmouth, Princeton, Harvard, Brown, Trinity, Cornell and Colgate among others. At the same time boys begin arriving from these places for mixers and parties. From Friday to Sunday, it's a man's world.

Starting in the early fall there are big all-class mixers which attract boys from most, if not all, of the aforementioned schools. The same is true of the smaller mixers held throughout the year by individual dorms, clubs and other groups. Chartered buses also travel to boys' schools every weekend for mixers there.

Blind dates are frequently supplied by upperclassmen in the dorms or friends at boys' schools. Good or bad, they're always interesting at least. Lately computer matching programs which attempt to supply you with your "ideal man" have been very popular.

A date at Amherst involves going "over the Notch" for a movie or play, a sports event, dinner at Valentine Hall, and, usually, a dorm or fraternity party. At other schools, from Dartmouth to Princeton, it's more of the same — only the atmosphere varies from school to school.

An essay on dating from the 1968 Mount Holyoke freshman handbook.
(Mount Holyoke College Archives and Special Collections)

1

Uncommon Women and Others (1977)

The End of an Era

We [are] living in a time which presents greater possibilities of choice to more people than ever before. It is such choices which present you with the dilemmas of the educated woman . . .

—David Reisman

When seventeen-year-old Wendy Wasserstein made her way on Route 95 North to dorm 1837 at Mount Holyoke College in bucolic South Hadley, Massachusetts, from the Upper East Side of Manhattan in the fall of 1967, the leaves were turning. President Richard Glenn Gettell presided over 103 female faculty, mostly wearing skirt suits, their hair in buns, and 95 male faculty, often bearded with horn-rimmed glasses. Tuition was $1,850, room and board $1,200. Wasserstein was registered for Principles of Zoology, Introduction to Literary Forms, Fundamentals of Regional Geography, Introduction to Music, Fundamentals of Politics, Introduction to Sociology, and Introduction to Arts of the Theatre. Based on her performance on the college entrance exam, she carried with her six credits in history from the Calhoun School. Her passion for history would define not only her major in college, but also her vocation as a social and historical playwright.

Before the semester, 100,000 young people had congregated in Haight-Ashbury to challenge American culture and politics in the Summer of Love. The hippie movement, however, seemed a million miles away from this elite women's college. Young women with strict curfews

Wendy Wasserstein at twenty in the 1971 Mount Holyoke College yearbook. (Mount Holyoke College Archives and Special Collections)

Students walking on the Mount Holyoke campus, in a 1968 *Mount Holyoke College Bulletin.* (Mount Holyoke College Archives and Special Collections) and neatly coiffed hair or headbands walked to class through wooded trails carrying Betty Friedan's *The Feminine Mystique* (1963). They wore skirts or dresses and Weejuns (loafers made by Bass), rode Schwinn bicycles with metal baskets, went canoeing on Upper Lake, and studied (and sometimes smoked) late into the night. At night, in their Lanz of Salzburg flannel nightgowns, they congregated for milk and cookies after Gracious Living, a formal tea hour with their housemothers in their dorms. The sounds of Leonard Cohen's "Suzanne" and James Taylor's "Fire and Rain" blared into the quad. On weekends, buses of boys from Yale, Dartmouth, Amherst, and Williams arrived for mixers, or the girls would visit them. In either case, women were hoping to be "pinned," a practice popular in the sixties and seventies in which a fraternity brother would give his pin to his girlfriend as a sign of serious commitment.

Wasserstein's good friend from the Yale School of Drama, playwright Chris Durang, then an under-graduate at Harvard, remembers those years as follows: "The whole history of college dances, and women from all-girls schools being 'bused' to men from boys' schools for these 'mixers' was very much a dominant social fea-ture of that era, and was sort of the only way girls and guys could meet each other—but they were clearly tense-making for shy or insecure people." Wasserstein's imagination was registering this social scene for *Uncommon Women and Others*.

Women—both as playwrights to be studied and as faculty—were conspicuously missing from the MFA program at the Yale School of Drama when Wasser-stein arrived in the mid seventies. But Wasserstein, who had already written a play called *Any Woman*

Milk and cookies in a Mount Holyoke dorm in 1963. (Mount Holyoke College Archives and Special Collections)

Can't at CUNY's MFA program in 1971, under the direction of Israel Horowitz and Joseph Heller, was determined to place women on stage. She recalls:

> When I was a playwriting student at the Yale Drama School in 1976 my thesis play was a piece I wrote for eight women, which was called *Uncommon Women and Others.*
>
> I wrote the play partly because I'd spent my graduate years reading a great deal of Jacobean drama in which men kissed the poisoned lips of women and promptly dropped dead. . . . This particular experience was not familiar to me or to any of my friends. Simultaneously, there were all these posters for *Deliverance* around New Haven. I thought to myself, "I'd really like to write the flip side of *Deliverance.*" I worked backwards and thought, "I want to see an all-female curtain call in the basement of the Yale School of Drama."

(James Dickey's *Deliverance* depicts a Hemingwayesque male canoeing trip.) Moreover, Wasserstein recalled that after *Uncommon Women* had its first performance in the basement of the Yale Drama School, a male student responded, "I can't get into this. It's about women." She whispered to a friend, "I've spent my life getting into *Hamlet* and *Lawrence of Arabia.* Why doesn't he just try it?" She did, however, have a male comrade who understood her well, Chris Durang. Over late-night milkshakes at their favorite diner near the New Haven airport, Durang and Wasserstein would discuss early drafts of *Uncommon Women.* They wrote a musical together at Yale, *When Dinah Shore Ruled the Earth*, and became lifelong friends.

In the summer of 1977, the O'Neill Theater Center's National Playwrights Conference in Waterford, Connecticut selected *Uncommon Women* from over eight hundred submissions to be workshopped. It was a pivotal moment in Wasserstein's career. From there, *Uncommon Women* went to the Phoenix Theatre in New York—with Jill Eikenberry as Kate, Ann McDonough as Samantha, Alma Cuervo as Holly, Ellen Parker as Muffet, Swoosie Kurtz as Rita, Josephine Nichols as Mrs. Plumm, Cynthia Herman as Susie Friend, Anna Levine as Carter, and Glenn Close as Leilah. When the play appeared on *Great Performances* on public television in 1978, Meryl Streep replaced Glenn Close. In 1984, it moved to the Lucille Lortel Theatre with Forrest Sawyer as the college

The cast of the 1978 PBS production of *Uncommon Women. Left to right, standing:* Cynthia Herman, Meryl Streep, and Anna Levine; *seated:* Ellen Parker, Jill Eikenberry, Ann McDonough, Alma Cuervo, and Swoosie Kurtz. (PBS/Photofest)

president. Since its 1977 production, *Uncommon Women* has been produced in regional and university theaters across the country.

The Graduate for women, *Uncommon Women and Others* explores the lives of five twenty-seven-year-old women who meet at a New York restaurant and then travel back six years to their senior year at Mount Holyoke College, where they perform the ritual of "Gracious Living"— the formal tea hour led by their housemother, Mrs. Plumm. The voice of a male college president of Mount Holyoke frames each flashback by pronouncing the ideal of this elite women's college—to produce "uncommon women"—which stands in ironic contrast to the humorous action of the play. In the end, however, the male voice fades into a woman's voice that pronounces the real obstacles women faced as they entered a workplace dominated by men. Despite the 1967 expansion of President Johnson's 1965 affirmative action policy that ensured equal educational and employment opportunities for women and minorities, the class of women in 1971 walked onto an unequal playing field.

Outside the iron gates of Mount Holyoke, women were demanding equality. In 1966, Betty Friedan and a group of feminists founded the National Organization for Women (NOW), which sought to end sexual discrimination, especially in the workplace, through lobbying, litigation, and public demonstrations. When Wasserstein was a sophomore in 1969, the Boston Women's Health Collective published a pamphlet that became a landmark book, *Our Bodies, Ourselves: A Book by and for Women.* Nineteen-seventy marked the "great media blitz" for the new women's movement. Pat Mainardi, a major voice of the second wave of feminism, proposed "wages for housework" in her essay that appeared in *Redstockings,* a publication by an early women's liberation group centered in New York. (California had just become the first state to adopt "no-fault" divorce, which resulted in the impoverishment of older women without skills.) Feminists staged sit-ins at *Newsweek* and *Ladies' Home Journal* and filed an antidiscrimination suit against *Time, Life, Fortune,* and *Sports Illustrated.* It was also the year that the Feminist Press began, and major classics appeared: Germaine Greer's *The Female Eunuch,* Vivian Gornick and Barbara Moran's *Woman in Sexist Society: Studies in Power and Powerlessness,* Shulamith Firestone's *Dialectics of Sex,* Robin Morgan's *Sisterhood Is Powerful,* and Celestine Ware's *Woman Power.* Nationwide, women participated in a "Strike for Equality"; in Wisconsin, the AFL-CIO conference met to discuss the status of women in unions; and the National Organization of Women sued 1,300 corporations, while other women's organizations filed class action suits against more than 100 colleges and universities. Nineteen-seventy also marked the year Bella Abzug was elected to the U.S. House of Representatives.

Between Wasserstein's graduation in 1971 and the writing of *Uncommon Women* in 1977, the women's movement had made progress: Congress had passed the Equal Rights Amendment, and Title IX banned sex discrimination in schools, increasing the enrollment of women in athletic programs. Despite these victories, women were feeling confused.

Wasserstein says, "I just didn't know what I wanted, and it didn't seem to me that my friends knew, either." In the play each character finds herself short of where she would like to be in life, and so in a Chekhovian refrain they look forward to a time when they will be "pretty amazing," though the age when they expect to attain their success moves from twenty-five to thirty-five to forty-five.

As young women in college, Kate, Leilah, Samantha, Holly, Rita, Susie Friend, Muffet, and Carter discuss their future careers, men, sex, and marriage within a patriarchal society. In the present, some have found their way while others have not. Kate has become a successful lawyer, and Leilah, Kate's academic and social rival, has become an anthropologist and married in "Mesopotamia" (Iraq) after earning her Ph.D. Like Leilah, the intellectual Carter does not appear at the reunion. Shy and bulimic, the only freshman in the flashback scenes, Carter followed through on her plan to make a film about Wittgenstein after graduation. In contrast, Samantha, the daughter of the mayor of Naperville, appears at the reunion married, having fulfilled the old adage that "Smith is to bed and Holyoke is to wed." Rita, winner of the 1966 D.A.R. (Daughters of the American Revolution) Scholarship, has also married and has been trying unsuccessfully to write a novel. She claims to be "into women's things." Susie Friend, the all-collegiate girl, who organizes and leads everything, has entered the corporate world. Muffet, having reexamined her "younger tenets that men were more interesting than women and life would simply fall into place," has become an insurance seminar hostess and is proud that she can support herself. Holly, on the other hand, is an overweight underachiever with a good sense of humor who has found neither a career nor a husband, announcing that she is "in 'transition'" and was therefore reluctant to attend the reunion. Her parents harass her about losing weight, finding a career, and marrying.

In short, the action and conflict consist of young women expressing their confusion about their lives, and for this reason alone, *Uncommon Women* was a landmark; it was the first time that contemporary women's issues were staged Off-Broadway and then on public television. Since Lillian Hellman had written for Broadway in the fifties and sixties, plays by women had been conspicuously absent. As Emily Mann, artistic director of the McCarter Theatre at Princeton, told me, "Wendy opened the way for other women to be heard. In 1979, women were not getting their plays produced, nor getting directing jobs on or Off-Broadway. *Uncommon Women* made a difference."

The women, especially Holly and Muffet, miss the female cama- raderie they shared in college. In this way, *Uncommon Women* belongs to a tradition of "female buddy" stories like Mary McCarthy's novel *The Group*. First published in 1954, *The Group* depicted, in what was con- sidered a sexually outspoken way, eight Vassar graduates in the thirties. It followed the group of friends through their first sexual experiences, marriage, and domestic duties as they encountered the political and social trends of their time. The link with *Uncommon Women* is clear, and Alma Cuervo, who played Holly, told me, "During rehearsals, everyone was reading *The Group*." *Uncommon Women* is also a parent of Candace Bushnell's Sex and the City, her sex column in the *New York Observer* that became the basis for the 1998 HBO hit series that explores single, professional women in Manhattan and their relationships with men. It is also the grandparent of her 2006 novel, *Lipstick Jungle*.

The play documents a transitional time for women. Yet no one has located it in its accurate historical context, which is 1967–71, the years its author was a student at Mount Holyoke, rather than the later dates that she artificially imposed on the play—1972 and 1978. Wasserstein was documenting life at Mount Holyoke College during her undergrad- uate years and dramatizing what had become of her peers after gradu- ation. Her classmate and good friend Mary Jane Patrone reminisced:

> Each character has a real-life prototype (except Susie Friend, who is more of an amalgam.) But the descriptions, the autobi- ographical details, the personalities—even the boyfriends are based on actual people. The dialogue and the interactions, of course, are all Wendy, but the play feels like a documentary in its representation of Mount Holyoke. For instance, Harriet is the prototype for Kate in *Uncommon Women* who remained a life- long friend of Wendy.

The play itself provides a cultural history of the time period, a reading list for understanding the play: Betty Friedan's *The Feminine Mystique* (1963), documenting the predicament of the suburban housewife in the fifties; *Mabel Dodge's Diary*—frequently assigned in colleges in the late sixties, it chronicles the life of Mabel Dodge Sterne Luhan (1879–1962), an American patron of the arts, associated with artist colony in Taos, New Mexico (at her weekly "salon" in Greenwich Village, she hosted Carl Van Vechten, Margaret Sanger, Emma Goldman, Charles Demuth, "Big

Mary Jane Patrone and Harriet Sachs, two of Wasserstein's classmates.
(Mount Holyoke College Archives and Special Collections)

Bill" Haywood, Lincoln Steffens, and John Reed, who proposed to her in 1916); Kate Millet's *Sexual Politics* (1968), which attacked patriarchy in literature and art, romantic love, and monogamous marriage, fueling feminism's second wave and changing women's perceptions of themselves; Germaine Greer's *The Female Eunuch* (1970), which argued that the traditional suburban, consumerist, nuclear family represses women sexually, and that this devitalizes them, rendering them eunuchs; and Jacqueline Susann's *Valley of the Dolls* (1966), the best-selling novel that grew out of Susann's failed attempt to make a name for herself in show business. With graphic depictions of sex and drugs, *Valley* exposed the exploitative, self-destructive side of success, and therefore the "downside" of women's liberation.

The popular culture touchstones within the play include *Let's Make a Deal,* the most popular game show of the sixties and seventies, in which contestants had to choose between Monty Hall's cash and a mystery prize (or booby prize) behind a curtain, a predicament Wasserstein uses as a metaphor for women's lives at the time; *Car 54, Where Are You?* (1961), the misadventures of a Mutt and Jeff pair of cops in the 53rd precinct in the Bronx; Judy Collins's "Both Sides Now" (1967)—her rendition of the Joni Mitchell song appeared on her classic 1967 album, *Wildflowers;* James Taylor's "Fire and Rain" (1968, Top Ten in 1970), referencing Taylor's periods in psychiatric hospitals and the suicide of a friend; Leonard Cohen's "Suzanne" (1968), a poetic account of the "meeting of spirits" between Leonard Cohen and Beat activist Suzanne Verdal on the St. Lawrence River in the summer of 1965; Bob Dylan's "Lay, Lady, Lay" (1969)—released on his *Nashville Skyline* album, the song was originally written for the soundtrack of the movie *Midnight Cowboy;* the Dave Clark Five (1964–67), one of the most successful 1960s British Invasion bands; EST, or Erhard Seminar Training (1971), a large group awareness training program; Marshmallow Fluff, a World War I, Durkee-Mower Inc., New England marshmallow spread that became popular as a dorm snack in the sixties and seventies; the National Student Strike (1970)—after the American invasion of Cambodia on April 30, 1970 and the killing of students at Kent State and Jackson State, more than four million students participated in strikes; and the birth control pill (1963)—by 1965 the Pill had become the nation's leading method of reversible contraception. All of these references verify that the play is set during 1967–71, rather than in 1978.

The women's movement was a critical part of this moment in American history when young people questioned everything: sexism, racism, and American foreign policy in Vietnam. Earlier drafts of *Uncommon Women* included more references to the Vietnam War, but the final drafts focus on women. In both cases traditional ideas seemed to have brought us to the brink of a global disaster, causing students to distrust the establishment. Christopher Durang notes the change in sensibility from the fifties to the sixties through film:

> As a movie buff I really felt the shift in the sixties, so many things were questioned, certainly including women's expectations and roles. A big hit in the early sixties was the goody-goody *Sound of Music*, which seemed an extension of the fifties' square, "wholesome" values. And yet the same year, the scathingly dark *Who's Afraid of Virginia Woolf* was also a hit. And by the end of the sixties films like *The Graduate* and *Easy Rider* really challenged the conformity of the fifties that bled into the early sixties. (When I saw *The Graduate* in 1967 in a theatre full of college students, when Ben, post-college, is lolling in the pool,

unclear what to do with his life, and his father says crankily, "What was the purpose of all that college then," Ben's line is "Ya got me." And the whole audience cheered. I don't think that would've happened in the fifties).

Everything from clothing styles to music to psychology changed. Cognitive behavioral therapy replaced the old Freudian male paradigm that insisted that women really wanted to be men, and psychologists began looking to larger, societal forces to understand our psyche, enabling us to reshape it. *Uncommon Women* chronicles not only the general skepticism of graduates in the sixties, but also the conflict of being a female graduate in a male world.

Wasserstein's archives contain documents that reflect the situation of women at the time or historical representations of women: the Mount Holyoke 1967–71 course bulletins; Richard Glenn Gettell's speech "A Plea for the Uncommon Woman," delivered at his inauguration in 1957; Harvard sociologist David Reisman's 1968 commencement speech, called "Dilemmas of the Educated Woman," and George Eliot's *Middlemarch*, the Victorian novel about the conflict between marriage and vocation. The playwright deliberately took her title from Mount Holyoke's course bulletin and its mission. "Uncommon Women" is the way the college refers to its students, whom Mary Lyon, the founder of Holyoke in 1837, told to "go where no one else will go; do what no one else will do."

However "uncommon" are the women in this play, they are representative of a transitional moment in American history, when wo-

Betty Friedan in the 1970s. (Photofest)

men women were caught between the feminine mystique of the fifties and the feminist movement of the sixties and seventies. Betty Friedan's 1963 *Feminine Mystique* challenged the conventional roles of the American woman as devoted wife and mother. A Smith College graduate from the class of 1942, Friedan writes: "Since the end of World War II . . . there was a strange discrepancy between the reality of our lives as women and the image to which we were trying to conform, the image that I came to call the feminine mystique." Through her research and interviews with women, she found "the problem that has no name":

> A strange stirring, a sense of dissatisfaction, a yearning that women suffered in the middle of the twentieth century in the United States. Each suburban wife struggled with it alone. As she made the beds, shopped for groceries, matched slipcover material, ate peanut butter sandwiches with her children, chauffeured Cub Scouts and Brownies, lay beside her husband at night—she was afraid to ask even of herself the silent question— "Is this all?"

The "feminine mystique" told women that their destinies were as wives and mothers, and that having careers and independence was "unfeminine." A woman's chief concern was getting and keeping a husband, while men made the major decisions, fought the political battles at work, and earned the money.

If a woman felt dissatisfaction in the fifties and sixties, she looked within her marriage or within herself. Psychiatrists did not understand why women were not fulfilled waxing the kitchen floor. Women desperately started telling each other about feeling "empty," "incomplete," lacking identity, feeling "tired," "angry," "sad." Housewives developed bleeding blisters, which had emotional causes. This spiritual ache was inscrutable through the lens of material problems, like poverty or sickness. It was a middle-class woman's problem, but it was not solved by more wealth. Seven years before Wasserstein and her classmates became freshmen, "the problem that has no name burst like a boil through the image of the happy American housewife." Therefore, they grew up with mothers who lived the mystique that was defined by the following facts: The average marriage age of American women was twenty "and still dropping into the teens." The proportion of women attending college in comparison with men dropped from forty-seven percent in 1920 to thirty-five percent in 1958. A century earlier, women had fought for higher education; by the mid fifties girls went to college to get an "MRS," and sixty percent of women dropped out of college to marry, or because they thought too much education would be a barrier to marriage. Colleges built dorms for "married students," but the students were usually the husbands. Wives earned "PHTs," "Putting Husband Through." Others began getting married in high school, causing high schools to institute courses on marriage and the family.

By the late sixties, *Uncommon Women* reveals, some women rejected the feminine mystique and viewed marriage differently. Rita expresses her reservations about marriage at graduation:

> Well, God knows there is no security in marriage. You give up your anatomy, economic self-support, spontaneous creativity, and a helluva lot of energy trying to convert a male half-person into a whole person who will eventually stop draining you, so you can do your own work. And the alternative—hopping onto the corporate or professional ladder—is just as self-destructive. If you spend your life proving yourself, then you just become a man, which is where the whole problem began, and continues. All I want is a room of my own so I can get into my writing.

Although Rita later marries, in college she embraces Virginia Woolf's belief that a woman needed her own room and financial security to write. As a student, Rita believes that marriage negates a woman's sense of self. Still, she does not see a career as a solution, because it encourages the very competition that she identifies as male. To address this problem within marriage at this time, Susan Edmiston wrote "How to Write Your Own Marriage Contract" in the first issue of *Ms.* magazine in 1971. She instructs couples to split *everything* equally in "The Utopian Marriage Contract": names, birth control, the decision to have or adopt children, how the children will be raised, where the couple will live, housework, finances, sexual rights, abortion. In other words, unbalanced domestic roles were a national problem that had its roots in the biological difference between men and women.

If heterosexual marriage was flawed, scene eight of *Uncommon Women* humorously conveys that so, too, would marriage be between women, because women impose the same standards on each other as men do on women. With Judy Collins's "Both Sides Now" playing late at

Music for the Mount Holyoke Drinking Song. (Mount Holyoke College Archives and Special Collections)

night, the girls drinking sherry, Rita invites them to play a game: "If we could marry any one of us, who would it be?" Selecting from their "own uncommon pool," each woman refuses her friend's proposal. Rita chooses Samantha "'cause she'd make the best wife, and in a matrimonial situation I could admire her the longest." While Rita is convinced that Samantha is "the perfect woman," Samantha does not feel the same way about Rita. She feels "really badly 'cause I wouldn't have picked you and it would have been nice if everything worked out." Realizing that "Kate probably has the best future," that Susie Friend would never be home because of "too many committee meetings," and that Holly is "sweet and funny"—but that she could not support her, nor would Holly be able to join the country club (the implication is that Holly is Jewish)—Samantha decides that she would marry Muffet because she is glamorous, does not scare her, and "could get on with the outside world." Holly confesses that she would be "most comfortable being married to Leilah or Rita," because she would "never feel [that she had] to impress them." Her ideal mate, however, is Kate: "I would consider living through your accomplishments, Katie, and besides, I'm sure if we got married my parents would approve, and one of us would get our picture in the Sunday *Times*."

Assuming the female subservient role of the time, Holly qualifies her proposal to Kate: "You don't have to marry me, Katie. I understand. Maybe you have to settle your career first." Pre-law, Kate knows she would be the main source of income in a marriage, "excluding the possibility of trust funds," so she chooses to support the future filmmaker, Carter. "If I'm going to be a boring lawyer, then I'd want to be married to someone who would stay home and have an imagination. Anyway, Carter would *need* me." Rita wants to celebrate that none of their marriage proposals have been reciprocated. The scene, therefore, conveys that incompatibility, unrequited feelings, and unbalanced power relations are not just true of male-female relationships, but of relationships in general. The play's view of feminism is too complex to accept simple reversals as viable solutions.

Uncommon Women captures the fallout of the feminine mystique. By 1967, it seemed unquestioned that women should get the best possible education, but what would become of those women was a larger question. There was a fifties hangover in the air; the class of 1971 was still experiencing the problems that Friedan described. They enrolled for a BA or a BS, but society still said, "Do not leave without an MRS." Wasserstein told me that when she first arrived at Mount Holyoke, it was expected that women would marry upon graduation. By graduation, the rules had changed, and you were expected to have a career. Then, *after* graduation, women returned to conventional values and decided to get married after all. The fluctuating rules confused the playwright. Similarly, her classmate Mary Jane Patrone told me: "When we got to Holyoke there were rules galore—dress codes (including mandatory skirts at Gracious Living on Wednesdays), parietal hours (no men allowed above the first floor), curfews, and countless others, but as seniors, all those rules were gone."

In just four years, women's lives changed radically and with them the notion of an "uncommon woman." In his 1957 inaugural speech, President Richard Glenn Gettell told students: "Mount Holyoke . . . has tried to foster and to develop the *uncommon woman*." Gettell's statement became part of the college's mission statement, which Wasserstein mined for her play's title:

> [I]n this age of the common man, I should like to present a plea for the uncommon woman. . . . In an earlier day, woman's life was [like man's] considered two-phased: first a growing up period requiring some training, generally in the home, then an adult lifetime of home-making, devoted and subservient to the husband and family. This concept of the role of women is vastly outdated—particularly so for the uncommon woman. Mount Holyoke, and its sisters among great women's colleges, have long since proved the point. Like the Nineteenth Amendment they stand as monuments to the long struggle towards the emancipation of women. . . . [They have demonstrated] . . . that intelligence has no gender. . . . Another principle has been established, though it [is not fully] accepted in practice: the right of women to careers outside, or inside of marriage. . . . Most must still do battle uphill against lingering prejudice and masculine assumptions of superiority . . . [but] the able and determined woman—the uncommon woman—can win out.

Gettel's speech was progressive, especially for 1954. In order to increase the female workforce and raise the level of performance in all occupations, he called for more widespread use of part-time workers, the granting of maternity leaves, greater willingness to hire and retrain mature women, fuller recognition of the ultimate utility of the delayed and interrupted careerist. The play, however, documents a disconnect between these feminist ideals and some of the anachronistic rituals of the college. It is also striking that all of Wasserstein's sources for *Uncommon Women,* except for George Eliot and Emily Dickinson's poem, come from men, not women—even with a women's college as her laboratory. Gettell shaped the mission statement: to produce "uncommon women" with "intellectual curiosity, hard work, and the spirit of adventure": "The college *produces* women who are persons in their own rights: uncommon women who as individuals have the personal dignity that comes with intelligence, competence, flexibility, maturity and a sense of responsibility. This can happen without loss of gaiety or charm" (emphasis mine).

Why would being an individual woman be *uncommon*? In addition, the suggestion is that gaiety and charm are usually at odds with intelligence, and that these feminine qualities must be maintained. The double standard is apparent. Would men's colleges say that intelligence does not interfere with their masculinity? Gettell continued:

> Throughout its long history Mount Holyoke has graduated women who helped, each in her own way, to make this a better and happier world. Whether their primary contributions were in the home or the wider community, in avocations or vocations, their role has been constructive. The College makes its continuing contribution to society in the form of graduates whose intellectual quality is high and whose responsibility to others is exceptional.

An "avocation" refers to "a hobby, a subordinate occupation," whereas a "vocation" denotes "a calling," "a summons to a particular course of action; work in which one is regularly employed." Such a distinction reflects the play's historical quality. Both the women's movement and the cost of living have made the option of working primarily at an "avocation" impossible for the majority of women. The division between home and society began to dissolve as more and more women dropped their kids at day care and headed to the office.

The Emily Dickinson poem inscribed in each edition of Holyoke's college bulletin erases the tension between aspirations and practicality.

> The Heart is the Capital of the Mind—
> The Mind is a single State—
> The Heart and the Mind together make
> A single Continent—
>
> One—is the Population—
> Numerous enough—
> This ecstatic Nation
> Seek—it is Yourself.

The heart is "the capital," the major force. However, it is incomplete without the intellect. The poem calls for uniting heart and mind in order to become a complete individual. Mount Holyoke, by way of Dickinson, was instructing students to combine their dreams with their abilities in order to become an "ecstatic Nation." In figuring the self as the nation, the poem magnifies the importance of the individual in an Emersonian way. Dickinson was, after all, writing in New England. But the poem conceives of the self apart from the nation; in fact, the self *is* the country, as Whitman would have it. As a nineteenth-century poet living in her father's house, Dickinson has no need to worry about worldly matters in this poem. Feminism, however, could not happen without adjustments in society. *Uncommon Women* says that women's hearts and minds had never before been so divided in America. Wasserstein appropriates many of the exact words from the bulletin and gives them to the male narrator. The action that follows often satirizes or ironizes those words.

For this reason, it is helpful to look at the juxtaposition of the action with the narration it follows. In scene one, the Man's Voice says, "The college produces uncommon women who are persons in their own right: Uncommon Women who as individuals have the personal dignity that comes with intelligence, competence, flexibility, maturity, and a sense of responsibility. This can happen without loss of gaiety, charm or femininity." Then we see Rita, in the present, trying to choose between bread baking, consciousness raising, and macramé. She has done nothing with her life but claims, "When I get it together I'm going to have a great novel." Six years earlier, in college, she says, "When the candy machine is empty, that's when I'm going to start my novel." She is Ms. Incomplete.

Later, after the Man's Voice asserts, "Miss Lyon's Seminary . . . was to do for women what Harvard and Yale were doing for men," someone says Mrs. Plumm has syphilis, another that there will be sherry and finger sandwiches. We then learn about the ritual of folding napkins for Gracious Living, about which Holly mockingly says, "When I get out of here, I'm never going to have dinner by candlelight in the wilderness with thirty-eight girls in hostess gowns. Unless I train for Amazon guerrilla warfare at the Junior League." Gracious Living began in 1950–51, when it is first mentioned in the freshman handbook. Historically, then, it belongs to the era of the feminine mystique. (By the 1969–70 academic year, the tradition was most often called "Gracious Dining." "Gracious Dinners" are still held in dorms on occasion.)

In addition, the college's high ideals are juxtaposed with the Holyoke song "Saving Ourselves for Yale":

Score for "We're Saving Ourselves for Yale." (Mount Holyoke College Archives and Special Collections/Wallace Literary Agency, Inc.)

Though we have had our chances
For overnight romances
With the Harvard and the Dartmouth male,

And though we've had a bunch in
Tow from Princeton Junction,
We're saving ourselves for Yale.
[solo] Mildred, Maud and Mabel
Were sitting at their table
Down at the Taft Hotel.
Working on a plan to
Catch themselves a man to
Brighten up their lives a spell. . .

Carter responds, "I knew we had a purpose." The juxtaposition is not only funny, but it reveals the tension between two worlds, between saving oneself for Yale on the one hand, and the professional goals pronounced by the president on the other, between the feminine mystique and the feminist movement.

In the next voice-over, the male voice articulates the predicament that these graduates will face in 1971, one that contemporary students have difficulty understanding:

The real problem for many educated women is the difficulty they have in recognizing whether they've been a success. . . . Women will be part-time mothers, part-time workers, part-time cooks, and part-time intellectuals. When scholars point out that even the best cooks have been men, the proper answer is, "But what man has been not only the second-best cook, but the third-best parent, the seventh-best typist, and the tenth-best community leader?" . . . an educated woman's capacity for giving is not exhausted, but stimulated by demands.

While telling women to be pioneers, the college paradoxically prepares women to serve others. Wasserstein adds the double standard to the voice-over: because women have traditionally juggled their work as homemakers with other kinds of work, they have not been able to excel in one profession the way men have. Or, as Samantha says, "I'm just a little talented at a lot of things." This part-time trend was representative of women at the time, as documented in the Holyoke bulletin:

Mount Holyoke graduates, like college-trained young women everywhere in the United States, marry. By the time a class has

Scene Four   20

The real problem for many educated women is the difficulty
they have in recognizing whether they have been a success..
Women will be part time daughters, part-time mothers, part-
time wives, part-time workers, part-time cooks, and part-time
intellectuals. When scholars point out that even the best
cooks have been men, the proper answer is, "But what man has
been not only the second best cook, but the third best parent,
the seventh best typist, the third most considerate child,
and the tenth best community leader. Just like the pot of
honey that kept renewing itself whenever any was taken from it,
an educated woman's capacity for giving is not exhausted but
stimulated by demans.

                    Muffet in negligee and argyle socks
                    lies on a bed. Carter is silent and
                    sits on the floor in baggy pants and
                    shirts.
          Muffet
I'm so tired. Why doesn't someone just take me away from all
this?.....(Noticing Carter for amoment) Ush, what's wrong with
your leg? How come it's so pink? Is that a bite or a fungus?
(She extends her leg towards the ceiling) I don't like the
way hair looks on my leg, do you? But I've taken a stand
body hair. ~~I don't want to be manipulated by the cosmetic establishment~~
Oh, well. (She sings and taps her finger on the bed.) I'm a
little acorn round, sitting on the cold, cold, ground. Everyone
steps on me. That is why I'm squashed you see. I'm a nut.
I'm a nut." That's a ditty Samantha taught me. Did you ever
notice how walking into Samantha's room is like walking into
a clean sheet. She's very sweet, but after two conversations
the baby-talk and rhyming couplets run pretty vapid. (laughs
to herself.) She and Susie Friend celebrate Piglet's birthday. (Pause.) Kate's says you're very bright. She's sort of
hipless and I'm better in the chest. XXXXXXXXXXXXXXXXXXXX
Actually, I'm pretty happy I'm not in the world's 2% mutants.
     Did I tell you what happened in Chip Knowles's women's
history class today? Do you know Chip Knowles? He's the
young Mr. Chips around here. He always wears tweed jackets with

Typed page from a draft of *Uncommon Women* explaining the "real problem for educated women." (Courtesy of the Wendy Wasserstein estate)

been out ten years, more than nine-tenths of its members are
married and many of them devote a number of years exclusively
to bringing up a family. But immediately after commencement,
nearly all Mount Holyoke graduates either get jobs or continue
studying. . . .

In 1968, when David Reisman gave Holyoke's commencement speech, he offered a solution for the inevitable conflict between career and marriage. Women, he argued, should be allowed to have their careers "simmer" while raising families, during which time they can study, and then return to work in a serious part-time way when their children go to school. Further, he observed, women often have thirty years left in their career at this point, because they live longer than men. Although most women feel unconfident about returning to work after a long absence, "it's not difficult to catch up, especially when women learn how to learn":

> What many young women coming out of colleges like Mount Holyoke desire is motherhood PLUS, not career MINUS. My interest is in exploring the nature of that plus. . . . There are many occupations our culture assigns largely to men—those careers, which I am convinced women could do better [those in the medical, dental, and legal professions].

The same women who were solving chemistry problems, reading literature, performing in plays and on the field, went on to serve their families, without adequate time to devote to themselves and to their communities. Reisman warned against such subservience by calling for a reversal of stereotypes. He concluded, "As American society becomes less demanding of men, it will become 'freer for women' in a post-industrial culture where a good meaningful life becomes more important than survival or getting ahead." In the play, the narrator echoes this idea when he says:

> Mary Lyon, sending her early students out across the plains and seas as teachers and missionaries, said, "Go where no one else will go. Do what no one else will do." Some of her 25,000 "daughters" have blazed new trails. . . . Today alums and students are serving their families and communities with generosity and imagination . . . ready to meet the unknown with steadiness and gaiety.

The structure of the action, however, belies these values: Carter's elf (a senior who provides surprises) sets her up on a double date; Kate wishes she could leave college; Chip Knowles, a male professor, teaches the women's history course; the college has a male president. After reading about suffragettes, Muffet reports that a French student has not prepared her report on Rosie the Riveter—the female icon of American labor during World War II when women entered factories to replace men at war. Rosie symbolizes all women who worked long, hard hours, "ensuring our boys had the necessary tools of war." The French student claims instead that the women in the class should focus more on their sexuality than on their intellect. While Rita and Holly protest her sentiment, Muffet agrees with it:

> I suppose this isn't a very impressive sentiment, but men are very important to me. . . . I would really like to meet my prince. Even a few princes. And I wouldn't give up being a person. I'd still remember all the Art History dates. I just don't know why suddenly I'm supposed to know what I want to do. . . . I just hate going to bed alone . . . I'm not even worried about next year. I just have to make sure something happens to me.

Muffet's version of being an independent woman is memorizing facts, and self-definition is a burden. She longs for more conventional values, but she is not the only woman in the play who waits for "Male L.D.s"— male long-distance calls that punctuate the action.

Rita's feelings forecast the first issue of *Ms.* magazine in which Vivian Gornick explains "Why Women Fear Success." Contrary to the belief that "women simply do not have the constitution for normal competition," she used Harvard psychologist Matina Horner's research that proved "unusual excellence in women was clearly associated for them with the loss of femininity, social rejection, personal or societal destruction or some combination of the above." Moreover, Horner found that "the fear of success manifested itself mainly in women of high intelligence" who came from homes where high achievement was valued. But by junior year in college, if not before, parents admonished their daughters "to be securely married, rather than take the unconventional and risky course of becoming a serious working person." Therefore, young women received a contradictory message: if they are too smart, too independent, and, above all, too serious about their work, they are unfeminine and will therefore never get married. The apparent liberation that women had achieved since the mid sixties did not diminish this "avoidance of success." The feminine mystique was still deeply entrenched in our society. Accordingly, the action of the play contradicts the college's mission to produce women who are ready to meet the unknown with courage.

In the next male voice-over, we hear, "A student should examine not only her academic interest, but also her conception of the good life, and the kind of community she would like to fashion." The action that follows consists of Kate sneaking a reading of a Jacqueline Susann novel about a man's seduction of a woman, while claiming to be reading *The Genealogy of Morals,* and Holly filling a diaphragm, which she compares with a yarmulke, with Ortho-Creme. In addition, the conflict between Kate and Leilah emerges, revealing that a women's college is not necessarily a sisterhood but a fierce competition—for grades, men, beauty, and popularity. Leilah and Kate, who roomed together for three years, have lost their former closeness. Kate asks Leilah whether she is angry over the two men who fell in love with her during their junior year in Greece, and whether Leilah is giving up further study in philosophy "because I'm Phi Bet and you're not?" Leilah later explains her feelings about Kate to Muffet:

> Sometimes when I'm in the library studying, I look up and I count the Katies and the Leilahs. They're always together. And they seem a very similar species. But if you observe a while longer, the Katies seem kind of magical, and the Leilahs are highly competent. And they're usually such good friends. . . . But I find myself secretly hoping that when we leave here, Katie and I will just naturally stop speaking.

Leilah wants to go to Iraq "to be in a less competitive culture." In terms of the structure of her scene with Kate, then, the presidential "conception of the good life" turns out to be the female locker room—full of sex-talk and competition. Trying to console Leilah, Muffet proposes that they go out on the town, like "two Uncommon Women, mysterious but proud."

The male presidential voice tries to be feminist when he asserts that "anatomy is not destiny," contradicting Freud's view. Rita strongly disagrees. Demonstrating with her hand the vertical and horizontal qualities of the buildings and roads, she mocks Freud's patriarchal theories:

> This entire society is based on cocks. The New York Times, Walter Cronkite, all the buildings and roads, the cities, philosophy, government, history, religion, shopping malls—everything I can name is

Gloria Steinem on *The Phil Donahue Show*, 1970. (NBC/Photofest)

male. When I see things this way, it becomes obvious that it's very easy to feel alienated and alone for the simple reason that I came into the world without a penis.

The play asks whether well-educated women can transcend a patriarchal society. As Rita says, "Our entire being is programmed for male approval," for which she wants vengeance: men "should be forced to answer phones on a white Naugahyde receptionist's chair with a cotton lollipop stuck up their crotch." But she is convinced that even if men experienced the same biological process as women, they would never really understand women. Rita's sentiments echo Gloria Steinem's article called "If Men Could Menstruate—A Political Fantasy," in which she humorously but earnestly argued the following:

> Menstruation would become an enviable, boast-worthy, masculine event: Men would brag about how long and how much. . . . Sanitary supplies would be federally funded and free. . . . Military men, right-wing politicians, and religious fundamentalists would cite "men-struation" as proof that only men could serve in the Army. . . . In fact, if men could menstruate, the power justifications could probably go on forever. If we let them.

In the same spirit, Samantha wants to know if men have breast and womb envy, to which Kate humorously responds, "If they have it, they just become creative or cook dinner every now and then." Holly also alludes to a patriarchal literary tradition that Wasserstein's plays attempt to subvert when she says boys "write with their cocks." She resents the fact that men have the confidence and options that women lack.

Accordingly, in 1968, David Reisman reminded Holyoke graduates that "women have to be better than men to get half as good opportunities." Of course, that academic double standard reflected a social double standard. Holly does not want to fall in love, because, she says, "If I fall in love it will be because I think someone is better than me. And if I really thought someone was better than me, I'd give him everything and I'd hate him for my living through him."

However, by the end of the scene, Holly sneaks off to a phone in the corner and leaves a desperate message with the answering service of a Dr. Mark Silverstein, whom she fleetingly met at the Fogg Museum in Boston, giving her name as Simone de Beauvoir and asking to be treated like an adult. Published in 1952, de Beauvoir's *The Second Sex* would have been a staple on Mount Holyoke's syllabi. De Beauvoir's revolutionary book revised the way women talked and thought about themselves. Drawing on interviews with women of every age and on her research about women's bodies and psyches, as well as their historic and economic roles, *The Second Sex* verified that "since patriarchal times women have been forced to occupy a secondary place in the world in relation to men" and that this subordination results from "strong environmental forces of educational and social tradition under the purposeful control of men." The desperate search for the doctor, of course, could not be farther from Simone de Beauvoir's goals for independent women, except perhaps that Holly initiates the call, which would have been considered inappropriate by the standards of the feminine mystique.

After the college president's voice announces that the college "places at its center the content of human learning and the spirit of systematic disinterested inquiry," Holly dials Dr. Mark Silverstein again from her dorm room, with systematic, *interested* inquiry. James Taylor's "Fire and Rain" plays in the background, echoing Holly's "thought I'd see you one more time again" feeling, her mournful loneliness. In the public television production of *Uncommon Women,* a poster of James Taylor looms on Holly's wall. Alone on her bed, wrapped in her raccoon coat,

Holly says into the phone, "I'm having trouble remembering what I want." Freud famously asked, "What do women want?" and failed to answer the question. Holly's confession conveys the confusion that many women were feeling in the early seventies, when their choices were not as simple as they once had been. In addition, she articulates the female self-effacement that becomes one of the play's central concerns: "I guess women are just not as scary as men and therefore they don't count as much . . . I guess they just always make me feel worthwhile." Samantha similarly subordinates herself to her fiancé and wants to live vicariously through him. In love with an actor, Robert Cabe, she says: "He's handsome and talented, and he's better than me and he'll love me. . . . I want to be his audience, and have my picture behind him in my long tartan kilt, in the *New York Times* Arts and Leisure section." When she is with her husband's friends, she says, "I think I haven't done very much of anything important. So I don't talk." Rita, too, needs external validation about her identity, wishing she could be herself "without any embarrassment or neurosis, and since that's practically impossible," she confesses she'd like to be Samantha. They are all uncomfortable in their own skin.

Accordingly, sociologist David Reisman spoke to Holyoke's class of 1968 about "women as they looked forward to careers where they face discriminations more subtle than those of a traditional Jim Crow pattern, but hardly less destructive of accomplishment and feelings of personal worth." While interviews with 1967 Holyoke students conveyed that coed classrooms were more vivacious than all-female classrooms, Reisman understood "that coed colleges and perhaps academic culture in general suffer from largely unconscious male hegemony, and this imposes subtle constraints on the coeds who are admitted on the men's own terms." The Seven Sisters colleges, therefore, represented the solution. Mount Holyoke, he maintained, "belongs to that group of women's colleges which has sought to overtake and surpass men academically. Women study as if their very lives depended on it even though they know that it will make them less adaptable to the interests and the career of the man whom they will marry." Kate and Leilah exemplify this fact. Reisman's research found that women were outperforming men in coed colleges, and yet in 1968, women "have to be better than men to get half as good opportunities."

In the play, the juxtaposition of the male voice-over and the action that follows it reveals that the fathers of these women continued to perceive educated women as sexual objects: Muffet receives an Easter bunny from Susie Friend's CEO father—right after the male voice pronounces that the college not only instills knowledge but prepares women for "learning unfamiliar techniques." The play affirms that this is the world that awaits smart women in 1971.

The goals of the college, as articulated in the student handbook, continue to contrast humorously with the anachronisms of the students' lives when the male voice speaks over the Milk and Crackers hour as the students slather "large globs of Fluff on their fingers and crackers." The president's voice says, "Students at the college are expected to encounter a wide range of opportunities—that is to say, uncertainties. A maturing mind must have an ethical base, a set of values, and wonder at the unknown." Moreover, in that scene Samantha announces her engagement to the man she will stand behind, Robert Cabe, and Carter reveals her problem with bulimia. Further, when the male voice announces in scene four, "the college fosters . . . the necessity for strenuous and sustained effort in any area of endeavor," Samantha's words again undermine the president's:

> Robert says that I never grew up into a woman. That I'm sort of a child woman. . . . Women who are wives of artists and actors . . . believe their husbands are geniuses, and they are just a little talented. Well, that's what I am. Just a little talented at a lot of things. That's why I want to be with Robert and all of you. I want to be with someone who makes a public statement. And . . . if I'm going to devote my uncommon talents to relationships, then I might as well nurture those that are a bit difficult. It makes me feel a little special.

This is exactly the problem Betty Friedan talks about in her chapter called "The Crisis in Woman's Identity" in *The Feminine Mystique*. She writes:

> When we were growing up, many of us could not see ourselves beyond the age of twenty-one. We had no image of our own future, of ourselves as women. . . . The feminine mystique permits, even encourages, women to ignore the question of their identity. The mystique says they can answer the question "Who am I?" by saying, "Tom's wife . . . Mary's mother."

While Rita speaks out against marriage as subordination, she understands its attraction, telling Samantha, "At least you made a choice. . . . None of the rest of us has made any decisions." Fraught with indecision, Rita has *Let's Make a Deal* nightmares, where the audience tells her to forget the unknown prize behind the curtain and "TAKE THE BOX!" The game show becomes a metaphor for uncertain decisions and a mysterious future. Kate has just been accepted to law school but does not think she should go: "I don't want my life simply to fall into place." Still, she has "a stake in all those Uncommon Women expectations." Unlike Samantha, for Kate becoming an attorney is fulfilling her uncommon duty. She tells Carter, who is priming for her typing test, "If I didn't fulfill obligations or weren't exemplary, then I really don't know what I'd do." In this way, Samantha and Kate represent two ends of the spectrum for this transitional period for women.

Their housemother, Mrs. Plumm, based on Mrs. Camilla Peach, who was actually the housemother for Wasserstein's freshman dorm, marks the end of an era when she embraces the decision to abolish the ritual of Gracious Living in 1972. The vote acknowledges the beginning of a more progressive era for women—a difficult transition. It seems no historical accident that Wasserstein's graduation coincides with the first issue of *Ms.* magazine, folded into *New York Magazine* in 1971. On its bold red cover, *Ms.* featured a woman with eight arms holding an iron, a steering wheel, a mirror, a telephone, a clock, a dust

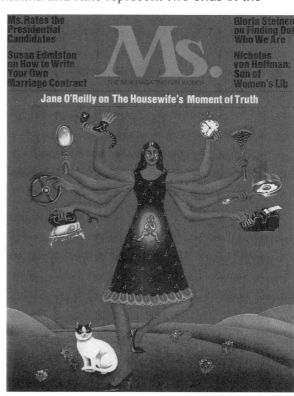

Ms. magazine cover of 1972, symbolically depicting the overworked housewife. (Reprinted by permission of *Ms.* magazine, © 1972)

broom, a pan with a fried egg, and a typewriter—and a fetus in her stomach. As she stands on a manicured lawn, complete with flowers and pet cat, tears drop from her eyes. This issue featured "Sisterhood," by Gloria Steinem, "The Housewife's Moment of Truth," by Jane O'Reilly, Nicholas von Hoffman's "My Mother, the Dentist," and "Rating the Candidates: Feminists Vote Rascals In or Out." This last article rated the candidates in the next presidential primary—Muskie, Nixon, Mills, Chisholm, Kennedy, Lindsay, Jackson, Humphrey, McGovern, McCarthy, and McCloskey—according to feminist standards. "Making Waves" signified "independence, the ability to challenge the status quo." "The Machismo Factor" meant "personal rejection of the traditional 'masculine' role and opposition to militarism and violence." The research conveyed that Richard Nixon and Henry Jackson received the worst rating for all categories, while Shirley Chisholm, Eugene McCarthy, and George McGovern earned the most points. An African-American presidential candidate and two men who voted progressively made 1971 a progressive year. They coincide perfectly with the end of Gracious Living, making *Uncommon Women* not just a play about Mount Holyoke College, but also a barometer of American politics. For both the graduates and the nation, this new era would not be easy, as indicated by the red marks next to Nixon and Jackson.

Like the graduates in the play, Mrs. Plumm, too, is in transition, heading to Bolivia on an ornithological expedition with her old friend, Dr. Ada Grudder. She never had this choice when she was a student; instead, her father, forbidding her to buy the rifles that she and her friend believed were necessary to protect them on bird-watching trips, urged her to get married and teach bird watching at the high school. Rebellious, she and her friend set up a firing range on campus, but she still married two years later.

Although Mrs. Plumm is ready for a new chapter in women's history, the students do not feel prepared for the new world outside. Muffet humorously says, "I am prepared for life. I can fold my napkin with the best of them." Wasserstein reflects, "That one gesture [of folding their napkins and placing them carefully in a cubby hole after every meal] says a lot about what women were thinking, how they saw themselves, their limitations." In college, at least, some of the women challenge these limitations with energy, like Rita, who shouts to her friends that she has met Germaine Greer's test of a liberated woman by tasting her menstrual blood. After graduation, she reads Doris Lessing and delights in having her husband wait on her. The other women at the reunion marvel that a classmate has joined a lesbian rock band; Muffet takes a stand on birth control pills, because she does not want to be controlled by the pharmaceutical establishment; and Kate, the successful attorney, declares that she is a feminist. Yet she also reflects, "I guess it never occurred to me in college that someone would not want me to be quite so uncommon."

Such discussions and others elicited outrage from Holyoke alums who felt the play denigrated their college when it aired on public television in 1978. The generation gap was striking in every way. The play was not an indictment of Mount Holyoke, but rather a satiric representation of an American society, reflected in colleges nationwide, that was not ready for its uncommon women. Although President Gettell announced in his 1957 inaugural speech, "Uncommon Women have broken the ice by entering many occupations formerly reserved to men," the ice, nevertheless, was still mostly frozen.

When Wasserstein departs from the actual words of the Holyoke college bulletin in scene eight, and the male voice-over fades out into a female one, the true predicaments of being a woman become honestly articulated: "Women still encounter overwhelming obstacles to achievement and recognition despite gradual abolition of legal and political disabilities. Society has trained women from childhood to accept a limited set of options and restricted levels of aspiration." Carter, for instance, who aspires to make a documentary of Wittgenstein, crams for her typing test, because she says, "I need fifty words a minute to get a good job when I get out of here." In fact, Carter represents the realities of the 1972 job market for women, documented by *New York Magazine:* "June is the month when a woman graduating from college discovers that whatever she studied in school, and however equally she and her classmates have been treated in class, she has to take a typing test to get a job." The typing test symbolizes the ironic situation that awaited women when they exited the gates of the college where they had grappled with philosophy, literature, math, and chemistry. Women with college degrees earned significantly less money than degree-holding men.

In scene seven, the male president's voice pronounces the career options for female graduates in 1971: "Today all fields are open to women, and more than fifty percent continue in professional or graduate school. Any one of a variety of majors may lead to a position as girl Friday for an eastern senator, service volunteer in Venezuela, or assistant sales director of *Reader's Digest.*" A liberal arts education allowed a young woman to assist a man, rather than be a professional in her own right. Telling graduates that they could aspire to become a girl Friday meant that they could look forward to being the woman behind the scenes, facilitating the work for her male employer. In Howard Hawks's 1940 film, *His Girl Friday*, news reporter Cary Grant lures his ex-wife, Rosalind Russell, away from her marriage to another man in order to return as his partner in journalism. Without her, he cannot uncover the Chicago murder mystery. Thirty years before Wasserstein's uncommon women graduated from Mount Holyoke, Russell's character was torn between career and marriage but managed to get both the career and the guy. Having it all, however, seemed only the province of movies. In real life, women with diplomas could become assistants or volunteers. (After the 1969–1970 bulletin, however, the term "girl Friday" disappeared.) In this context, the Emily Dickinson poem that Mrs. Plumm recites during "Gracious Living" reads ironically. Could the heart be capital of the mind when the nation at large placed limitations on women? Perhaps Samantha's suggestion, at the end of the play, that they see *Cries and Whispers*, Ingmar Bergman's 1972 dark film about the reunion of three sisters, oddly resonates with the situation of American women at the time. It dramatized "painful revelations and long-suppressed emotions." In 1971, according to Wasserstein, the women's movement sounded like cries and whispers.

Women of subsequent generations, however, regard the play as something of a "period piece." Of course it is. Holyoke students in recent years have said, "The women at your time were so confused about sex and graduate school. We're not confused. We know we're going to professional school, and we know all about sex." Wasserstein reflects on this reaction in her essay "Mrs. Smith Goes to Washington":

> These students, most of them only twenty years old, seemed both competent and confident—already pretty amazing. In fact, most of them already had life plans mapped out. Blue for long-term personal goals, red for short-term career decisions. . . . I wonder what will happen to those students who seem so secure, so certain, when they discover that a piece of the pie doesn't fit. What happens if they fall out of the norm and life gets messy, unbalanced just a bit?

Each phase of progress comes with new challenges. Sociologist Reisman's 1968 commencement address to Holyoke students speaks equally to today:

> We [are] living in a time which presents greater possibilities of choice to more people than ever before. It is such choices which present you with the dilemmas of the educated woman, providing you with the education to ponder the dilemmas without being paralyzed by them, while moving toward destinations that will be interesting, often troublesome, and remarkably unforeseen.

Mary Lyon, the founder of Holyoke, had encouraged students to embrace the unknown years earlier. Both Lyon and Reisman were encouraging women to be courageous in the face of the uncertainty that came with change. Lyon wished that "our daughters may be as cornerstones, polished after the similitude of a palace." She was envisioning women as the foundation of society, and for Wasserstein, having tea in hostess gowns did not seem the best way to prepare for that role. The end of Gracious Living marks the end of an era. When the class of 1971 walked through the campus gates with their diplomas, books, fraternity pins, and hockey sticks, they waved good-bye to hostess gowns and Gracious Living. They were confused as they loaded their trunks into their parents' cars. The world outside would neither resemble a Seven Sisters college, nor would it be ready for its uncommon women. *Uncommon Women* is about that gap.

The Brooklyn Bridge and Manhattan at night. In *Isn't It Romantic*, Brooklyn symbolizes Jewish identity as opposed to the "Babylon" of New York. (Andreas Feininger)

2

Isn't It Romantic (1983)

Can Women Have It All?

You mean having it all? That's just your generation's fantasy.
—Lillian Cornwall

By 1983, some of the graduates from *Uncommon Women* had unpacked their trunks in New York City, searching for love and professional fulfillment. Janie Blumberg is the daughter of Jewish parents who worry about her safety and desperately want her to get married, while Harriet Cornwall is the daughter of a professional, divorced WASP mother, Lillian, who encourages her to pursue her career before marriage. Janie meets Marty Sterling, originally Murray Schlimovitz, a Jewish doctor with a specialty in kidneys, who wants to marry her and move to Brooklyn. But she feels suffocated by him because he views her as his future wife, rather than as an individual with her own aspirations.

While Janie takes a part-time job at *Sesame Street*, Harriet, a Harvard MBA, gets promoted at Colgate-Palmolive. Harriet has an affair with her boss's boss, "the sadist vice president," then leaves him for the headhunter who found her the Colgate job. (Headhunters, executive recruiters who matched professionals with corporations, became popular in the early eighties.) After a whirlwind courtship, she decides to marry the headhunter, Joe Stine. Janie feels abandoned and betrayed by her best friend, who always insisted on the importance of independence and considered herself Janie's "family." In this way, *Isn't It Romantic* anticipates *The Heidi Chronicles*, in which Heidi feels her peers have abandoned the ideals of the women's movement. According to Wasserstein, *Isn't It Romantic* is about "women being told how to live their lives, with the rules changing every six months."

In earlier drafts of the play, Harriet returned from Italy, where she escaped after college, to look for jobs at Proctor and Gamble, General Foods, and advertising agencies. Harriet was without job or home, and the conflict between her and her mother was more central. In the finished play, however, it is Janie who learns to insist that her overprotective parents treat her like "a grown woman" who must and can make her own decisions.

While Janie and Harriet are trying to figure out their relationships with men and with each other, we hear the phone messages of Janie's old friend, Cynthia Peterson (originally played by Meryl Streep), desperately recording her rejection by the Upper West Side male population, and messages from Janie's parents singing "Sunrise, Sunset" from *Fiddler on the Roof.* Wasserstein borrows the theatrical device of the answering machine from the seventies television detective drama *The Rockford Files*, which Lillian Cornwall watches after work. Like the television drama, each scene begins with a recorded message. In an early draft, Janie says about the "Sunrise" message, "They're practicing for the wedding," because in *Fiddler*, the song accompanies the traditional Jewish wedding ceremony. Moreover, *Fiddler* resonates with *Isn't It Romantic*'s concern about the need to break tradition in order to be true to oneself. But here the tradition is marriage altogether, not just marrying within one's faith.

Isn't It Romantic, then, explores relationships between women, between mothers and daughters, and between men and women. Frank Rich saw the conflict between Janie and Marty as archetypal. On the night he saw the play, he hand-wrote an impassioned letter to Wasserstein in which he said, "You've hit on something fundamental about the choices we all make. . . . I really think *Isn't It Romantic* will speak to everyone, or at least everyone sensitive. . . ." Moreover, writing about relationships meant exploring the situation of women in 1983 and whether women could "have it all" in a society that continued to be sexist. This theme recurs throughout Wasserstein's canon, as do questions about Jewish-American identity in a WASP culture. Being female in a patriarchal society, it seemed, was not unlike being Jewish in an Anglo-American one.

Wasserstein chose New York—the financial, intellectual, and artistic capital of the United States—as the setting for *Isn't It Romantic* for im-

FRANK RICH
30 BEEKMAN PLACE
NEW YORK, NEW YORK 10022

Thursday night

Dear Wendy,

It was impossible to tell you at La Rousse how overwhelmed I was by your play. Partially because of the circumstances – but just as much because of the strong feelings the play aroused. Indeed, comparisons between the old "Isn't It Romantic?" and the new one ludicrous – for it seems to me that the cuts, narrative changes and so on (the improved carpentry of the play) are beside the point. What's really important about the new version is that you said honestly and exactly what you wanted to say — and said it so eloquently that the play hit home to me in a way it never had before. Which is to say that I now really understand what Janie wants — and who she is — and what Marty wants — and who he is. And in that conflict you've hit on something fundamental about the choices we all make. I found it devastating — just as I did the conflict between Janie and Harriet, which crystallized and moved me in a more forceful way than it did before. I really think "Isn't It Romantic?" (excuse me for adding the question mark — I'll stop) will speak to everyone, or at least everyone sensitive, quite apart from their feelings about nouvelle cuisine.

Frank Rich's letter to Wasserstein admiring *Isn't It Romantic*.
(Courtesy of Frank Rich)

portant reasons. It has been the home of the largest Jewish population in the United States ever since the first Jewish settlers landed in New Amsterdam in 1654 and a gateway for immigrants in general. The Upper West Side, where Cynthia Peterson lives, as did Wasserstein, has also been a largely Jewish neighborhood, populated with German Jews who moved there at the turn of the century, and Jewish refugees escaping Hitler's Europe in the thirties. In 1983, the Upper West Side is not only where Janie spills horseradish on Marty's sister-in-law and small nephew, Schlomo, at Chanukah, but also an upscale home to New York City's liberal, cultural, and artistic workers.

Janie says, "I scream here on Central Park South." This section of 59th Street along the southern end of Central Park, bound by Columbus Circle to the west and Fifth Avenue to the east, reflects the wealth of the characters in *Isn't It Romantic.* Central Park South is the home of the Ritz-Carlton and former Plaza Hotels. Harriet and Lillian Cornwall dine at the Four Seasons restaurant, famous for its wooden bar, bubbling marble pool, and New York celebrities. They eat ice-cream sundaes and buy stuffed animals at the legendary Rumpelmayer's Ice Cream parlor, which was located in the St. Moritz Hotel. The Blumbergs eat brunch at Oscar's at the Waldorf Astoria on Park and Forty-ninth just across the street from Colgate-Palmolive, where Harriet works—near Morgan Stanley and Botticelli's as well as the Princeton and Columbia Clubs. Janie's prospective wedding was going to take place at the Carlyle Hotel on East Seventy-sixth Street, where Bobby Short played regularly for socialites. An early draft of the play referenced the Empire Diner on Tenth Avenue and Twenty-second Street, but Wasserstein decided to confine her setting to the most elite neighborhoods of Manhattan. The farthest north we go is Rye, New York, where Marty's patient, Mrs. Rosen, lives and Harriet visits. With Central Park in its center, Manhattan is pastoral and romantic, yet quintessentially urban and unromantic, representing the ambiguous and ironic nature of romance that the play presents.

Moreover, as Frank Rich observes, Manhattan started out being the nation's capital and is more representative of America's political values than Washington, D.C.:

> Manhattan has . . . been . . . the site of classic American battles between money and values, between commerce and art, between powerful interests and upstart citizenry, between past and future—all staged on America's largest urban frontier. And, New York is a place where neighborhoods reinvent themselves faster than anyone can keep count . . . the byproducts include hyphenated talents, melting-pot families, a . . . laboratory for social, political and cultural change in which the experiments . . .

succeed big and fail catastrophically in full public view. Manhattan is a city in perpetual renewal, pursuing creation and demolition with equal abandon, always testing the limits.

Accordingly, New York is the perfect setting for chronicling the difficult transition that women were experiencing in the early eighties.

Cynthia Peterson's Upper West Side is full of frustration and disappointment for a single woman. She desperately leaves messages on Janie's answering machine about her search for an eligible bachelor: "Everything is awful. I'm getting divorced. I'm looking for a job. There are no men. Call me." In fact, sociologists determined that by the end of the eighties, two-thirds of all first marriages in the United States would end in divorce. The more economically independent women were, the more optional marriage became. More Americans were finding personal services, satisfaction, and leisure outside the family. Scholars of the family also noted a shift from a communal sensibility to an individual one, resulting in "a flight from commitment."

Later, Cynthia records on Janie's answering machine, "I have been rejected by every man on the Upper West Side," and her last phone message laments a *New York Post* report that "There are 1,000 men for every 1,123 New York hubby hunters." Wasserstein was registering a sociological fact: in 1983 there were 55 million singles over eighteen in the U.S., compared to 4 million never-married adults in 1950. The number of never-married singles grew from 10.9 million in 1970 to 19.4 million in 1982, a seventy-eight percent increase. According to the Census Bureau, the increasing number of unmarried people in the pivotal thirty-to-thirty-four age bracket suggested "that an increasing proportion of persons may never marry." Whereas in 1957 American culture regarded the failure to marry "as a pathology," by the mid-seventies being single could increase one's happiness. Many Americans began focusing on the burdens and restrictions of marriage, rather than on its opportunities.

By 1983, being single had become a positive choice for many women that enabled them to pursue careers, increase their freedom, and develop friendships like Janie's and Harriet's, which improved self-esteem. It is significant to note that in 2007, the Sunday *New York Times* ran an article called "Why Are There So Many Single Americans?" and concluded that "the 'marriage gap' isn't about men and women. It's about class and education." But the demographics have changed. It used to be the case that the more educated the woman, the higher her earning power, the more culturally liberal her values would be, and therefore the less likely that she would marry. More recently, however, statistics reveal that "economic resources are conducive to stable marriages." The stereotype of the competitive career woman collapsing on her desk alone at night with Chinese take-out has apparently changed. Instead, according to the *Times*, "women who have more money or the potential for more money are married to men who have more stable incomes." Moreover, marriages with more stable income seem happier. "Better educated husbands and wives tend to share intellectual interests and economic backgrounds, as well as ideas about the division of household roles." In addition, there are more single women now than before, because so many women are financially independent. Therefore, the relationship between education, marriage, and career, as dramatized in *Isn't It Romantic*, has changed.

In 1983, however, Janie decides to remain single because of Marty Sterling's sexism. He calls Janie "Monkey," claims that his female colleagues in medicine, like Harriet, "bite your balls off," and wants Janie to mother him: "Be sweet. I need attention. A great deal of attention." Trying to convince Janie to marry him, he patronizes her without even being aware of it. He tells her that his sister-in-law, who is bright but has "less direction than Janie," married his brother blindly: "She'll go back to work in something nice. She'll teach or work with the elderly— and she won't conquer the world, but she'll have a nice life. Monkey, I don't want to be alone." Marty reduces a woman's work to "something nice," to a social service that will never have a large impact on the world. When Janie chooses to go to her *Sesame Street* interview instead of to Marty's brother's anniversary party, he responds, "Don't let it take over your life . . . our life. That's a real trap. You don't want a life like that." He envisions her alone, staying up late to write, choosing artificial insemination, "com[ing] home to Cynthia Peterson's phone calls," and warns her that that life "isn't right for me. And I'll tell you something, Janie: it isn't right for you either." As psychologists observe, men like to initiate action, and Marty characterizes Janie as "a little disorganized" and himself as "a little bit of a nudge. So if I don't make the arrangements, what's going to happen?" He is "trying to move forward" according to traditional values that are beginning to disappear: "All I want is a home, a family, something my father had so easily and I can't seem to get started on. Why?" According to him, "All [Janie has] to do is put your crates that you never unpacked on that truck and get on the Belt Parkway" to join him in their new home. He never considers what Janie will do or become beyond the Parkway. This missing connection between men and women in the eighties becomes a metaphor when, on one of the answering machine recordings, the operator says, "There seems to be a receiver off the hook." Janie can only marry someone who "will listen." She tells Marty, "You have all the answers before I ask the questions." Marriage, she believes, would interfere with her work, which she enjoys. "I may have stumbled into something I actually care about. And right now I don't want to do it part-time and pretend that it's real when it would actually be a hobby. I want a life too." She concludes that Marty is "not right for [her]."

When Marty and Janie exchanged these lines in 1983, a new study called *American Couples* by Blumstein and Schwartz affirmed that for men, money [and career] represent identity and power, while for women, careers represent "security and autonomy," which seems to be the dynamic in the dialogue above. Women who work, they reported, "have more clout in their marriages than those who don't," and Marty is uncomfortable with female power. He believes that Janie makes "everything . . . harder than it has to be." In a society that continued to view women's careers second to men's, it was still difficult for women to meet men who understood their professional aspirations.

Harriet also battles male chauvinism. Her boss tells her that her ideas are "too theoretical" and then sells those very ideas the next day as his own. Her mother assures her that chauvinism in the workplace is no worse than having "your husband steal your ideas." Her boyfriend Paul Stuart also displays sexism. After Harriet announces that she no longer wants to see him, he dismisses it by snapping his fingers "as if to say see you later." He tells Harriet that he cannot be the nurturing kind of male that she wants, one who sees her as " a potential mother, but also is someone who isn't threatened by [her] success and is deeply interested in it . . . but when you need him, he should drop whatever it is he's doing and be supportive." He explains his frustration: "Everything is a negotiation . . . the girls I date now . . . the MBAs from Harvard—they want me to be the wife. They want me to be the support system. Well, I can't do that. I just wasn't told that's the way it was supposed to be." Harriet and Paul are at a standstill, not wanting to be alone, not wanting to move forward, "blocking each other's lives." Once again Wasserstein catches America in transition, when men like Marty and Paul Stuart feel insecure about professional women and are unable to bridge the gap between their conventional values and the more liberal ones they need to accommodate independent, successful women.

Marty and Paul's discomfort with feminism could be understood as a reflection of a national conservatism marked by the election of Ronald Reagan in 1980. It was the first time more men than women had voted for a president. According to journalist Susan Faludi, the evangelical right produced a backlash in the seventies that brought a fundamentalist ideology to the White House of the early eighties and encouraged traditional gender roles. The New Right was telling America that "women's equality is responsible for women's unhappiness," that it "turned women into greedy yuppies," and that it "dismantled the traditional familial support system." Faludi maintains that Reaganomics, the recession, and the expansion of a minimum-wage service economy undermined women's progress in the job market. In fact, women working full-time made only sixty-four cents to a man's dollar—the same gap they faced in 1955. In the corporate world, where Harriet works, women experienced "inequity and intimidation." In the entertainment industry, where Janie works, women were not surviving in high-level positions. Moreover, the Republican platform no longer supported the Equal Rights Amendment (which after a ten-year battle had still not been ratified), and it officially opposed a woman's right to choose. In 1983, feminist Alice Schwarzer agreed with Faludi that America was blaming women's problems on feminism when the real problem was that women had not achieved parity with men.

Beneath the chauvinism that Harriet Cornwall faces at Colgate-Palmolive lurked the problem of competition that Suzanne Gordon called "the new corporate feminism" in a 1983 article in the *Nation:*

> a brand of feminism designed to sell books and magazines, three-piece suits, airline tickets, Scotch, cigarettes and, most important, corporate America's message, which runs: Yes, women were discriminated against in the past, but that unfortunate mistake has been remedied; now every woman can attain wealth, prestige and power by dint of individual rather than collective effort.

Many of the women who once hoped to revolutionize the system were being trained as its administrators, and they needed a corporate education and an ideology that enabled them to reconcile the hopes of the past with the realities of the present. The women's movement grew out of a critique of male power and of the price men pay for their dominant position. According to some feminists, men had failed to balance their personal and professional lives, which made equality between men and women impossible. In 1983, driven women in business seemed to follow that male pattern, causing "progressive politics" to fragment. Women were becoming "company women." In the play both Marty and Paul believe that Janie and Harriet are working like one of the guys. Here this perception interferes with their relationships, but feminists were noting that it was interfering with the larger goal of equality.

Susan Faludi argues that the timing of the backlash "coincided with signs that women were believed to be on the verge of breakthrough." *Isn't It Romantic,* then, is set in the middle of that wave of conservatism. Janie feels caught in the current, while Harriet moves with the backlash. The backlash blamed the women's movement for the "feminization of poverty"—while the backlash's own instigators in Washington implemented the budget cuts that helped impoverish millions of women, fought pay equity, and undermined equal opportunity laws. In short, to blame feminism for women's "lesser life" misses the point of feminism, which is to gain a wider range of experience for women. Feminism asks for equal rights to participate in the world, not to "choose" between public justice and private happiness. It asks that women be free to define themselves, instead of having male society define their identity. The cultural battles of the eighties, played out by Wasserstein's characters, verify that women still had a long way to go before reaching equality.

Psychologist Carol Gilligan observed the conflict that Wasserstein presents between men and women in psychological terms in her 1982 book, *In a Different Voice*: "Men often speak as if they were not living in connection with women." She also pointed out that "women often sensed that it was dangerous to say or even to know what they wanted or thought" for fear of upsetting others, being abandoned, or experiencing retaliation. Gilligan marks the 1973 *Roe v. Wade* decision, establishing women's right to an abortion, as the moment when women began speaking for themselves rather than being the selfless "Angel in the House." She found that many women acted and spoke only for others, in order to have relationships. Marty Sterling speaks as though he were the answer to Janie's life, and Gilligan affirms that "by restricting their voices, many women were wittingly or unwittingly perpetuating a male-voiced civilization" based on disconnection from women.

Published in 1982, a year before *Isn't It Romantic, In a Different Voice* would have been part of Wasserstein's and Janie's consciousness, making it impossible for Janie to marry a man who wants to dictate her life. Gilligan learned from Erik Erikson that "life-history, history, psychology and politics are deeply entwined," and social drama, like Wasserstein's, reflects the intersection of those forces. Marty wants to marry, to control, and to dominate Janie. In asking Janie to give up her career, he is, as Gilligan would put it, asking her "to give up [her] voice." "Moral problems are problems of human relations," says Gilligan. It is interesting to note that in a notebook draft of the play, Janie asks a therapist character, Stanley, whom Wasserstein later deleted, "It's all about control, isn't it? . . . Men and women?" Stanley responds, "I don't think you can make those separations." In her final, seventh draft of the play, Wasserstein omitted Stanley's dismissal of gender differences in behavior. In other words, *Isn't It Romantic* suggests that the imbalance of power between men and women was built into our culture. Harriet agrees with Janie that marrying Marty "isn't a solution" for Janie and that "there's nothing wrong with being alone. We can wait till it's right." She explains, "Maybe it's because I'm Lillian's daughter, but I never respected women who didn't learn to live alone and pay their own rent. Imagine spending your life pretending you aren't a person. To compromise at this point would be antifeminist—well, antihumanist—well, just not impressive."

Harriet sees no distinction between women's rights and human rights. When Janie asks her if she should marry Marty, she replies, "No matter how lonely you get or how many birth announcements you receive, the trick is not to get frightened." Both are responding to the traditional pressure to marry, to the stigma of "the spinster." Mary Daly, feminist philosopher and theologian, observed, "She who has chosen her Self, who defines her self, by choice, neither in relation to children nor men, who is Self-identified, is a Spinster, a whirling dervish spinning in a new time/space." Moreover, in "Working at Single Bliss," Mary Helen Washington notes that "unmarrieds" are "a pejorative, like coloreds," "women trying to rationalize lives of loss. Losers at the marriage game. *Les femmes manquées.*" Being married, she says, has always been considered more "socially acceptable," while society often regards singles as leading "selfish lives of freedom." Society asks single people to account for their choice, unlike married people, whose family structure provides protection. This social expectation leads Janie to imagine herself "at thirty-six driving cross-country to inseminate [herself] with a turkey baster," while Harriet's career mother urges her to have children: ". . . it's one of the few things in life that's worthwhile."

In the end, however, *Isn't It Romantic* affirms the power of the single woman, who, as Washington says, "may be more aware of the responsibility to discover and create meaning in her life, to find community, to honor her creativity, to live out her values, than the person whose life is circumferenced by . . . family life." The play challenges

> the myth that marriage must be the vertical choice in a woman's life—one that raises her status, completes her life, fulfills her dreams, and makes her a valid person in society. In the 1950s, all the movies, all the songs directed us to this one choice: to find our worldly prince and go two by two into the ark. Nothing else was supposed to matter quite as much. . . .

Janie Blumberg concludes that she cannot be herself if she marries Marty, and so she chooses to be on her own. Like Carrie Bradshaw in *Sex and the City,* who breaks out in a rash when she tries on a wedding dress, Janie feels suffocated at the prospect of marriage. She confides in Harriet:

> Driving along the Long Island Expressway I was fantasizing if we'd make the Sunday Times wedding announcements: "Daughter of Pioneer in Interpretive Dance Marries Popover Boy." And it was just as we were approaching Syosset that I thought, "I can't breathe in this car." . . . And then I found myself kissing his hand saying, "I love you."

She tells Harriet that she loves Marty, but "maybe I'm just frightened," to which Harriet responds, "I thought we had a pact. There's nothing wrong with being alone." In addition to her ambivalence about marriage, Janie also feels ill equipped for it, for which she blames her parents: "Did you teach me to marry a nice Jewish doctor and make chicken for him? . . . Did you teach me to go to law school and wear gray suits at a job that I sort of like every day from nine to eight? . . . Did you teach me to compromise and lie to the man I live with and say I love you when I wasn't sure?" She fits neither in a traditional marriage nor in corporate America. Still, she does not want to dismiss marriage and feels with Marty's proposal that she has "been accepted, not even on the waiting list."

Landing a Jewish doctor is like being accepted into an elite college, but ultimately Janie declines admission.

Still, Wasserstein "felt the tug of a conservative ending" to *Isn't It Romantic*. She had great difficulty deciding whether or not Janie was going to end up alone. Part of her wanted Janie "to get the guy," and so she kept rewriting the ending during the Phoenix run; in some versions Janie ended up with Marty, while in others she did not. She deliberately refrained from placing a question mark after the title to convey ambiguity about whether the play is romantic or ironic. In the original production, Janie was innocent, sweet, alienated, and insecure, badgered by her protective mother and her dominating boyfriend, and she spent her days postponing decisions and her life; even when she finally did try to stand up for her rights, she never really understood why. In the ending of the later production, however, Janie becomes a stronger woman who takes responsibility for her choices. In deciding not to marry, she affirms that she is unwilling to settle for someone who falls short of her ideals, even if it means being alone. Wasserstein commented, "You have to see the play as separate from yourself. When I first wrote the play, I was devastated that Janie did not marry [the doctor]. . . But I knew this time it was right for her to dance alone at the end." In other words, playwright and protagonist needed to accept the definition of "romantic" as "unrealistic," and reject its meaning as "idealistic, desiring chivalry."

In choosing to have Janie remain single, Wasserstein subverts the genre of the romantic comedy. From its earliest traditions in Plautus and Terence through Shakespeare, romantic comedies have dramatized the conflicting values between parents and children. In *Isn't It Romantic*, Janie's parents support, even demand, the marriage that she rejects, but here the older generation are antagonists for different reasons. Tasha Blumberg hounds Janie about getting married, recalling her first New York apartment when she was "much younger than [Janie]" and "already married" to Simon Blumberg. She hopes next year she and Simon will carry up four cups of coffee to her apartment on morning visits instead of three. Traditional comedies often staged a battle between father and son, but Wasserstein chooses the mother-daughter conflict. Tasha tells Janie, "You can have a nice life" with Dr. Marty Sterling, and Janie tells Harriet that the moment her parents find out she's met Marty, her mother "will have caterers on the other extension" because "Marty could make a girl a nice husband."

At the end of a traditional romantic comedy, the opposite sexes unite with a dance, achieving clarification about their place in the world. As

Tasha (Joan Copeland) and Janie (Christine Estabrook) in the 1984–85 L.A. Stage Company West production of *Isn't It Romantic*. (Showbill/Photofest)

Northrop Frye explains, "The tendency of comedy is to include as many people as possible in its final society," but Janie's solitary dance replaces the communal festivity of the wedding. The power of love no longer represents the natural rhythm of the universe, and Janie achieves her moment of discovery alone. In more contemporary romantic comedies, love challenges the characters, who must accept or deny the love that finally transforms them. The process tests values. Janie and Marty were never soul mates, but their relationship does challenge conventional ideas about marriage. In the archetypal romantic comedy, the younger generation usually reverses the social order, moving from one kind of society to another; the final society is the "real" one, while the other is "illusory." In 1983, *Isn't It Romantic* was telling us that the "real" and "new society" was the single woman, and that perhaps marriage was "illusory." The play was making a social and moral statement.

As being single became more popular in the eighties, so did dating. When Cynthia Peterson was leaving phone messages for Janie Blumberg about "a Lib/Men, Lib/Women mixer at the Unitarian church," single New Yorkers were looking for Mr. and Ms. Right by way of classified ads. No longer for "losers" or "mail-order brides," the personals became the province of everyone who wanted to "go for it." New Yorkers were holding up their criteria for a soul mate to the *New York Review of Books*, the *Village Voice*, the *Nation, Advocate,* and *Chocolate Singles.* Magazines were instructing singles about how to place and answer ads. Rule Number One was "Don't be too eager to please." This proactive experience empowered women "who grew up with the message that passivity, 'settling,' and adapting oneself to a man's goals and expectations are feminine virtues." For the first time, women as well as men could ask for what they wanted—before going on a date. Dating became a competitive sport.

Janie's parents already have their criteria for their daughter's future husband—"a nice Jewish doctor"—and believe such a match will bring "a little *naches.* . . . A little happiness." In Yiddish, *naches* means joy, and to *shep naches* means to derive pleasure. Jewish children are expected to provide their parent with *naches* in the form of achievement. Translated literally, then, nice Jewish daughters provide their mothers pleasure through the achievement of marriage, especially marriage to another Jew. Because of the loss of so many Jews during the Holocaust, marriage between Jews and perpetuating family became an important part of Jewish culture. In the old world, "the only way that marriages ever took place was when a *shadchen*, a matchmaker, arranged them." The matchmaker scrutinized the parents, determined how observant they were, "checked out their son and then found a girl for him." It is a role that Janie's parents cannot help playing. Traditional Jewish matchmakers still exist, and

August 1983 *Ms.* magazine cover. (Reprinted by permission of *Ms.* magazine, © 1983)

Mary Wells record cover
for "My Guy." (Photofest)

some encourage single
women "to settle for Mr.
Alright instead of Mr.
Right." One such
matchmaker says, "With
all the single people
around, I don't know if I
still believe in the Jew-
ish concept of *bashert*—
that there is someone
fated for each person."
Isn't It Romantic pres-
ents a similarly skepti-
cal view about finding
one's soul mate.

Nevertheless, Janie and Harriet grew up on traditional, romantic
values. Janie reminisces to Harriet about listening to Mary Wells's 1964
Number One single, "My Guy," as they ironed their hair before high
school dances: "Nothing you could say / Can tear me away from my guy
/ Nothing you could do / Cause I'm stuck like glue to my guy. . . ." Written and produced by Smokey Robinson of the Miracles, the song
proclaims a woman's dedication to her man. In addition, Harriet sings
Little Peggy March's 1963 song "I Will Follow Him" into Janie's answering machine. With these lyrics about fidelity in her mind, Janie reflects
on the marriage she envisioned for herself as a younger woman:

> When I'm twenty-eight I'm going to get married and be very much
> in love with someone who's poor and fascinating until he's thirty
> and then fabulously wealthy and very secure after that. And we're
> going to have children who wear overalls and flannel shirts and are
> kind and independent, with curly blond hair. And we'll have great
> sex and still hold hands when we travel to China when we're sixty.

Harriet, though, never aspired to that kind of marriage. With her
high-powered career mother as an example, she doesn't respect women

who do not learn to live alone and pay their own rent. "Imagine spending your life pretending you aren't a person," she tells Janie. Her confident stance influences Janie's decision not to marry Marty, and so Janie is confused when Harriet suddenly decides to marry Joe Stine: "I made choices based on an idea that doesn't exist anymore." Janie accuses Harriet of marrying because of social pressure and trends, rather than for love, and of renouncing her earlier call for independence:

> What do you do? Fall in with every current the tide pulls in? Women should live alone and find out what they can do, put off marriage, establish a vertical career track; so you do that for a while. Then you almost turn thirty and *Time* magazine announces, "Guess what, girls? It's time to have it all." Jaclyn Smith is married and pregnant and playing Jacqueline Kennedy. Every other person who was analyzing stocks last year is analyzing layettes this year; so you do that. What are you doing, Harriet? Who the hell are you? Can't you conceive of some plan, some time-management scheme that you made up for yourself? . . .You don't have to force yourself into a situation—a marriage—because it's time.

As in *The Heidi Chronicles*, Wasserstein's protagonist adheres to the ideals of the feminist movement and resists fads, while her peers' values are in flux. In fact, the playwright says she began writing *Isn't It Romantic* after being surprised by her own emotion when one of her best friends decided to get married. She was twenty-eight, and suddenly there was the question of biological time bombs going off:

> I had never thought about it before, because there was this pressure when I was getting out of Holyoke in '71 to have a career. If you said you were getting married back then, it was embarrassing. And then suddenly, all of these people were talking sheer madness about getting married and having babies. Things had somehow turned around, and I was trying to figure it all out. I decided it might be interesting to write a comedy about it.

The newly engaged Harriet, on the other hand, claims Janie is avoiding marriage out of a fear of making a choice and taking responsibility for it, and a desire to remain "girls" together. As she puts it, "It doesn't take any strength to be alone. It's much harder to be with someone else." Janie has decided she does not want to "turn someone into an answer for her" and feels betrayed by her friend, concluding that Harriet never listened to her or really told Janie about herself. But she defuses her argument in this scene by joking that she hopes to meet someone taking out the trash. Her mother's values prevail.

At the time that Wasserstein was writing about the conflict between Janie and Harriet, international films about the darker side of female friendships were appearing at the New York Film Festival: The French film *Entre Nous*, by Diane Kurys, depicted an incompatible couple who might have stuck it out but for the influence of a woman friend. *Sheer Madness*, by the German filmmaker Margarethe von Trotta, asked questions about the cost of independence and the presumption of liberating others.

In sociological terms, Harriet is "outer-directed," and in 1982, American women were being told that they could have it all. Helen Gurley Brown, author of *Sex and the Single Girl*, offered a prescription for health, love, marriage, and financial stability in her book, *Having It All*. Writing about diet, exercise, face, body, clothes, sex, love, marriage, friends, and money, she was selling a female version of Benjamin Franklin's program for self-improvement to American women: any woman could achieve anything through "action and self-discipline." She drew on the ideas of cognitive behaviorist Dr. Albert Ellis, whose *Guide to Rational Living* and *Reasons and Emotions in Psychology* (1973) helped Americans recognize that human happiness is internally caused, and that people can control their sorrows and disturbances. Similarly, Brown was encouraging women to take initiative, to "cope, climb, manage, endure" and to renounce their traditionally submissive and reactive roles. In so doing, she was also telling women that if they did not manage to achieve it all, it was not society's fault but their own. The play challenges this idea.

While Janie "lives from the inside out," as Wasserstein puts it, "Someone like Harriet is living her life from the outside in, almost like a checklist: you get the job, the apartment, then the husband and baby. In two years, she'll be on the cover of *Savvy* magazine (a women's magazine providing tips on beauty, lifestyle, money, and shopping) looking fantastic." In other words feminism could coexist with marriage. Harriet says, "Of course you should learn to live alone and pay your own rent, but I didn't realize what it would feel like for me when I became too good at it. I know how to come home, put on the news, have a glass of wine, read a book, call you. What I don't know is what to do when there's someone who loves me in the house."

Some sociologists of the time found that the emotional loneliness experienced by some single women caused feelings of anxiety and emptiness. Janie, however, concludes that the alternative to being discontented is "dependency." When Marty presumptuously decides to put down a deposit on an apartment in Brooklyn for them without consulting Janie, she asserts herself: "I don't want to sneak around you and pretend that I'm never angry. I don't want to be afraid of you. I guess to a man I love I want to feel not just that I can talk, but that you'll listen . . . ." Their unequal relationship collides with the romantic anticipation on their first dinner date when "Volare," playing in the background of an Italian restaurant, promises that they will "sing in the glow of a star . . . where lovers enjoy peace of mind." Another version of "My Guy," "Volare" ironically rhapsodizes about soul mates walking into the sunset.

Janie's assertion of her independence reflects some of the progress that the women's movement was making at the time. Between 1971—the real end of *Uncommon Women*—and 1983—the publication of *Isn't It Romantic*—women had made great strides, despite obstacles created by concervatives. In 1972, Congress passed Title IX, which mandated support of women's sports in schools, and the Equal Employment Opportunity Act, which prohibited sex discrimination in employment. The Equal Pay Act began to cover all employees. NOW launched an attack on sexism in schoolbooks with its pamphlet *Dick and Jane as Victims,* and in 1973 *Roe v. Wade* defended women's right to obtain abortions. Singer Helen Reddy won a Grammy for her song "I Am Woman," which became an anthem for the women's movement, the same year that the National Black Feminist Organization was formed. Conservative Judaism permitted women to be counted as part of the ten people needed for congregational worship, and Dr. Mary Daly's book *Beyond God the Father* rejected male divinity. On the tennis court, Billie Jean King defeated Bobby Riggs in the "Battle of the Sexes" tennis match, enabling women to earn as much money as men in the U.S. Open. The Government Printing Office stylebook accepted Ms. as a prefix in place of Mrs. or Miss, because women did not want to be defined by the presence or absence of a man. *Isn't It Romantic* does not specifically refer to these events, but they shape the society in which Janie and Harriet live.

By 1974, women had made more strides: Congress passed the Equal Credit Opportunity Act, which allowed married women to obtain credit in their own name for the first time. Over a thousand colleges and universities offered women's studies courses, and eighty had full programs. Helen Thomas became the first female White House bureau chief for United Press International. Little League Baseball, for the first time, allowed girls to compete with boys. Four thousand women attended the first National Women's Health Conference, sponsored by the Our Bodies Ourselves Collective at Harvard Medical School. Moreover, the National Congress of Neighborhood Women formed to upgrade the status of working-class women through education. Barbara Jordan became the first African American and the first woman to give the keynote speech at the Democratic National Convention.

In 1977, the president of the National Organization of Women, Eleanor Smeal, demanded that homemakers should have their own Social Security accounts. Women gained even more freedom when Congress passed the Pregnancy Discrimination Act in 1978, which prohibited discrimination against pregnant women in all areas of employment. And, for the first time, more women than men entered American colleges and universities. That same year, the first Take Back the Night march drew attention to a woman's right to walk the streets at night without fear.

In 1983, the year of *Isn't It Romantic,* U.S. feminist peace activists established a Seneca Falls encampment against nuclear arms, while Sally Ride was the first woman to rocket to the moon. In Chicago, 3,000 women met to form the Coalition of Labor Union Women. Moreover, a new breed of superwoman appeared in the form of female triathletes when Julie Moss and Kathleen McCartney joined the Iron Man race with men. In the literary world, two women took the Pulitzer Prize—novelist Alice Walker for *The Color Purple* and playwright Marsha Norman for *'night, Mother,* a play that dramatized the problems between mother and daughter, which ended with the daughter's suicide.

The film *Terms of Endearment* won an Oscar in 1984, and critics seemed to think that *Isn't It Romantic* echoed this drama about a mother and daughter searching for love; but the play feels closer to another 1983 movie hit, nominated for best screenplay, *The Big Chill*, about disillusioned baby boomers whose ideals have dissolved. Marlo Thomas and Alan Alda introduced *She's Nobody's Baby: A History of American Women in the Twentieth Century,* celebrating women's accomplishments. Elsa Dixler published a reading list in *Ms.* magazine for "feminist intellectuals" that included novels, literary criticism, psychology, motherhood, sexuality/health, theory, art/architecture, work, general history, and the history of feminism. Dixler highlighted Betty Friedan's *The Feminine Mystique* and Doris Lessing's *The Golden Notebook* as the books that "changed the way women over thirty-five looked at the world." In fact, upon seeing *Isn't It Romantic,* Friedan sent Wasserstein a letter about

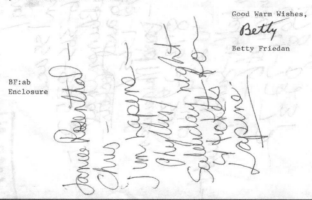

BETTY FRIEDAN
1 LINCOLN PLAZA
NEW YORK, NEW YORK 10023

January 21, 1984

Wendy Wasserstein
605 East 82nd Street
New York, NY 10028

Dear Wendy:

I saw your play the other night and loved it. It is witty, it is
wise, and it has real soul. In fact, I am going back to sit in the first
row so that I can get the few bits of dialogue I missed the first time---
and take my daughter and daughter-in-law.

I still think you would be a wonderful writer if I ever get this
project finalized for a T.V. Mini-Series dramatization based on my three
books, THE FEMININE MYSTIQUE, IT CHANGED MY LIFE and THE SECOND STAGE.
As I told you, the people interested in the project now are David Wolper
and Joan Micklin-Silver.

I am quite certain that while you are "hot" right now---and deserve
to be---that you are also very busy with your own projects. However, it
might be worthwhile to talk about the project I have in mind. So, just
in case you haven't read it, I am enclosing a copy of THE SECOND STAGE.

Thank you for helping me get the tickets. I am very proud of you
and hope you will keep evolving both personally and professionally in
your own beautiful direction.

Good Warm Wishes,

Betty

Betty Friedan

BF:ab
Enclosure

Letter from Betty Friedan praising *Isn't It Romantic* and suggesting
that Wasserstein adapt Friedan's books for television. (Copyright ©
1984 by Betty Friedan; reprinted by permission of Curtis Brown, Ltd.)

adapting her trilogy of books—*Mystique, It Changed My Life,* and *The Second Stage.* She intuitively addressed a gap in the *Ms.* list: there were no plays by American women, and a television miniseries drama just might be the best way to reach a wide audience.

Friedan had documented the emergence of the second wave of feminism, when women were mainly trying to get out of the house. Janie and Harriet concern themselves with the next stage, which asked whether women could "have it all." They feel the pressure of trying to have both careers and families. Harriet asks her corporate mother, "Do you think it's possible to be married or live with a man, have a good relationship and children that you share equal responsibility for, build a career, and still read novels, play the piano, have women friends, and swim twice a week?" Lillian responds, "You mean what the women's magazines call 'having it all'? Harriet, that's just your generation's fantasy." In contrast, Janie's stay-at-home mother romantically believes "you can have a family, you can have a career, you can learn to tap-dance!" In an unpublished, notebook draft of this scene, a therapist humorously tells Janie, "A woman can wear elongated leotards and have the perceptions of Heidegger." But Harriet's mother believes that "life is negotiation":

> You think the women who go back to work at thirty-six are going to have the same career as a woman who has been there since her twenties? You think someone who has a baby and leaves it after two weeks to go back to work is going to have the same relationship with that child as someone who has been there all along? It's impossible. And you show me the wonderful man with whom you're going to have it all. You tell me how he feels when you take as many business trips as he does. You tell me who has to leave the office when the kid bumps his head on a radiator or slips on a milk carton. No, I don't think that what you're talking about is possible.

Lillian Cornwall voices the way it was for many professional women who began working in the sixties: career women with families made domestic sacrifices, while women who entered the workforce after their children were grown could not compete with those whose work had not been interrupted.

In 2009, however, professional women consider Lillian's perspective dated. An accomplished MBA, Jeanne Athos, with her own business and family, commented, "You can have it all but maybe not all at once. The key is sequencing, placing more emphasis on different parts of your life at different times. And the men in your life can help you sequence—be more flexible to help with the kids when their job is stable but lean on you more when they are at a challenging point." Wasserstein's plays continue to be time capsules. Harriet's idealistic perspective lacks the ambiguity of contemporary women: "I'm going to try to do it: have it all." Still, both Janie and Harriet are caught between two worlds: the one in which Lillian Cornwall asks Harriet to pick up the check with her American Express Gold Card, and the other in which Janie's mother tells her to comb her hair. In an earlier draft, Janie joked about the absurdity of the perfect life: "We could order the kids from the L.L. Bean catalogue."

The mother-daughter conflict is a central part of the feminist conflict. Representative of an earlier generation of stay-at-home mothers, Tasha Blumberg does not understand the tension experienced by her daughter's generation. She tells Lillian Cornwall, "Harriet will find a nice boy, she'll get married, she'll work, she'll have a nice life. I don't understand why they're fighting it so hard." Janie feels that her mother is measuring her success according to marriage, weight, and career, a combination of demands not placed on men. Therefore, she answers her mother's calls with: "Hello, Mother. This morning I got married, lost twenty pounds, and became a lawyer." Tasha defends herself, saying that she calls Janie because she misses her and "want[s] to know she's well," but "to give her a little push too." Mothers, especially those who came of age before the women's movement, naturally measured their success by their children's success, and the family was a business whose products were children. ("We both worked very hard," says Tasha to Lillian. "That's why we put out such nice products.") For some mothers, that kind of success required intervention. "If I could take her by the hand and do it for her I would," Tasha tells Lillian. While Tasha "would love for Janie to take over" her father's business, she has traditional values: "Nixon did all right for himself. Both his daughters married well."

The play challenges the values of Tasha Blumberg, just as the women's movement did. In the beginning, American feminists saw the nuclear family as "a source of women's oppression" that interfered with a professional life. But it failed to acknowledge the satisfaction it provided many women, and it had not found a solution to the stress experienced by women who were trying to combine careers and family. After all, most American women's lives were still "rooted in family life" and their identities were connected to their domestic roles. Betty Friedan noted in her 1981 book *The Second Stage* that though "the women's movement was being blamed . . . for the destruction of the family," feminists were not trying to dismantle the family. As Anne Roiphe wrote, "a truly feminist position does not mock the family, and a Jewish feminist position must by definition cherish the home and value the work that is done there." Like Janie Blumberg, Jewish-American feminists wanted to embrace a broader definition of family to include singles, single parents, and gay couples in order to honor "Jewish concepts of communal responsibility." Jewish-American matchmakers, however, still existed in the eighties, and they encouraged their clients to place marriage and family before career. One, Irene Nathan, remarks:

> If I had a daughter who was willing to listen to me, I would tell her: Find a loving partner, establish a family, and then pursue a career. I don't think super-moms are happier—they work all day, then they run home to do everything for everybody. Men might appreciate a talented and driven woman, but don't they also really want a woman who's less harried and more nurturing?

The play holds up a mirror to an American society that did not accommodate super-women, because it did not provide the resources necessary for women to have careers and family.

The conflict between being Jewish and being American in *Isn't It Romantic* is as significant as the tension between the feminine mystique and feminist values. Because Wasserstein chose to make Janie and Marty Jewish Americans, it seems important to understand the feminist movement in the context of being Jewish. Paula Hyman writes, "Misogyny and 'separate but equal' . . . characterized many rabbinic attitudes toward women." While Janie is more American than Jewish, Marty wants to be more Jewish than American. Hyman notes:

> Once Jewish-American women . . . realiz[ed] that female inferiority was a cultural construct . . . Jewish women became acutely aware of the inequities women suffered in Jewish law, in the synagogue, and in Jewish communal institutions. By 1974, articles analyzing the patriarchal nature of Judaism had appeared, a group called Erat Nashim had issued a call to the Conservative movement to count women in the minyan and to ordain women as rabbis, and the Jewish Feminist Organization had formed as a result of two successful conferences in New York City, in 1973 and 1974.

Though Janie does not participate in Jewish feminist politics, and we do not see Marty going to shul, Judaism's patriarchy defines their heritage, as it does most religions. Like the American women's movement, Jewish feminists understood prescribed sex roles as a mode of social control—specifically the ways in which women had been excluded from education and positions of power because of their gender. Jewish feminism wanted to achieve "the full, direct, and equal participation of women at all levels of Jewish life—communal, educational, and political." Many feminists, Christians as well as Jews, had determined that their patriarchal religions "were simply a source of oppression" and therefore "irrelevant to their lives" and so they turned to Eastern religions for their spirituality. Mary Daly's *Beyond God the Father: Toward a Philosophy of Women's Liberation* had been in the air for ten years when Wasserstein wrote *Isn't It Romantic*. Daly "formulated a rationale for a woman-centered spirituality that would undermine the hierarchic thinking characteristic of patriarchy, which she believed would provide the basis for human liberation." She called on women to refuse to be co-opted by institutions like the church and synagogue "whose sexism is direct and explicit but whose ideologies, policies, and goals are not defined exclusively or primarily by sexism." The characters in the play, of course, do not speak in these terms, but they act within this social matrix. Erika Monk of the *Village Voice* argued that this "TV play stripped Judaism [and Protestantism] of all religious and ethical meanings," but it is the critic's job to fill in the play's context, not the characters'.

In *Isn't It Romantic,* and later in *The Sisters Rosensweig,* Wasserstein's Jewish-American characters are either trying to efface their Jewishness or to retrieve it. In *Romantic,* Marty went to Camp Kibbutz with Janie's brother, Ben Blumberg. The second time he dropped out of medical school, Marty worked on a kibbutz, an Israeli collective community that combines socialism and Zionism; this was a trend for some young American Jews in the eighties. He is also considering opening his kidney practice in Tel Aviv. Wanting to perpetuate his Jewish identity, he tells Janie, "Israel's very important to me," and "Jewish families should have at least three children. It's a dying religion. Intermarriage, Ivy League colleges, the *New York Review of Books*." Marty's urge to affirm his Jewishness reflects a historical fact: the founding of the State of Israel in 1948, the growing awareness of the Shoah/Holocaust, and the 1967 Six Day War bolstered Jewish-American consciousness, secular and religious, "even as the postwar opening of society to Jews in all arenas ensured their Americanism." Wasserstein was documenting Jewish-American experience from the fifties, when these characters were born, through the eighties. Significantly, at the time that *Isn't It Romantic* was playing in New York, Chaim Potok's *The Chosen*—about the conflict between assimilated and Hasidic Jews—was playing in movie theaters, and so was *Sophie's Choice,* a film about the horrors of the Holocaust. The play's references to *The Sorrow and the Pity* and to *Fiddler on the Roof* also reinforce the historical oppression of the Jews, which informs Marty Sterling's appreciation of his Jewish identity.

As Samuel Heilman notes, in the fifties Holocaust survivors were beginning a new life in America that promised democracy and economic opportunity. The Holocaust infiltrates *Isn't It Romantic* in small details like Tasha Blumberg's comment that "Steiff toys at F.A.O. Schwartz" are undesirable because "they're made in Germany." Holocaust survivors felt strongly about perpetuating their Jewish identity. As Alfred Kazin put it in *New York Jew*, "The farther we got away from the Holocaust in time, the more it took up residence right on New York's West Side." New York and Boston were becoming the New Jerusalem—but to sociologists, Jewish cultural integrity seemed more precarious than ever before. The second half of the twentieth century, a time of lessened anti-Semitic prejudice in America, brought extraordinary assimilation and swelling rates of intermarriage for American Jews. Hence, from 1950 to 1990, while America grew by over two-thirds, American Jewry grew by only one-fifth. By 1990, the number of Jews in America had shrunk to about 4.4 million. Although Jewish Americans were prospering, fewer were going to synagogues, writing Jewish scholarship, studying Judaism or Hebrew, visiting or living in Israel, or working for the Jewish community.

Marty Sterling responds to this demographic and sociological fact. He decides that he and Janie should live in Flatbush or Brighton Beach, "where people have real values," and he regrets that his father never sees "those people" anymore, "the alta kakas in Brooklyn, the old men with the accents who sit in front of Hymie's Highway Delicatessen." He also laments the fact that his father no longer goes to Miami but to Palm Springs or Martinique with their friends from the Westchester Country Club: "My father thought my brother was crazy when he named his son Schlomo." It was Marty's father who changed the family name from Schlimovitz to Sterling, but Marty wants to open his kidney practice under his Jewish name. (In an early draft, Marty's original name was

Moise Scharfman "when he went to Yeshiva," and he changed his name when he went to Harvard. In a crossed-out, handwritten notebook page of dialogue Janie says, "Believe me. Most people would not think of Martin Sterling as British.") Returning to Brooklyn means returning to Jewish roots. Those who lived in Brooklyn's "golden age" describe a small-town American life where stoops, streets, alleys, parks, school-yards, and lots were places of bonding. Candy stores were community centers, and egg creams were "the elixir of life." Wasserstein's references to Brooklyn, then, have historical and mythic significance. In 1917, Christopher Morley wrote, "If New York is Babylon; Brooklyn is the true Holy City. New York is the city of envy, office work and hustle; Brooklyn is the region of homes and happiness." Despite its seventeenth-century Dutch origins, Brooklyn became "a central switchboard of the Ameri-can population," according to Ilana Abramovitch. Called "cosmopolitan" by Arthur Miller, "universal" by Bernard Malamud, and "individualistic" by Carson McCullers, Brooklyn has been a place where immigrants have dropped their bags when they arrived in America. Brighton Beach, Flatbush, and Williamsburg have had thriving local Jewish lives and institutions, and Brooklyn's Jewish community is one of the most creative in the world, including Lenny Bruce, Sandy Koufax, Beverly Sills, Mel Brooks, Woody Allen, Arthur Miller, and Alfred Kazin.

Brighton Beach, in particular, has been a mecca for eastern European Jewish immigrants, like Wasserstein's family, for most of the twentieth century. Annelise Orleck writes that "Brighton Beach, more than any of its larger neighbors, retains the taste and feel of an immi-grant ghetto." Along the wooden boardwalk you hear "a stage-whispered mix of Russian, Yiddish, and English." Marty wants to leave the assimilated Upper West Side for old-fashioned Brighton Beach where "live carp still swim in fish store windows, pickles are sold from barrels; women in headscarves squeeze melons . . . and music in minor keys drifts from narrow dark doorways." "Portal for the massive exodus that brought half a million Jews from the Soviet Union to the United States since 1967," Brighton Beach has been called "Little Odessa," reflecting the Ukrainian origins of many of its residents. Beneath its Russian sur-face, it has Yiddish roots, "remnants of the first and second waves of eastern European Jewry to settle this bit of urban Atlantic seashore." Since the late 1940s, hundreds of Holocaust survivors have lived there. In 1937, as news of Hitler's increasingly frightening anti-Jewish policies made its way to Brighton Beach, Dr. Maxwell Ross said, "Brighton Beach, not Europe or Palestine, is the real promised land for Jews . . . where we may practice the religion of our forefathers without interference from narrow-minded bigots. . . ." After World War II, next to Miami Beach, Brighton Beach had the largest population of senior immigrants. On the grounds of the old Brighton Beach Hotel were the Brighton Beach baths, "an urban Jewish equivalent to the country club [with] three saltwater pools, lockers for rent, and the live big-band performances by Benny Goodman." Brighton Beach, then, represented freedom, tradition, solidarity, and entertainment for Jews.

Marty Sterling/Schlimovitz is also considering moving to Flatbush, which was ninety-five percent Jewish at the time. He is nostalgic for the traditions of Flatbush: latkes, lox, pickles, Bialystok kuchel, Ebinger's baked goods, seltzer, the iceman, the milkman, pinochle, shul, Ebbets Field, and Prospect Park. In effect, Marty and Janie are reacting against their parents. While Marty's father is trying to assimilate, Mrs. Blumberg wants to be Jewish. She calls her Christian daughter-in-law "Christ" instead of Chris, revealing her concern about the fact that her son has married a shiksa. The Blumbergs spoke Yiddish at home when Janie was growing up, and instilled Jewish tradition in her to the extent that Harriet celebrates Janie's new apartment with "challah bread for the staff of life," "kosher salt for spice," "sugar for sweetness," and "a candle to light the way." Of course, Marty's father was not assimilated at first. He "started out in show business" and "used to tell jokes at Grossinger's," the famous nightclub in the Catskills. In the forties, fifties, and sixties, Jewish New Yorkers vacationed in these "Jewish Alps" or "borscht belt" in bungalow colonies, summer camps, and *kuchaleyns* (a Yiddish name for self-catered boarding houses), where they ate borscht and heard stand-up comics like Woody Allen, Morey Amsterdam, Milton Berle, Mel Brooks, Lenny Bruce, George Burns, Sid Caesar, Rodney Dangerfield, Phyllis Diller, Totie Fields, Shecky Greene, Carl Reiner, and Joan Rivers. Marty's father, then, would have been trying to break into an accomplished group of Jewish comedians. With the decline of discrimination against the Jews at vacation spots and elsewhere, the broad installation of air conditioning in New York City, and the end of rail service to the Catskills in the sixties, the borscht belt disappeared as a major vacation destination for Jews.

Comedy is not just a reference in *Isn't It Romantic*; it is Wasserstein's way of examining middle-class life, and it is a uniquely Jewish way of looking at the world. Humor has been a way of "coping with the challenges of modern life, of dealing with vulnerability in oppressive situations, of self-criticizing and self-affirming, of expressing discomforts, of defusing fears," and of challenging power. Centuries ago in Eastern Europe, satirical jesters called "'badchens' performed at social functions for important people in the community. So Jews, often politically powerless, challenged the status quo with 'shtoch,' or jab humor, which deflated pomposity." Moreover, French philosopher Henri Bergson says that laughter can temporarily resolve the conflict of two opposing conceptions of being human, and in this way, humor enables Wasserstein to make fun of dated conceptions of being a woman. At the same time, *Isn't It Romantic* expresses the anxiety that came with this transitional period, reflecting Freud's definition of humor in playing out forbidden actions or desires that either the individual wishes to be fulfilled or that could produce anxiety. Furthermore, Freud notes that "stories created by Jews are often directed against Jewish characteristics. . . . I do not know whether there are many other instances of a people making fun to such a degree of its own character." *Romantic* pokes fun at Jewish customs and speech.

Wasserstein herself links comedy with being Jewish. She told me, "I think in many ways my idea of show business comes both from temple, not that I really practice, but that sense of community and melancholy, and spirituality is there. My folks used to travel every year to Miami, twice a year, Christmas and New Year's, and to San Juan, and the entertainment that I knew was those Jewish comics." Skepticism, cynicism, self-criticism, and the desire to give and participate in pleasure appear in *Isn't It Romantic*. The dialogue is fully of witty one-liners: Harriet tells Janie, "People named Homo and Schlymie! I feel our move back to New York has been very successful. I've met a sadist vice-president, and you've become involved in a shtetl." Janie makes fun of Marty's father's restaurant chain, "Ye Olde Sterling Tavernes," and of her father's perfumed envelopes business. *Woman's Work* magazine rejects her because she "has not experienced enough pain." Janie, too is frustrated with her own laziness, self-absorption, fat thighs, inability to change, and lack of courage. Making fun of herself, she tells Marty, "Whenever I get most depressed, I think I should take charge of my life and apply to medical school. Then I remember that I once identified a liver as a heart." Fluffing her hair, she tells Harriet that she deeply resents "having to pay the phone bill, be nice to the super, find meaningful work, fall in love, get hurt" . . . but the alternative, she jokes, is "dependency."

After Janie spills horseradish on Marty's sister-in-law at Chanukah, Marty says, "My mother says you're shy and a little clumsy because you're angry with your family. But she says don't worry, you'll grow out of it." Janie responds, "I'm reflective and eager to please, and my mother is a pioneer in interpretive dance." She also makes fun of the prolonged adolescence of her boomer generation, telling Marty, "It's weird going to someone's parents' house. Shouldn't we have mortgages and children?" Harriet also has a sense of humor about her relationships, telling Janie that Paul Stuart is only a temporary boyfriend: "It's similar to the case method. And he's great in bed." Wasserstein's humor has much to do with the fact that she is writing about middle-class characters. As she has said, "there's something comedic about bourgeois human nature because it has to do with surviving." Judaism's tradition of Talmudic study means that all of life was open to examination.

In addition to verbal wit, *Isn't It Romantic* derives its humor from comic situations and timing. Mrs. Blumberg enters in a cape with an attaché case, singing "Sunrise, Sunset," turns on her Jazzercise tape, takes off her cape to reveal a tie-dyed leotard, awakens Janie, and hassles her about unpacking. Later, just as Janie calls Harriet to ask her how to cook a chicken, perhaps inspired by Katharine Hepburn in *Woman of the Year,* her parents arrive, followed by the Russian taxi driver who wants to see *The Sorrow and the Pity*, then by the Jewish doctor with the chicken. Janie unwraps it on the coffee table, lifts it up by two wings over her head, and stares at it.

Wasserstein juxtaposes the play's Jewish references and geography with a WASP world, represented by Harriet and Lillian Cornwall. In the play, the Blumbergs are originally from eastern Europe, while the Cornwalls are northern European. To draw the contrast, Janie says that Harriet looks like "a Vermeer," a seventeenth-century Dutch painter of blonde women, while Janie looks like "an extra from Potemkin," the 1925 silent film about the 1905 Russian uprising against the Tsarist regime on the battleship *Potemkin*. Janie sees herself not only as part of an oppressed Russian group, but further marginalized as "an extra" on the movie set. In addition, Marty's father exemplifies the Jew who wants to assimilate into Anglo-American culture through his chain of medieval English–sounding Sterling Tavernes, with a specialty in popovers (an Americanized version of Yorkshire pudding). To become more American, Mr. Schlimovitz hoped to Anglicize his identity in order to assimilate himself into the business world and his son into an Ivy League education.

In various essays, Wasserstein has written about WASP culture in contrast to Jewish culture. She associates WASPs with Saab cars; lacrosse sticks; Darien, Connecticut; names like Ed, Rick, and Jim; faded cardigans; Lilly Pulitzer dresses; egg salad sandwiches; Pappagallo shoes; prep schools; running and sculling; cocktails; candy dishes (and uneaten candy); and headbands. This is Harriet's world, and she is the foil to Janie. When Harriet enters in scene one, she sings the 1976 commercial for Revlon's "Charlie" fragrance, which featured the WASP-y looking Shelley Hack. The "Charlie Girl" arrived at a swanky hotel in a Bentley convertible, tossed her hat to the doorman, spun around with her boyfriend in the cocktail lounge, and sank into a chair with him as Bobby Short sang about the fragrance for the "kinda young, kinda now, kinda free, kinda wow." Charlie was the cologne for women who "lived in the fast lane." A Harvard MBA, Harriet is "attractive, bright, charming, and easily put together." She also comes from money, and her interviewer at Colgate Palmolive is impressed that she "took a year off to look at pictures in Italy." Harriet is a pedigree WASP.

Popularized by sociologist Digby Baltzell in his 1964 book *The Protestant Establishment: Aristocracy and Caste in America,* the term WASP originally referred to the white, Anglo-Saxon, Protestant segment of the U.S. population whose ancestors had founded the nation and who traced their heritage to England or to western Europe. Now, with only twenty-five percent of the population being WASP, the term has come to mean "the Establishment," or privileged white Protestants. Wasserstein is not using WASP in the derogatory sense that it has acquired, but rather as a sociological marker of affluence in a culture that differed from the Blumbergs'. WASP culture included social registers that listed the privileged who mingled in the same private clubs, attended the same churches, and lived in neighborhoods like Philadelphia's Main Line, New York City's Upper East Side, and Boston's Beacon Hill, which separated the well bred from the merely wealthy. It is not surprising, then, that class and wealth become the central issues in Wasserstein's 1990s play *Old Money.*

Class and gender are inextricably connected in *Isn't It Romantic,* as they are in all of Wasserstein's work. The Blumbergs sent their daughter to the Helena Rubinstein Charm School, where Janie learned everything from how to put on makeup to how to charm a date—in other words, feminine style and grace. Rubinstein's etiquette for meeting, pleasing, and keeping a man was something that even the first All-American Girls

Professional Baseball League studied from 1943 to 1954. The pioneer of skin-care creams, cosmetics, perfumes, sunscreens, day spas, and manners, Rubinstein banked on women's quest for beauty and youth in order to attract men. Her charm school sought to instill "femininity" and "the highest ideals of womanhood" in young American women. Rubinstein proclaimed, "There are no ugly women, only lazy ones." In all respects, it was a school where Janie did not feel at home. Her mother recalls that Janie always arrived late "with your hair in your eyes and your hem hanging down."

Similarly, the mink coat that her parents give her at the end, which fits her mother "perfectly," represents a world and a lifestyle that do not fit Janie, so she rejects it. She tells them, "If I was thirty-six and married to a doctor and a size three, this would be perfect for me." The coat does not fit and neither do its values. Janie feels that her parents expect her to call saying, "Everything is settled. Everything has worked out wonderfully," because Janie's father believes, "Everything presses itself out." In 1983, however, American women were far from being settled. "Going on location with the letter C" for *Sesame Street* does not represent the ultimate professional achievement for women, but could be read as stereotyping women's work with children. Janie is not off writing her own work. *Isn't It Romantic* registers this transitional period for women in 1983. In doing so, it subverts unrealistic notions of romance, romantic comedy, and traditional definitions of womanhood. While Janie rejects "the feminine mystique," she recognizes that it may work for some women. She tells her parents, "There's nothing wrong with that life, but it just isn't mine right now." She adds, "I don't see how I can help you understand what I'm doing. Neither of you ever lived alone; you never thought maybe I won't have children and what will I do with my life if I don't."

Like the nineteenth-century utopian socialist and feminist revolutions that Ellen Dubois explored in her 1983 book *Eve and the New Jerusalem,* the feminism of *Isn't It Romantic* calls for revolutionizing marriage and the family. Janie's parents want to know "who's going to take care of you when we're not around anymore." Janie responds, "*I* will." She is neither at home in her parents' house nor willing to marry someone whom she does not love. In an early draft, Janie tells her parents, "Your house isn't my home," and in the final draft, "All you have to do is trust me a little bit." Only at the end of the play does she begin unpacking the crates that we saw at the beginning when she first moved to her apartment. She is beginning to unpack herself, to find out who she is, and to start an independent life.

In the margins of a spiral notebook draft of the play in which Janie was speaking to a psychiatrist, Stanley, she quotes Bob Dylan's lyrics: "How does it feel to be on your own with no direction home, just like a rolling stone." Although these words did not end up in the final play, Dylan's lyrics speak to the uncertainty that women faced in 1983. Like another Janie in Zora Neale Hurston's 1939 novel *Their Eyes Were Watching God,* Janie Blumberg decides "to find out about living for [herself]." This was not an academic issue but a social one, and Wasserstein

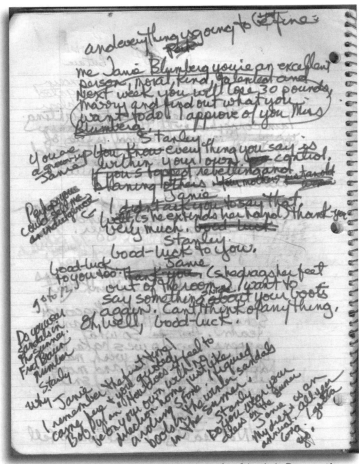

Notebook page from unpublished draft of *Isn't It Romantic.*
(Courtesy of the Wendy Wasserstein estate)

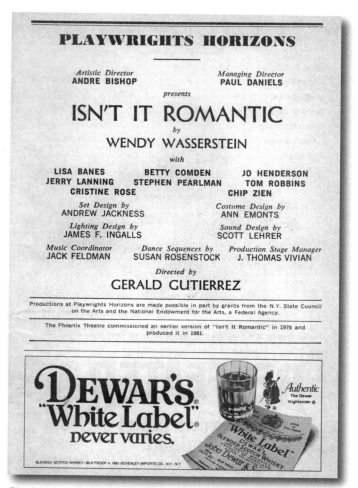

Playbill for 1983 Playwrights Horizons production of
Isn't It Romantic. (Photofest/With permission of Playbill, Inc.)

wanted to reach broad audiences by adapting the play to the screen for
Robert Shapiro Productions. Unfortunately, the film was never produced.
Nevertheless, the play was saying that life is "as shaky as a fiddler on the
roof," but that without change, life cannot progress. *Isn't It Romantic* is
not just about anachronistic values, but also about ones that never fit
certain women like Janie Blumberg.

PLAYWRIGHTS HORIZONS

Artistic Director
ANDRE BISHOP

Executive Director
PAUL S. DANIELS

presents

THE HEIDI CHRONICLES

by

WENDY WASSERSTEIN

CAST

(in alphabetical order)

JOAN ALLEN	**JOANNE CAMP**	**PETER FRIEDMAN**
BOYD GAINES	**ANNE LANGE**	**DREW McVETY**
ELLEN PARKER	**SARAH JESSICA PARKER**	

Set Design by
THOMAS LYNCH

Costume Design by
JENNIFER VON MAYRHAUSER

Lighting Design by
PAT COLLINS

Sound Design by
SCOTT LEHRER

Production Stage Manager
ROY HARRIS

Production Manager
CARL MULERT

Directed by

DANIEL SULLIVAN

This production has been awarded a grant from the Fund for New American Plays, a project of the John F. Kennedy Center for the Performing Arts, with support from the American Express Company in cooperation with the President's Committee on the Arts and the Humanities.

Playwrights Horizons is supported, in part, by public funds from the National Endowment for the Arts, the New York State Council on the Arts and the Department of Cultural Affairs of the City of New York.

47

Playbill for the Off-Broadway Playwrights Horizons production of *The Heidi Chronicles.* (Photofest/With permission of Playbill, Inc.)

The Heidi Chronicles (1988)

The Dissolution of the Feminist Movement, from Liberal Ideals to Conservative Backlash

I wrote this play because I had this image of a woman standing up at a women's meeting saying, "I've never been so unhappy in my life. . . ."

—Wendy Wasserstein

The Heidi Chronicles dramatizes a romantic, witty, unmarried art history professor at Columbia University, Heidi Holland, approaching middle age and becoming disillusioned with the collapse of the idealism that shaped the sixties. Spanning twenty-three years, the play begins with Heidi's slide lecture about the neglect of women artists and then travels back to a 1965 Chicago high school dance, where she meets the lifelong friends whose feminist values fluctuate. In college, Heidi and her friends become passionate feminists and liberals: we see them at a 1968 Eugene McCarthy rally in New Hampshire, a 1970 Ann Arbor consciousness-raising session, and a 1974 protest for women artists at the Art Institute of Chicago.

While Heidi remains committed to the ideals of feminism, her friends become swept away by the materialism and narcissism of the Reagan eighties, leading the vacuous lives they once denounced. Heidi feels stranded. At her 1986 high school alumni luncheon, the climax of the play, she confesses her feelings of abandonment and her disappointment with her peers: "I thought the point was we were all in this together." By the end of the play in 1989, however, Heidi feels a little less alone and depressed in her New York apartment, having adopted a daughter as a single parent. She hopes that her daughter will feel the confidence and dignity that were the aims of the women's movement.

The play grew out of Wasserstein's strong feminist sentiments: "I wrote this play because I had this image of a woman standing up at a women's meeting saying, 'I've never been so unhappy in my life. . . .' The more angry it made me that these feelings weren't being expressed, the more anger I put into that play." A comedy of manners, satirically depicting the concerns and conventions of a group of yuppies and a pair of witty lovers—Scoop and Heidi—the play exposes the marginalization of women artists, sexism in general, women's loss of identity, an unromantic view of marriage, and the lost idealism of the second wave of feminism that began in the early sixties.

Unlike the first wave of feminism of the nineteenth and early twentieth centuries, which focused on officially mandated inequalities, like gaining women's suffrage, the second wave encouraged women to understand the psychological implications of sexist stereotypes and opened the eyes of American women to careers and achievement, which they had lost in post—World War II America.

From the start, Heidi, standing in a lecture hall showing slides of paintings, addresses the neglect of women artists. She then points out the difference between the male and female sensibility: "Clara Peeters used more geometry and less detail than her male peers." This aesthetic difference becomes a metaphor for gender conflict throughout the play. Although female characters are frustrated that they derive their identities from men, they frantically seek boyfriends. Heidi treats this problem with humor as she segues from the art history lecture back to a 1965 high school dance: "This painting has always reminded me of one of those horrible high school dances. And you sort of want to dance, and you sort of want to go home, and you sort of don't know what you want. So you hang around, a fading rose in an exquisitely detailed dress, waiting to see what might happen."

During the 1965 dance, we hear the "The Shoop Shoop Song," whose lyrics answered the question of anxious young American women: "How can I tell if he loves me so?" with "It's in his kiss." The song became a hit with Betty Everett's 1963 album *It's in His Kiss*. During this song, Heidi declines the All-American Chris Boxer's invitation to dance the "Hully Gully"—a sixties line dance consisting of a series of quick steps called out by the MC. Her friend Susan, however, advises her on how to get a guy to dance with her: "Don't look desperate. Men don't dance with desperate women." Eyeing a Bobby Kennedy lookalike, who is "twisting and smoking" in his "vest, blue jeans, tweed jacket and Wee-juns," Susan quickly unbuttons her sweater, rolls up her skirt, and pulls a necklace out of her purse. She cautions Heidi, ". . . you're going to get really messed up unless you learn to take men seriously," and "The worst thing you can do is cluster. 'Cause then it looks like you just wanna hang around with your girlfriend."

Heidi is quick to point out that men are not such a big deal, that the only difference between men and women is biology: ". . . he can twist and smoke at the same time and we can get out of gym with an excuse called 'I have my monthly.'" As Peter Patrone approaches Heidi, who is now reading a book, the Rolling Stones' 1965 song "Play with Fire" plays, suggesting that Heidi is playing with fire by choosing not to be the representative 1965 girl. In another sense, playing with Peter Patrone is also "playing with fire"; although he may be Heidi's soul mate, he is unattainable, because, we later find out, he is gay. Peter and Heidi enact their own melodrama, pretending they are star-crossed lovers on a *Queen Mary* cruise. Their meta-drama ironizes the 1965 high school dance; the sanitarium replaces the church wedding (Heidi declines Peter's proposal, saying she covets her independence), and Peter and Heidi never kiss.

Two years after *The Feminine Mystique* (1963) and one year before the establishment of the National Organization of Women in 1966, the scene represents two kinds of women—those who seek the chapel of love (which Susan identifies as the culmination of the journey begun on the dance floor) and those, like Susan and Heidi, who want independence. In fact, the song "The Chapel of Love," written by Jeff Barry, Ellie Greenwich, and Phil Spector, and made famous by the Dixie Cups, spent three weeks at Number One on the *Billboard* Hot 100 in 1964. While some women had their eyes fixed on marriage, others were protesting the United States' bombing of North Vietnam on college campuses. That same year the Supreme Court declared that married couples had a right to birth control based on their "right to privacy" in *Griswold v. Connecticut.*

Heidi, however, is not unconditionally independent. In fact, her judgment about men is sometimes questionable. She drops everything for "a charismatic creep," Scoop Rosenbaum, at the 1968 Eugene McCarthy rally. Sexist and obnoxious, Scoop assaults Heidi's dignity by telling her,

Peace protest on Mount Holyoke's campus, as shown in a 1968 *Mount Holyoke College Bulletin*. (Mount Holyoke College Archives and Special Collections)

unprovoked, that she is "being very difficult" and devalues her intelligence by saying, "The changes in this country could be enormous. Beyond anything your sister mind can imagine." He quickly dismisses Heidi's aspirations to be an art historian as "really suburban" and he condescendingly labels women who go to "Seven Sister schools" as "concerned citizens." Furthermore, he reduces the whole fight for women's equality to "equal pay, equal rights, and equal orgasms." Heidi insists that all people deserve to fulfill their potential: "I mean, why should some well-educated woman waste her life making you and your children tuna sandwiches?" While Scoop agrees that neither should "a badly educated woman" be wasting her life, he continues to patronize Heidi by correcting her word choices, and confesses that his real goal is to get her to go to bed with him. He frankly admits Heidi has little reason to like him but predicts she'll tolerate him anyway because he is "very smart." This prompts the exasperated Heidi to ask what mysterious thing "mothers teach their sons that they never bother to tell their daughters. I mean . . . why . . . are you so confident?" The women's movement sought to rectify this double standard.

During the above scene, we hear Janis Joplin's 1968 "Take a Piece of My Heart," a song about a woman who feels she has "had enough" of the man who takes pieces of her heart, but keeps coming back for more, because "a woman can be tough." The lyrics echo Scoop's exploitative behavior in the scene, while also conveying Heidi's resilience in the face of his chauvinism. Cultural critic Ellen Willis noted that when Aretha Franklin sings "Take a Piece of My Heart," it is a challenge: "No matter what you do to me, I will not let you destroy my ability to be human, to love." In contrast, Joplin's rendition suggests, "If I keep taking this, if I keep setting an example of love and forgiveness, surely he has to understand, change, give me back what I have given." Therefore, Joplin used blues conventions not to transcend pain, but "to scream it out of existence." "Take a Piece of My Heart," then, represented the problem of unequal power between men and women.

Women were working hard for equality in 1968: New York feminists buried a dummy of "Traditional Womanhood" at the all-women's demonstration against the Vietnam War in Washington, D.C. led by Jeanette Rankin (a pacifist and the first woman elected to the U.S. Congress). For the first time, feminists used the slogan "Sisterhood Is Pow-

Scoop (Tony Shalhoub) and Heidi (Christine Lahti) at a Eugene McCarthy rally in the Off-Broadway production of *The Heidi Chronicles*. (Photofest)

Eugene McCarthy rally in 1968. (Time & Life Pictures/Getty Images)

erful." In Chicago, the First National Women's Liberation Conference met, while women created the National Abortion Rights Action League and the Women's Equity Action League. Nineteen-sixty-eight also marked the year that the Equal Employment Opportunity Commission ruled that sex-segregated help wanted ads in newspapers were illegal, opening the way for women to apply for higher-paying jobs that used to be open only to men. In 1969, women picketed the Miss America Pageant on Atlantic City's Boardwalk, protesting the objectification of women that feminists had declared unacceptable.

Nineteen-sixty-eight was also a year of worldwide political protest. From the Paris Commune to Prague to Mexico City to Cape Town to Columbia University, students and workers were questioning white men in power. In America, women's rights, the Vietnam War, and civil rights were really all part of the same revolution. Scoop and Heidi are at the Eugene McCarthy rally, because McCarthy represented change, crusading for reform of the CIA, the FBI, and the draft boards. Competing with McCarthy for the Democratic ticket was Robert Kennedy, who also appealed to the antiwar movement, to African Americans, and to the disenfranchised. When RFK was shot in 1968, the same year Martin Luther King, who was trying to take us to the promised land of racial equality, was assassinated; it became "the year the dream died" for America. The liberal hope that they represented, started by JFK, ended. As one historian put it, "We became *might have beens.*" Richard Nixon defeated Hubert Humphrey by less than one percent of the popular vote in 1968, appealing to what he called the "silent majority" of socially conservative Americans. Before the election, feminists rated Nixon among the worst candidates for women's issues. Scoop, attending the rally as a journalist rather than a McCarthy supporter, claims, "McCarthy is irrelevant. He's a C+ Adlai Stevenson." (Stevenson had also been an advocate of liberal causes in the Democratic party.) While Scoop acknowledges the potential of the women's movement, telling Heidi, "You're the one whose life this will all change significantly. Has to," in the same breath he adds, "You'll be one of those true believers who didn't understand it was all just a phase." His words highlight the play's central concern about the collapse of the women's movement in the eighties.

The sparring between Scoop and Heidi concludes with Heidi agreeing to spend the night with Scoop as "White Rabbit" plays. The psyche-

A protest outside the Miss America Pageant in 1968. (Getty Images)

delic rock song from Jefferson Airplane's 1967 album *Surrealistic Pillow* underscores the irrationality of her decision. The White Rabbit is a fictional character in Lewis Carroll's *Alice's Adventures in Wonderland* whom Alice follows down the rabbit hole into Wonderland. With its enigmatic lyrics, "White Rabbit" became one of the first songs to sneak drug references past censors on the radio. Sometimes compared to Ravel's *Bolero*, "White Rabbit" evokes the distorted perception of a dreamworld. ("One pill makes you larger and one pill makes you small. . . .") For the sixties generation, drugs were part of mind-expanding and social experimentation. First performed by composer Grace Slick with her band the Great Society in 1966, the song makes connections between the hallucinatory effects of LSD and the images in Carroll's 1865's *Alice's Adventures in Wonderland* and its 1871 sequel, *Through the Looking-Glass.* Janis Joplin sang "White Rabbit" at Woodstock in 1969, making it representative of the social revolution and its consciousness-altering impact on a whole generation. Just as Alice follows a mysterious white rabbit into a rabbit hole to enter "Wonderland," an absurd and improbable world inhabited by many strange characters, at the end of scene two of *The Heidi Chronicles*, the song signals Heidi's entrance into a new world. Like Alice, by the end of the play in 1989, she comes out the other end of the social revolution with a sobering realization that it was a transient dream.

In order to combat the sexism that Scoop represents, women began joining consciousness-raising groups in the late sixties. Scene three represents a seventies version of such a group in which Aretha Franklin's "Respect," adopted as an anthem by the civil rights and feminist movements, blares in the background. Seated in a circle, the group represents a broad spectrum of women—preppy, feminine, lesbian, tomboy, young, and middle-aged: Jill, forty, in whale turtleneck and pleated skirt; Fran, thirty, in army fatigues; Becky, seventeen, in poncho; others in hiking boots and down jackets. They embrace, tell one another, "I love you," and call each other "lamb." Fran, having overcompensated for her effacement, is trying to "work through coming on a little strong." Jill confesses that when she first joined, she was "a Hostess cupcake" because she subordinated herself to every man, and Fran tells Heidi, who is visiting, not to judge them, because they spend their lives being judged by men. Becky's relationship with her boyfriend has rendered her voiceless and subordinate: "I mean, I try to be super nice to him. I make all his meals, and I never disagree with him. But then he just gets angry or

Consciousness-raising group in the Off-Broadway production. *Left to right:* Marita Geraghty, Anne Lange, Deborah Hedwall, Christine Lahti, and Amy Aquino. (Photofest)

stoned. So when I need to think things through, I lock the bathroom door and cry. But I try not to make any sound."

Heidi, who at first is reluctant to share her relationship troubles because they are "personal," finally admits that she allows her off-again, on-again relationship with Scoop to determine her feeling of self-worth. She knows she is not as powerless as she feels—"The problem isn't really him. It's me. I could make a better choice"—and that it is not only male behavior, but the way that women have been socialized to relate to men, that results in a lack of self-esteem for women. As Heidi says, "I keep allowing this guy to account for so much of what I think of myself. I know that's wrong. I would tell any friend that's wrong." Aware of the problem, she cannot solve it for herself: "If I decide to get better and leave him, he's unbelievably attentive." Or, as Jill puts it, "'Personal' means I know what I'm doing is wrong, but I have so little faith in myself, I'm going to keep it a secret and go right on doing it." Heidi hopes that their "daughters never feel like us," that they feel "worthwhile." Fran echoes the problem of women's subordination to men and becomes a spokesperson for women's equality:

Heidi, every woman in this room has been taught that the desires and dreams of her husband, her son, or her boss are much more important than her own. And the only way to turn that around is for us, right here, to try to make what we want, what we desire to be as vital as it would undoubtedly be to any man. And then we can go out there and really make a difference!

In order for men and women to compete fairly, the male establishment needed to be reformed, and the play documents this dilemma. Susan, who might be Kate from *Uncommon Women,* considers beginning a law journal devoted solely to women's legal issues, but after heavy deliberation decides to "work within the male-establishment power base to change the system." Fran, however, claims that Susan is compromising, that it would be like Fran "dating Tricia Nixon": "You either shave your legs or you don't"; you are either a feminist or not. The play asks whether women are selling out if they do not abandon the system that oppresses them. Fran represents the prevailing radical view of the time. Susan moves with the trends, not from an internal set of values, like Harriet in *Uncommon Women.*

The fight for equality was still slow in 1970, and with the consciousness-raising scene, Wasserstein dramatizes an important ritual of the feminist movement. "CR" groups were pioneered by New York Radical Women, an early women's liberation group in New York City, and quickly spread throughout the United States. As in the play, meetings involved "going around the room and rapping" about issues in their own lives. Feminists adopted the phrase "consciousness raising" from the Old Left, who had adopted it to awaken workers about their oppression. The groups began in America as a result of early radical feminists' belief that women were isolated from each other, and that many problems in women's lives were misunderstood as "personal," as the results of conflicts between the personalities of individual men and women, rather than as systematic forms of oppression. Raising consciousness meant helping oneself and helping others to become politically conscious. The groups aimed to better understand women's oppression by bringing women together to discuss and analyze their lives, without interference from men. Weekly meetings of a small group of women, held in one of the members' living room, usually involved going around the room and having each woman "rap" about a predetermined subject, speaking from her own experience, without a formal leader or rules. Feminists believed that their feelings would lead them to ideas and then to actions.

Critic Iska Alter argues that Wasserstein reduces the consciousness-raising group to a kind of twelve-step self-help organization that supplies a sense of personal wholeness to women, instead of working toward any larger social change. Fran cannot promise her friends that their daughters will feel worthwhile, so she offers Heidi instead her love and a hug, reducing the consciousness-raising group to parody. Alter is convinced that Heidi's unrealistic demand "reveals Wasserstein's insular view of feminism, drained of political context, ideological analyses, and intellectual rigor, the very tools necessary to understand and change the social hierarchies and cultural systems that have created and sustained the gender imbalance that Heidi articulates only in personal terms." The personal, however, is political; as Fran says at the CR meeting, "nothing is going to change until we really start talking to each other." When Jill invites Becky to move in with her, her decision stands for a national feminist solidarity. At the end of the scene, Aretha Franklin's "Respect" replaces the friendship song.

The play continues to track the women's movement in scene four. Outside the Chicago Art Institute, the Chicago Women's Art Coalition pickets for equal representation of female artists in front of a banner for "The Age of Napoleon" in 1974. Though Peter insists on protesting, they refuse to allow men to participate, and he is ousted from the march after comically acknowledging the patriarchal tradition of art history, and all history, with the cry "No more master penises!" Heidi explains to Peter, "No man really plays on our team. And no man isn't threatened

Aretha Franklin on one of her album covers.
(Photofest)

Robert Curtis-Brown, Amy Irving, and Michael Sandels at a Women in Art protest in an Off-Broadway production. (Photofest)

by our potential." If women were going to gain equality, they could not count on men to help them. Wasserstein set this scene in Chicago for historical reasons: 1974 was the year in which more than 3,000 women from fifty-eight unions attended a Chicago meeting where the Coalition of Labor Union Women was formed. In addition, Heidi's assertion occurs in a scene that also includes references to Watergate. In 1974, America was insisting that not only men in general, but also the man in the White House be held accountable for cheating.

Gay liberation, like the women's movement, was young in 1974. Peter tells Heidi, "*My* liberation, *my* pursuit of happiness is just as politically and socially valid as yours." He does not feel that Heidi really understands his situation or his community: "I know you think that my world is small and personal and yours resonates for generations to come." It seems surprising that although the gay and feminist characters are such good friends, they do not seem to empathize with the discrimination that each faces. When Heidi decides to move to the Midwest to teach at Carleton College, in part because she feels sad about her life in New York City, Peter responds that after losing so many friends from AIDS, "a sadness like yours seems a luxury." Equal rights are hardly a luxury, but in light of AIDS, they seem that way to Peter. All liberation should be equal, but the play suggests that people are primarily interested in their own cause.

Along with the struggle of the feminist and gay movements, the play chronicles the collapse of marriage, represented by Scoop and Lisa's 1977 wedding, set at the Pierre Hotel (a Taj Hotel and New York landmark since 1930, on Central Park at Fifth Avenue and Sixty-first Street). When Susan's girlfriend from the "Montana collective" arrives at the Pierre, she notes a cultural and psychological shift, alluding to *The Wizard of Oz*:

"I have a feeling we're not in Montana anymore." The Midwest is always another country in Wasserstein's plays—innocent and conservative, while New York represents experience and liberalism. When Peter asks Scoop if he is in love, he retorts, "Sure, why not?" For Scoop, marriage is a pragmatic contract: "Makes sense. Lisa marries a nice Jewish lawyer; Heidi marries a warm Italian pediatrician. It's all interchangeable, isn't it?" Later in scene four, the "divorced Senate wives modeling coats for spring" who follow Peter, Scoop, and Heidi on *Hello New York* also represent the breakdown of family and politics. In the wedding scene, however, Lisa, unlike Heidi, places marriage and family before her career: "I've always known I wanted to be a mom. I guess that's pretty embarrassing." Still, she wants to "keep up" her "illustration work," but Scoop patronizingly responds, "We'll see." He assumes control of her life decisions, while she confines her power to a smaller scale, telling Heidi that "it's so much fun to push [men] around"—that is, to elicit a reaction from them, as opposed to threatening them on a deep level. Scoop admits to Heidi, who is now writing a book hyperbolically called *And the Light Floods in from the Left and Other Overcommitments*, "I don't want to come home to an A+. A− maybe, but not A+ . . . I couldn't dangle you anymore. . . . You want other things in life than I do. . . . Self-fulfillment. Self-determination. Self-exaggeration. . . . Then you'd be competing with me." Equating self-determination with self-exaggeration, he tells Heidi that her ambition will leave her frustrated:

> On a scale of one to ten, if you aim for six and get six, everything will work out nicely. But if you aim for ten in all things and get six, then you're going to be very disappointed. And, unfortunately, that's why you "quality time" girls are going to be one generation of disappointed women. Interesting, exemplary . . . but basically unhappy. The ones who open doors usually are.

Social revolutions and visionaries inevitably fall short of their ambitious goals, but Scoop is patronizing Heidi by warning her not to aspire to be her best. The effort is the victory. In contrast to the sixties, when women hoped to be superwomen, both homemakers and professional powerhouses, by 1977 American women realized that they could not have it all and chose to make compromises. Scoop tells Heidi, "It's either/or" and that she has made "life choices"; "otherwise we'd be getting married." Though they end the scene slow-dancing to Sam Cooke's number

Ronald Reagan and George H. W. Bush campaigning in 1980. (Ronald Reagan Library/Photofest; © Ronald Reagan Library)

one 1957 soul song "You Send Me," as if they were a married couple, Heidi could never marry someone who does not want women to compete and achieve their best. Scoop's lack of progressive values seems to match Lisa's, but their marriage does not work out, suggesting that unequal power relations are doomed. According to Wasserstein, by 1980, the feminist movement began dissolving, and the play reflects this shift. The opulent Pierre Hotel wedding, celebrating the convention of marriage and later family, echoes a national conservatism that called for family values. Later, at Lisa's baby shower, we learn that Scoop is having an affair with the graphics assistant of his magazine, who is notorious for her leather miniskirts and fishnet stockings. Having opinions about everything without having done anything, Scoop's mistress represents a phony feminist. Set in 1980, the baby shower scene coincides with the conservative wave that came with Reagan's presidential election.

Breaking new ground in a patriarchal world was difficult. Accordingly, *Savvy*, a new magazine for executive women that previewed in *New York Magazine*, provided one response to this 1977 scene about frustrated women. It featured an article called "The New Girl Network: A Power System for the Future" that called for "ending isolation and passivity among ambitious women" through a "new girls'" network, just as the old boys' network had always done. Women at the top of their game needed professional solidarity, because they were not one of the boys, nor were they just one of the girls.

This conservatism is also reflected in the talk show scene, *Hello New York*. The topics include social conscience, Reaganomics, careers, the "death of the ERA," and kids. Scoop calls the eighties "a decade defined as sexy and greedy." In fact, in the eighties, Wall Street experienced "merger mania" as antitrust laws were not enforced and a wave of corporate takeovers—mergers and acquisitions—junk bonds, and insider trading began. Each business merger required brokers, lawyers, and bankers, creating a new class of businesspeople known as "young urban professionals," or yuppies—the people Wasserstein writes about. David Wright describes yuppies of the eighties as follows: "People saw money as power. Young executives consumed 'power lunches' while wearing fashionable 'power suits.' Labels crept from the inside to the outside of clothes, as designer fashions boosted egos and fattened the cash registers of swank stores."

Reagan's $43 billion in budget cuts to domestic programs and cutbacks in regulations that affected business and the environment defined "Reaganomics." Wealth was supposed to trickle down from the wealthy to the poor, but, in fact, the gap between rich and poor grew wider. As Kevin Phillips, assistant attorney general in the Nixon administration, writes,

> The 1980s were a triumph of upper America—an ostentatious celebration of wealth, the political ascendancy of the richest third of the population and a glorification of capitalism, free markets, and finance. But while money, greed, and luxury had become the stuff of popular culture, hardly anyone asked why such great wealth had concentrated at the top, and whether this was the result of public policy. Despite the armies of homeless sleeping on grates, political leaders had little to say about the Republican party's historical role, which has been not simply to revitalize U.S. capitalism but to tilt power, policy, wealth, and income towards the richest portions of the population.

The Michael Milkens of the eighties gave way to the Bernie Madoffs of the early twenty-first century. In the eighties, Reagan also instilled opti-

An iconic photograph of John Lennon. (© Bob Gruen/bobgruen.com)

mism in the public with statements like "There are no such things as limits to growth, because there are no limits on the human capacity for intelligence, imagination and wonder." That wonder differs from Scoop's reference to a Ferlinghetti poem about "awaiting the rebirth of wonder." Ferlinghetti urged writers to engage with politics, and his San Francisco City Lights bookstore published the works of Beat writers like Allen Ginsburg and Jack Kerouac who advocated antiestablishment values.

The liberal values of the sixties and the conservative ones of the eighties, then, provide the two bookends for *The Heidi Chronicles*. Accordingly, in scene four, Wasserstein chooses John Lennon's 1980 assassination and memorial as the occasion for Lisa's baby shower and the end of liberal values. The soundtrack for the party is Lennon's "Imagine," whose lyrics imagine a world free of war, prejudice, possessions, and hunger at a time of corporate greed and social cutbacks. Social standing replaced solidarity and peace, leading Peter to say that the standard for success for their generation is being on *Hello, New York*. With Lennon's death, hippies gave way to yuppies, and the play documents this transition. During the *Hello New York* scene about Boomers, Scoop wants to distinguish his generation from the yuppies:

We're serious people with a sense of humor. We're not young professionals, and we're not old lefties or righties. We're unique.

We're powerful, but not bullies. We're rich, but not ostentatious. We're parents, but not parental. And I think we had the left magazines in college, we had the music magazines in the seventies, and now we deserve what I call a "power" magazine in the eighties. We're opinion- and trendsetters, and I hope *Boomer* is our chronicle.

After college, Scoop abandoned the *Liberated Earth News* for *Boomer* magazine, which tracks the trends of the eighties. "An arbiter of good taste in a decade defined as sexy and greedy," Scoop and his magazine "helped get a few people elected and a few people investigated" and "was responsible for a chintz renaissance." Peter tells him, "People like you run the world. You decide what it's all for." Scoop and the characters in the play represent the Baby Boomers.

Daniel Yankelovich divides the Boomers into two categories: the first comprises those born from 1946 to 1954, whose memorable events were the assassinations of JFK, Robert Kennedy, and Martin Luther King; political unrest; the first walk on the moon; the Vietnam War; antiwar protests; social experimentation; sexual freedom; the civil rights movement; the environmental movement; the women's movement; protests and riots; and experimentation with mind-altering substances. Experimentalism, individualism, free-spiritedness, and involvement in social causes characterize them. The later Boomers, born from 1955 to 1964, have a different set of memorable events: Watergate, Nixon's resignation, the Cold War, the oil embargo, raging inflation, gasoline shortages. They are less optimistic, more distrustful of government, and more cynical than their predecessors. The characters in *The Heidi Chronicles* have a foot in each group.

At the end of the play, Peter tells Heidi he might "do something crazy like announce I'm running for Congress . . . Gay men and single mothers for Rosenbaum. . . . A man for all genders." It is hard to imagine that the guy who jokes about selling *Boomer* according to whether he "could get the lemon soufflé at Lutèce without ordering a day in advance" and has his "secretary" choose a gift for Heidi's daughter will really become a liberal congressman. If he is sincere, then the ending can be read as an attempt to redeem the conservative backlash that the play chronicles.

According to Wasserstein, part of this backlash included women who wanted to "have it all" but realized that they could not and then blamed their frustration on the rights they had won. When Heidi appears on the talk show with Peter and Scoop, who constantly cut Heidi off, the interviewer, April, tells Heidi, "A lot of women are beginning to feel you can't have it all. Do you think it's time to compromise?" Heidi does not have a chance to reply, because Scoop interrupts her. Early eighties history reveals that women were led to believe that their problems came from having achieved equality with men, when in truth equality still eluded them. Wasserstein set the *Hello New York* scene in 1982, the year that Gloria Steinem articulated an agenda for the women's movement: to reintroduce the ERA, to retire Superwoman, to make "our own" economy, and "to turn out our own vote." Women could not afford to "compromise" on needed progress.

Heidi's friend Denise exemplifies wanting "it all." She complains of a shortage of men, since "Once my career's in place, I definitely want to have my children before I'm thirty. I mean, isn't that what you guys fought for? So we could 'have it all'?" Although Heidi turned down a marriage offer in England for a job at Columbia University, the other women at the shower lament that there are no eligible men for "such fabulous attractive" women. Later, Denise says, "Our girls have a plan. They want to get married in their twenties, have their first baby by thirty, and make a pot of money." Robert Brustein argued that "the feminist movement, instead of reforming society, has succeeded largely in introducing women to the ravening competitiveness of the eighties, adapting women to the worst qualities of men." Wasserstein, too, was dismayed by the direction that the feminist movement had taken, as she told me in conversation: "It was that whole idea of the We Generation, and then suddenly everyone was going off in their own direction. . . . Was the purpose of all this so that twenty-year-old girls can get MBAs?" For Wasserstein, feminism goes astray when it becomes "about being acquisitive." In addition, she was troubled by the inordinate demands placed on women. As she told me, "I think there are wonderfully energetic people who manage to have children and careers. I've always thought that you do different things at different times in your life. But I think there's always been this pressure on women that you have to have children, a family, a career, a really good body; you have to stay young forever."

Heidi expresses the frustration of trying to have it all in her speech at the Miss Crain's School East Coast Alumnae Association in 1986. She suggests that she may have neglected to prepare a written speech because she was too busy being the bionic professor—going to a low-impact aerobics class, picking up her gifted children from school, prepar-

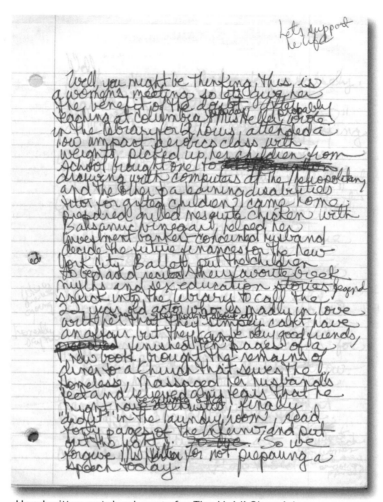

Handwritten notebook page for *The Heidi Chronicles:*
"Well, you might be thinking . . ." (Courtesy of the Wendy
Wasserstein estate)

ing grilled mesquite free-range chicken, advising her investment-banker
husband on future finances for the City Ballet, reciting her kids' favorite
Greek myths and sex-education legends at bedtime, calling the twenty-
two-year-old squash player who has a crush on her to tell him they can
only be friends, writing ten pages of a new book, taking the remains of
the mesquite free-range dinner to a church that feeds the homeless,
massaging her husband's feet, "doing it" with him in the kitchen to re-

lieve any fears that he might be getting old, reading forty pages of *The Inferno* in Italian, taking a deep breath, and putting out the light. The hyperbolic list conveys how overwhelmed some women were feeling. Heidi confirms the impossibility of having it all at the end of the play when she says that her daughter will "never think she's worthless unless [men let] her have it all." Since it's not possible to do everything, women feel inadequate; hence, more freedom comes with more problems. The more opportunity, the greater the frustration.

Scoop offers an important solution to the "superwoman" problem, the problem of trying to have it all: "If we're asking women to compromise, then we also have to ask men to compromise." His idea resonates with Pete Hamill's 1986 call for a new family structure in which men participated equally with women in raising families, for government's responsibility for child care and support of single parents. According to Hamill, for equality to happen, America needed a social revolution that the women in *The Heidi Chronicles* need but are unable to name. It would require that men go against their American upbringing of being competitive, driven to fame and power, and instead be compassionate and responsible. And this would require compromise for men in a world where the traditional family structure no longer exists because of economics and divorce:

> Having It All is a desire for perfection, and . . . the notion of the perfect is the enemy of all human beings. There are no perfect marriages, perfect children, perfect careers, perfect living arrangements, because there are no perfect human beings. Mr. and Mrs. Right do not exist. The ethos of the Reagan era urges us to tend our private gardens. But willed isolation from the real leads to disaster. . . . Conservatives act as if the traditional American family exists; but only 12% of American families are built on the old structure of husband as breadwinner, wife as homemaker. . . . Statistics indicate that 50% of American marriages will still end in divorce. There's a sunny impression that a booming stock market, the fall in oil prices, the growth of a service economy have created abundance and prosperity for all; but 1986 *Newsweek* says that to maintain a middle-class lifestyle of twenty years ago, husbands and wives must both work. . . . Of 1 million people 700,000 of them are women and children on welfare. . . . The traditional family, beloved of the American right

wing, is as dead as the big bands, and having it all is an adolescent slogan.

Accordingly, *Ms.* magazine, featuring a handsome young man with arms full of baby, briefcase, and bottle, decided that it was time to ask whether men could juggle their lives any better than women. In 1982, Scoop and Peter had not yet evolved into the kind of feminist male characters that Hamill and Wasserstein would have liked; perhaps that is why Heidi chooses adoption over marriage.

In a later 1984 scene in which Susan is trying to recruit Heidi to be her "consultant" about the art world for a television show about "three women turning thirty in a large urban center," Susan again represents an eroding feminism: "I'm not political anymore. I mean, equal rights is one thing, equal pay is one thing, but blaming everything on being a woman is just passé." In fact, in 1984, *Ms.* concluded with an article about the "sting of the liberal backlash," citing the following reasons: Men feared female competition for scarce jobs, and some men were angry at feminism for taking women out of the home, since homemakers economize during times of scarcity. The need for a second income did not always overcome resentment that women were "neglecting" their homes in hard times. Moreover, men who resisted change felt punished, angry, and sometimes guilty. The woman whom a man married became a different person once she had a career. Men who tried to share parenting and housework could not devote the time required to advance their careers; women with children found they could not get enough time off to enjoy them, could not find adequate child care, and also could not put in the hours necessary to get the professional recognition that would make it worthwhile. While research showed that despite these frustrations, women who worked for wages generally expressed more satisfaction with their lives than those who did not, *Ms.* pointed out that "it's easy for harassed egalitarians, both men and women, to blame feminism rather than the demands of work or the lack of adequate child care." Susan represents a popular misconception of the time.

According to some journalists in the late eighties, some women who were in their late twenties and early thirties in 1984 felt stranded by their success. They were the women who triumphantly entered law school, medical school, and business school throughout the seventies and later quickly advanced in their careers. But as they reached their thirties and started to think about having children, it became evident that having a family would be difficult given the demands of their successful careers. Those who were unmarried found eligible men resistant to women who had "made it." America had not changed to accommodate egalitarian families, and so these women faced the "the frightening realization that their hard-won careers might be at risk." For those young women, and even more for their husbands, the argument that women themselves *wanted* to stay home with kids had "a certain appeal. . . . It resolved a personal dilemma without challenging institutional realities." *Ms.* concluded that the backlash tried to make real problems of work and family go away by pushing us back to traditional solutions that do not work. It attempted to redirect our energies away from equalizing and humanizing our world by dismissing feminism's accomplishments and making our goals seem impossible. Its cruelest side was that it exploited what some women value most—their legitimate desire to have families, to preserve something of the emotional side of life. It implies that for women there must be a choice between equality and humanity, between work and family. Instead, satisfying lives for men and women depend on equalizing women's access to work and men's involvement in family. And this requires a long struggle to change basic institutions in society.

Although Heidi does not identify these sociological reasons behind her frustration, she refuses to believe that her generation "made mistakes" as one of her friends believes. Denise claims that "a lot of women your age are very unhappy. Unfulfilled, frightened of growing old alone." At the time, Jennifer Crichton wrote about the detrimental impact of the pressure to marry on women's self-esteem. Without discounting marriage, she wanted to impress on young women that marriage did not necessarily mean happiness in her article "Who's Winding the Matrimonial Clock?"

> The last thing we need again is for a woman alone to be deemed worthless or for women to be viewed as grasping creatures conniving to hook a man—single-mindedly bent on marriage as men allow themselves to be trapped—or for women to start believing they ought to be grateful to the men who agree to marry them. None of these elements "seem" to add up to a future of domestic bliss. . . . The people who wind up happily married, at all ages, are people who were happily unmarried: optimistic, assured, outward-looking and forward-thinking people who never lost the art of living or waited for marriage to start up their lives

for them. Most women who want to be married can contrive to marry someone. . . . But anxiety about one's marriage ability seems only to decrease one's chances of marrying happily. . . . Never underestimate the serendipity of love . . . how much the vagaries of human nature and chance factor into love relationships. In the meantime, be fearless. Don't be afraid of dying alone, of having missed out, of asking someone you're in love with to marry you.

Crichton's voice was not representative of the majority of American women in 1984, or of the women in the play—except for Heidi.

In addition, American women were frantically trying to start families later than at any time in history, a phenomenon reflected in the play. Susan tells Heidi, "Every other woman I know is either pregnant or just miscarried. Honestly, I've been to more fertility lunches." Heidi is planning to start her family at sixty: "I hear there's a hormone in Brazil." In vitro fertilization became a viable option for women once the first test tube baby was born in England in 1978. Part of this process included monthly peer support lunches for women who were trying to conceive. The play registers the fact that biological clocks were causing identity crises for many women in the eighties. In the above scene in which Susan is trying to recruit Heidi to be a consultant for a new television show about women, Heidi refers to the paradox of being female when she asks Susan, " Do you ever think that what makes you a person is also what keeps you from being a person?" If Heidi means that the ability to have children can also interfere with a woman's freedom, Susan does not get it. She responds, "By now I've been so many people, I don't know who I am. And I don't care." She has changed careers four times: from lawyer to radical shepherdess/counselor living on a Women's Health and Legal Collective in Montana to getting an MBA in New York to accepting a job in L.A. as an executive vice-president for a new production company. The play dramatizes the fluid state of values in the eighties, not only for women, but also for men. There were few constants like Scoop's reference to Smokey Robinson's three decades on his personal top ten list. Looking for meaning in the midst of transient values, Scoop asks Heidi at the end, "What's it all for?" Lost, he wants to marry Heidi, who declines, knowing she would never stay married to him, unlike his conventional wife, Lisa. Heidi is too much of an idealist to get married for the sake of getting married.

Despite the backlash of the eighties, there were some advances for women: Reagan appointed Sandra Day O'Connor the first woman justice on the Supreme Court, calling it the "most awesome appointment" within his power, and Democrats also made history in 1984 when presidential candidate Walter Mondale selected New York congresswoman Geraldine Ferraro as his running mate. *The New York Times* finally agreed to use the title Ms. instead of Miss or Mrs. Barbara Mikulski from Maryland became the first Democratic woman elected to the U.S. Senate who had not succeeded her husband. The number of women in the Senate doubled from one to two. *Newsweek* polls revealed that fifty-six percent of women considered themselves feminists. Seventy-one percent said that the movement had improved their lives, and only four percent described themselves as antifeminist.

These political achievements, however, do not appear in the play, and Heidi feels stranded in a world of Denises, Susans, and Scoops. She addresses the collapse of feminist idealism in her alumnae speech, which she formulates in the locker room where she encounters the empty values of her peers: the mother with the son at Harvard Law school who married a Brazilian hairdresser not good enough for him; Mrs. Green with the perfect nails who complains about the hardship of throwing a dinner party the same night as a benefit at the Met; a naked gray-haired woman "extolling the virtues of brown rice and women's fiction"; twenty-seven-year-olds draped in purple and green leather; and a concerned discussion about where to buy Zeus low-impact sneakers. Observing their busy schedules, alligator date books, and extra-heavy weights, Heidi feels disillusioned by these frantic, soulless, unhappy careerists, asserting, "I thought the whole point was that we wouldn't feel stranded. I thought the point was that we were all in this together." Two of Heidi's friends, formerly feminists, now media manipulators, ask Heidi to be a consultant on a television sitcom, not because of her talents, but because "sitcom is big, art is big, and women are big." As Wasserstein told me, "Heidi plays by the rules. And life doesn't necessarily work by the rules. . . . Her melancholy results from her lack of connection."

Heidi's speech reflects Susan Faludi's meticulously researched book about the backlash against women in the eighties, *Backlash: The Undeclared War Against American Women*:

What has made women unhappy in the last decade is not their "equality"—which they don't yet have—but the rising pressure to halt, and even reverse, women's quest for that equality. The "man shortage" and the "infertility epidemic" are not the price of liberation; in fact, they do not even exist. The eighties supported the belief that women are unhappy precisely because they are free, that women were enslaved by their own liberation. They have grabbed at the gold ring of independence, only to miss the one ring that really matters. They have gained control of their fertility, only to destroy it. They have pursued their own professional dreams—and lost out on the greatest female adventure.

According to Faludi, the *New York Times* reported that childless women were "depressed and confused," and *Newsweek* said that unwed women were "hysterical" and crumbling under a "profound crisis of confidence." Health advice manuals informed us that high-powered career women were stricken with unprecedented outbreaks of "stress-induced disorders," hair loss, bad nerves, alcoholism, and even heart attacks. Psychology books advised that independent women's loneliness represented "a major mental health problem today." Even Betty Friedan spread the word that women now suffered from a new identity crisis and "new problems that have no names." From *Vanity Fair* to the *Nation,* the press indicted the women's movement with headlines like "When Feminism Failed—or the Awful Truth About Women's Lib." They held women's equality responsible for everything from depression to economic struggles to teenage suicides to eating disorders to bad complexions. Even the *Today* show blamed women's liberation for bag ladies, and the *Baltimore Sun* claimed that the violence of abortion propagated violent movies.

Hollywood told the same story. *Fatal Attraction* became the paradigm for those movies that represented emancipated women who "paid for their liberty with an empty bed and a barren womb." In *Surrender*, Sally Field cried, "My biological clock is ticking so loud it keeps me awake at night." Prime-time television shows like *Thirtysomething* and *Family Man* humiliated their single, professional, feminist women characters, who had nervous breakdowns and, by the final episode, renounced their independence. In popular novels like Gail Parent's *A Sign of the Eighties* (1987), professionally successful unwed women "shrink to sniveling spinsters." Even Erica Jong, who had written a radically feminist book for the seventies, *Fear of Flying* (1973)—the story of Isadora Wing and her desire to fly free—wrote *Any Woman's Blues* (1990), a book that the narrator says demonstrates "what a dead end the so-called sexual revolution had become." Further, the best-selling popular psychology manual *Being a Woman* presented the same diagnosis for contemporary female distress: "Feminism, having promised her a stronger sense of her own identity, has given her an identity crisis." And the era's self-help classic, *Smart Women, Foolish Choices* by Connell Cowan, announced that feminism created *a myth* that self-realization could be achieved only through autonomy, independence, and career among women.

In addition, President Reagan's spokeswoman Faith Whittlesey declared feminism a "straitjacket" for women in the White House's only policy speech on the status of the American female population. She called the speech "Radical Feminism in Retreat." Even law enforcers claimed that rising female independence led to rising female pathology, arguing that more freedom resulted in more crimes. Legal scholars criticized "the equality trap," and economists argued that well-paid workingwomen have created "a less stable American family." Everyone seemed sure that equality did not mix with marriage and motherhood. Women on the fast track of their professions, they claimed, were relegated "to solitary nights of frozen dinners and closet drinking."

Behind Wasserstein's dramatization of the collapse of the women's movement lay a dire economic fact. In 1986, women represented two-thirds of all poor adults; seventy-five percent of full-time working women made less than $20,000 a year, were still more likely than men to live in poor housing and receive no health insurance, and were twice as likely as men to have no pension. The average woman's salary lagged behind the average man's, and the average female college graduate earned less than a man with only a high school diploma. In short, American women faced one of the worst gender-based pay gaps in the developed world. If women had "made it" in the eighties, Faludi asked, then why were nearly eighty percent of working women still stuck in traditional "female" jobs—as secretaries, administrative "support" workers, and salesclerks? And why were they less than eight percent of all federal and state judges, less than six percent of all law partners, and less than one half of one percent of top corporate managers? Why were there only three female state governors, two female U.S. senators, and two Fortune 500 chief executives? Unlike virtually all other industrialized nations, the U.S. government still had no family leave and child care programs—and more than ninety-nine percent of American private employers did not offer child care either. Moreover, in the eighties, reproductive freedoms were in new jeopardy. Research for new birth control had halted. New laws restricted abortion—or information about abortion—for young and poor women—and the U.S. Supreme Court weakly defended the right it had granted women in 1973 with *Roe v. Wade*. Meanwhile, women's struggle for equal education was far from being won. And in their homes, women still shouldered seventy percent of household duties. In the late eighties, battering was still the leading cause of injury to women.

In poll after poll, overwhelming majorities of women said they needed equal pay and equal job opportunities, the right to an abortion without government interference, a federal law guaranteeing maternity leave, and decent child care services. How had women "won" the war for women's rights? "The man shortage," "the infertility epidemic," "female burnout," "toxic day care" originated in the media, popular culture, and advertising, but not in the real conditions of women's lives. Sex discrimination charges filed with the Equal Employment Opportunity Commission rose nearly twenty-five percent in the Reagan years, and charges of general harassment directed at workingwomen more than doubled. Government budget cuts in the first four years of the Reagan administration pushed almost two million female-headed families and nearly five million women below the poverty line. In national politics, the already small numbers of women in both elective posts and political appointments fell during the eighties. One theory about the backlash was that men felt that women were threatening "their economic and social well-being." In any case, Faludi maintained that backlashes are like viruses, and the eighties provided a perfect Petri dish for a resurgence of inequality that had always lurked beneath the surface. The year that Heidi gives her 1986 speech, Margaret Atwood published *The Handmaid's Tale,* a dystopian novel in which the religious Right had won electoral power. Playwright, novelist, and historian were all noting the same backlash.

Not all women, however, felt like Heidi. Emily Mann, artistic director of the McCarter Theatre, comments:

Many people who were fighting for social justice felt that the movements vanished on them . . . with Reagan in power. But really, many thought it prudent to just do the work and keep quiet. I know full well I wouldn't have gotten my job as artistic

director of the McCarter Theatre in 1990 without the help of the
women's movement . . . or my plays on Broadway for that matter.
I think for Wendy, her feeling of abandonment was more
personal. She was naming a real thing—the excitement, the idealism, the public banner waving of the women's movement had
diminished, just as the civil rights movement got quiet. But they
continued to work. Heidi's sense of abandonment was more
personal than political, I think—Heidi's women friends had on
some level abandoned her. . . . Heidi's character did not speak to
or for me, though I felt for her. Rather, I am grateful every day to
the women's movement for the life I've been able to live because
of it.

Many feminist critics assaulted the play, insisting that it was not really feminist because Heidi "sells out" in the end by adopting a baby.
They argued that "this unmotivated conclusion compromised Heidi's an-
tecedent values" and that the true cause of her depression was her
"manlessness." Some, like Laurie Winer, claimed, without explaining,
that Heidi let herself down and that the feminist movement, or its fail-
ures, were not to blame. Both Wasserstein and Heidi prefer being called
"humanist" to "feminist." But if what the larger women's movement
seeks is a transformation of the structures of a primarily male power
that now order our society, then *The Heidi Chronicles* is in some ways a
feminist play. Heidi's adoption of a baby in 1989 certainly subverts the
traditional family structure because she remains a single woman supporting herself as a professional.

When the play was being considered for film production in Hollywood, L.A. producers objected to the ending (also voicing concern about
"the second act" and "the main character" herself); Wasserstein retorted
that Heidi adopts a baby because that choice is consistent with her character. As she told me, "How can they say, 'We find the choice in your life
politically incorrect. Give your baby back'? I thought feminism was turning against itself. She is a woman who wants a baby. It takes enormous
courage to do what she does."

In addition to questioning Heidi's choices, critics argued that in general *The Heidi Chronicles* was perfect for a middle-class Broadway audience because it was not really subversive: it evaded serious feminist
issues because it never raised the question of abortion or of women's
rights in a real context. While it is true that no one in the play has an

abortion, characters do participate in feminist protests that actually occurred. Critics also maintained that Wasserstein's choice to depict her protagonist as an art historian undermined Heidi's validity because her profession has little effect on anyone's life. Who could have more impact on people than educators? Moreover, Heidi's training as an art historian enables her to address gender conflict not only within her discipline, but also in society at large. Lecturing to her students, she says, "What strikes me is that both ladies seem slightly removed from the occasions at hand. They appear to watch closely and ease the way for the others to join in. I suppose it's really not unlike being an art historian. In other words, being neither the painter nor the casual observer, but a highly informed spectator." It was an idea Wasserstein had encountered when she was a student of Kenneth Burke at the University of Massachusetts. According to Heidi, women, like art historians and writers, are detached observers. Wasserstein reflected, "Women have traditionally, until this century, eased the way for others, made the family, a home, made it possible for others to grow. The woman has been the nurturer."

Heidi gives her final art history lecture in 1989, a year when there was no visible progress in the women's movement, despite a major pro-choice demonstration on Washington on April 9. Gloria Steinem pronounced, "The right to choose whether, when, and with whom to have children is as fundamental as freedom of speech. . . . If Patrick Henry, Frederick Douglass, and Thomas Jefferson had ever been pregnant against their will, they would have been right there rebelling—and so will we." At the time, President Bush had endorsed the Human Life Amendment, which defined protectable human life as beginning at conception.

Nineteen-eighty-nine was also the year when feminists were "blowing the whistle on the mommy track"—meaning a lower-pressure, flexible, or part-time approach to work. Felice Schwartz, president of an organization that advised corporations on women's careers, argued that mothers had become a corporate liability because they "cost too much to employ." Accordingly, she proposed that mothers should be put on a special, lower-paid, "low-pressure career track—the now notorious 'mommy track.'" The "mommy track" story appeared in the *New York Times, USA Today, Business Week,* on dozens of talk shows, and in the *Harvard Business Review.* Schwartz intended "to urge employers to create policies that help mothers balance career and family responsibilities," but feminists found no evidence to back the claim that women were more costly to employ than men. Moreover, Schwartz assumed child-raising only involved mothers, that employment for married women was optional, that career mothers were "satisfied" and "willing" to forgo promotions; the study did not account for single mothers or wives of low-paid men and dismissed the glass ceiling and sexism altogether. In short, the 1989 "mommy track" article conveyed a backlash against America's workingwomen. In 1989, while women were working in numbers never before imagined, little had been done to assist them with their double roles. Women felt their personal and professional lives were falling apart. *Time*'s December 4, 1989 cover story asked whether feminism had a future:

> Hairy legs haunt the feminist movement, as do images of being strident and lesbian. Feminine clothing is back; breasts are back; motherhood is in again. To the young, the movement that loudly rejected female stereotypes seems hopelessly dated. The long, ill-fated battle for the Equal Rights Amendment means nothing to young women who already assume they will be treated as equals.

In addition, nonprofessional women, poor women, and minority women, not represented in the play, felt that the organized women's movement ignored their needs and values, because the movement grew out of white, middle-class women's discontent. Women of color were concerned about access to education, health care, and safe neighborhoods, which were not the priorities for the women's movement. And poor women had always been in the workplace, working for the middle class. So they never saw the feminist movement as liberating them from home. Stay-at-home mothers, who made up one-third of American women in 1989, also had their gripe with feminism because they felt it devalued motherhood. Nonetheless, seventy-seven percent of women in 1989 thought the women's movement had made life better, while only eight percent thought it had made life worse. So why did only thirty-three percent of women identify themselves as feminists at this time? There were still enormous obstacles ahead for American women to overcome. They were still only earning sixty-six cents to the man's dollar. The wage gap and the segregation of women into low-paying jobs, along with the lack of affordable child care, hurt unmarried women and single mothers the most. Moreover, no-fault divorce laws benefited men and impoverished women. And then there was the "second shift" of work that women did when they came home from their day jobs. Men were trying to have their wives' salaries and still have the traditional roles at home. Betty Friedan's 1981 book, *The Second Stage*, called on her feminist sisters to transcend the "sexual politics" that cast man as the enemy and denied women's connection to the family and instead to achieve a balance between the role of career woman and woman's traditional roles as mother and homemaker. In order to achieve that balance, Friedan called for a change in the structure of the workplace and the home, in which men must participate.

Despite the conservative climate in which the women's movement found itself in the eighties, Wasserstein wanted to write an affirmative ending to the play. Heidi "triumphantly" holds her daughter, as mother and daughter are photographed in front of a museum banner for a Georgia O'Keefe retrospective. Once again, the action of the play reflects the reality of its time: *Time*'s October 9, 1989 issue featured an article about the trials of adoption. Critics of the play, however, have discounted the feminist quality of the play's final image. Iska Alter reads it as a compromised feminism, because we are left with an image of triumph, not necessarily its reality or realization. Georgia O'Keefe, she argues, consistently acted against feminist expectation. It is unclear to me how O'Keefe's landscapes and still lifes, which launched a new American art; her travels; and her teaching career are not feminist. Moreover, while it is clear that the play is not radically feminist—even Heidi regrets that she never torched lingerie—it is a mistake to read the ending so literally. Heidi and her daughter represent future generations of women who hope to have a stronger sense of self in a more equal society. Feminism had hit some serious roadblocks in 1989, and *The Heidi Chronicles* was the first Broadway play to hold up a mirror to this backlash. Wasserstein continued to register the pulse of the women's movement like a social historian.

An ad for the Brighton Beach Baths, a traditional summer destination for entertainment and sports for Brooklyn Jews such as the Rosensweig family. (Brooklyn Public Library, Ephemera Collection)

The Sisters Rosensweig (1991)

"The Self-loathing Jew, the Practicing Jew, and the Wandering Jew"

My name is Sara Rosensweig. . . . I was born in Brooklyn, New York, August 23, 1937.

—Sara Rosensweig

Set on the historic weekend in late August 1991 when the Soviet Union collapsed and Lithuanians tore down the statue of Lenin in Vilnius, *The Sisters Rosensweig* tells the story of three middle-aged, Jewish sisters, originally from Brooklyn—Sara, Pfeni, and Gorgeous—as they reunite to celebrate Sara's fifty-fourth birthday at her chic apartment in Queen Anne's Gate, London, a year after their mother's death. In contrast to her earlier, episodic plays in which her female protagonists remain alone, Wasserstein wanted to affirm the possibility of love for middle-aged women, "in a culture that denies it," within one set, while observing the unities of time, place, and action. Moreover, the playwright observed, "Three middle-aged women on a stage who are accomplished and successful and not caricatures in our culture is still a surprise. And that's why I wanted to write this play."

The oldest sister, Sara Goode, divorced twice and recovering from a hysterectomy, is a successful banker at a Hong Kong bank, who has given up on love. She has moved to London to efface her Jewish identity by acquiring a British accent and an English last name from her second ex-husband, and by naming her daughter Tess, after Thomas Hardy's heroine in his controversial 1891 novel that explored class conflict and challenged the sexual mores of the time. Sara resists falling in love again until she meets Merv Kant (Mervyn Kantlowitz), a world leader in synthetic animal protective covering. After a night with Merv, Sara also begins to re-embrace her Jewish identity.

While Sara is a self-loathing Jew, her younger sister Gorgeous is a practicing Jew who encourages Sara to fall in love again. She is in London not just for her sister's birthday, but also to lead the Temple Beth El sisterhood on a tour of the crown jewels. Married to an attorney, who has lost his job and is writing mystery novels in their basement, she has the most conventional life of the sisters as the mother of four living in Newton, Massachusetts. Yet Gorgeous is also a kind of Dr. Ruth Westheimer with a call-in love counseling radio show and a great sense of humor.

The youngest sister, Pfeni, is a forty-year-old journalist, dating a bisexual theater director, Geoffrey, who leaves her because he misses men. The wandering Jew, Pfeni begins the play by arriving and ends it by leaving. She explains that she has renounced her political writing for travel writing because she feels that she is exploiting the people whose problems she records. Sara helps her understand that she is avoiding her true calling, and Pfeni returns to a study of Tajikistan.

Sara's daughter, Tess, is doing a biography of her mother's early years for her school summer project; when the action begins, Tess is recording her research on her mother's college singing group, and as it ends Tess is beginning an interview with her mother. Her exploration of her family history resonates with each character's quest for his or her identity. Her journey includes plans to go to Lithuania to support the Lithuanian independence movement with her working-class boyfriend, Tom Valiunus, but her mother opposes the relationship and the trip. In the end, Tess decides not to go to Lithuania, not because of her mother, but because she does not feel sincerely connected to the Lithuanian movement.

The larger political backdrop of Eastern Europe's democratization resonates with the evolving autonomy and liberation of each woman. Wasserstein likens her dramatic form to that of British political theater: "In a way, what I do is a lot like British theatre. It's a large canvas in which you see the social and historical change, and then the personal change, and how they reflect each other." In this way, Wasserstein is part of a political tradition in American playwriting that began in the thirties with Hallie Flanagan's Living Newspaper, part of the Federal Theatre Project. According to Flanagan, a playwright and professor at

Vassar College, the Living Newspaper sought "to dramatize the search of the average American today for knowledge about his country and his world." The Group Theatre continued this tradition in the thirties.

To write this kind of historical play, Wasserstein looked to Chekhov. In conversation, she said,

> Like Chekhov, I wanted to write a play dealing in time, obsessing about time. I wanted to write something about the end of the century when everything was breaking up. Setting it at the time of the Russian coup was important because there was great hopefulness then, before things fell apart. I also wanted to write about [the fact that] time has passed and you're not going to be all those persons you might have been; you have a history, you've chosen a road, and yes, you did know what you were doing.

More specifically, she based her characters on *The Three Sisters*. But while Chekhov's play opens on the anniversary of their father's death and the youngest sister's birthday, *The Sisters Rosensweig* opens a year from their mother's passing, and it is the oldest sister's birthday. Moreover, both sets of sisters are disappointed in love and both seek their "Moscow," an unattainable utopia. Sara tells Tess, "Pfeni has romanticized a world we never belonged to." While disapproving, she also envies Tess's devotion to a political cause. In addition, the Merv/Sara relationship echoes that of Vershinin and Masha in that both women enter into romance without wanting a permanent commitment; and the Geoffrey/Pfeni relationship is like Irina and Tuzenbach's: both Pfeni and Irina compromise their dream of ideal companionship, a gamble that ends in lonely heartbreak. Wasserstein also borrows exact lines from *The Three Sisters*: Pfeni laments, "Oh my God, my life is stuck. 'I've forgotten the Italian for window,'" and, most famously, "If I could only get to Moscow." Further, Gorgeous wishes that when all the children and men have gone upstairs, the three sisters could sit together ("around the samovar," Pfeni offers) and talk about life, and that each would be able to say she had "had a moment of pure, unadulterated happiness!" In focusing on the sisters' internal conflicts rather than on external ones, *Sisters* is especially Chekhovian.

Wasserstein's sisters are the feminist counterparts of Chekhov's nineteenth-century sisters with careers and choices that Masha, Irina, and Olga never imagined. Banker, travel writer, and radio personality

Notebook page with ideas for *The Sisters Rosensweig,* including a note to "read [Chekhov's] *The Three Sisters.*" (Courtesy of the Wendy Wasserstein estate) replace Chekhov's headmistress, telegraph operator, and wife. According to Gorgeous, "The decade of the bimbo is over. . . . This is the era of the strong but feminine woman." Some critics complained that "the affluence and success of the Rosensweig sisters undermine their self-proclaimed tragedies." But Wasserstein acknowledges that "these are not tragic lives" because middle-class stakes are not high enough—at least externally. The play balances comedy and melancholy as it examines serious questions about gender, Jewish-American identity, assimilation, relationships, family, the democratization of Eastern Europe, colonialism, and class conflict.

As much as *Sisters* is indebted to Chekhov, Wasserstein says that this old-fashioned drawing-room comedy also owes something to the comedies of George S. Kaufman, Moss Hart, and Noel Coward. Kaufman's satires about social class that addressed politics, urban life, and the theater appealed to Wasserstein. Like Kaufman, she wrote about wealthy New Yorkers for commercial Broadway audiences. Wasserstein must have been especially interested in *Dinner at Eight,* a romantic comedy about wealthy people losing their money (like Gorgeous and Henry) during the Depression, written by Kaufman and Edna Ferber. It also dramatized power dynamics in relationships (Sara and Nick, also Sara and Merv), blind love (Pfeni and Geoffrey), selfishness and unselfishness (Gorgeous), and class conflict (Tom and Tess). Kaufman's collaborations led to two musical comedies for the Marx Brothers, *The Cocoanuts,* written with Irving Berlin, and *Animal Crackers,* written with Morrie Ryskind, Bert Kalmar, and Harry Ruby. Therefore, there is a line that runs from the Marx Brothers—by way of Kaufmann—to Wasserstein.

In 1939, George Kaufman collaborated with Moss Hart to write *The Man Who Came to Dinner*, which taught Wasserstein about the conventions of a comic coming-to-dinner play. Sara alludes to the play when she calls Merv "the furrier who came to dinner." In addition, Geoffrey alludes to Hart's 1952 film, *Hans Christian Andersen*, in which bisexual actor Danny Kaye says, "You'd be surprised how many kings are only a queen with a moustache." In *Sisters*, gay theater director Geoffrey boasts, "I'm the only theatre director who can ignite the stage with true female sexuality" and insists, "Love is love. . . . Gender is merely spare parts. Just ask Danny Kaye." In England, Noel Coward's interest in gay culture, high society, class, comedy, farce, relationships, musicals, and popular music also had an impact on Wasserstein's only play set in London. While *The Sisters Rosensweig* is more of a social play than is

Coward's *Private Lives*, Coward, Kaufman, and Hart nevertheless influenced the comedy of manners in *Sisters*.

In addition, Philip Barry's *Holiday* (1929) provided Wasserstein with a paradigm for writing comedies about the problems of the rich and sophisticated. Like *Sisters*, *Holiday* is a drawing-room comedy, set in the home of a wealthy banker, exploring love, success, and happiness. While Barry was writing about the Roaring Twenties from the perspective of an Irish-American, and Wasserstein about the early nineties from a Jewish, American point of view, both were interested in the tensions between the outsiders and the insiders of society. In this way, they were doing through drama what Edith Wharton was doing in her novels of manners about class in America.

In *The Sisters Rosensweig*, comedy derives not just from one-liners, but also from the precise timing of lines, entrances, and exits, in the tradition of farce. After Sara's night with Merv, Gorgeous blurts, "Well I'm not shy. How was it?" to which Tom adds, "A good man is hard to find." Just when Pfeni and Geoffrey are breaking up, Gorgeous enters drenched, with an umbrella and a shopping bag, wearing one shoe of a brand new $400 pair, having caught and ruined the heel of the other in the subway. She reveals that her husband has been out of work. Pfeni lightens the mood by saying, "Tea time is over. We can now move into wine." In an earlier scene, Geoffrey appears in a plumed hat and rhinestone glasses, and Pfeni in a ballroom gown and tiara, to wish Sara a happy birthday. The juxtaposition of comedy with sadness also characterizes the play and a particularly Jewish kind of humor: Sara says, "When they send the tanks in, you and Tom can take in a quick hamburger and a show," and Tess says, "It's just like my mother to have a dinner party on the night the Soviet Union is falling apart."

Set on "that August weekend of 1991 when the Soviet Union was teetering on the revolution that was to turn it back into Russia," the play explores the democratization of Eastern Europe, which reaches back to 1982 when Poland's Lech Walesa was released from prison. In 1989, Poland had its first democratic election in forty years. Then on November 9, 1989, the Berlin wall, erected by the Soviets between West and East Germany in 1961, crumbled. For the first time since the end of World War II, Communist East Germany was physically united with free republican West Germany. The iron curtain around Czechoslovakia, Hungary, Poland, Yugoslavia, Romania, Bulgaria, and other regions dominated by the Communist Party of the USSR began to dissolve. In August

1991, the collapse of the Soviet Union was the biggest victory for freedom and democracy since the end of World War II.

The fifteen republics were demanding the same freedoms as the countries of Eastern Europe, and on August 29, 1991, the Soviet legislature voted to suspend all activities of the Communist party. By Christmas, the Soviet Union, seventy-four years old, had unraveled and been renamed the Commonwealth of Independent States. In the play, on the night of the momentous event, Frank Sinatra is playing in the background as if to say America has made its way to Eastern Europe. The Cold War ended when Yeltsin ordered the last Russian troops to evacuate the Baltic States and Germany, causing Nick Pym, Sara's British friend, to say, "You know the shocking thing about all this business with the Soviets is one questions what in God's name the entire twentieth century was for." McCarthyism and blacklisting, Korea and Vietnam now all seemed pointless. Where Wasserstein's early plays documented the ends of various eras for American women, *Sisters* depicts middle-aged women at the end of an era on an international scale. Part of this new era involved women's rights. Gorbachev was also calling for "glasnost for women," and he told the Soviet Communist Party Congress that "the working and living conditions of our women require considerable attention, radical improvement" and that "women must participate in political life."

The end of the Cold War, however, did not end oppression in Eastern Europe or make the region more prosperous or peaceful. While some countries made the transition to democracy, other former republics experienced chaos and political corruption. In other words, finding one's unique and independent voice would be a long road. For Wasserstein it seemed to echo a similar problem for middle-aged women who were trying to figure out their identities. While the women's movement created the possibility of change, self-determination, and liberation for women, in 1991 women were still fighting for equality in a sexist world: Anita Hill accused Clarence Thomas of sexual harassment; the American Association of University Women published a groundbreaking critique, *How Schools Shortchange Girls*; the President of NOW, Patricia Ireland, was vilified for living with a female companion; Susan Faludi published *Backlash*, documenting the backlash against the women's movement in the eighties; and feminist sociologist Kathleen Barry blamed the demise of feminism on "deconstruction," a literary and philosophical movement that claimed nothing has any inherent meaning or connection to anything else. The women's movement insisted that the personal and the political were inextricable.

In 1991, women were continuing their struggle against a patriarchal society, but they disagreed about how to wage their war. According to the predominant feminist literary critic of the eighties, Elaine Showalter, feminist critics became concerned with "developing a uniquely female understanding of the female experience in art, including a feminine analysis of literary forms and techniques." "Gynocritics" wanted to read women's literature by examining how the female body marks itself on a text through image and tone, how women use language differently from men, and how the female psyche creates a more fluid form than the rigid structure of male writing. Both Wasserstein and her characters, however, want to reject this academic interest in distinguishing women's writing from men's. Wasserstein preferred to document feminist concerns without being segregated as a "woman writer." "Separate but equal" did not work for her literary agenda.

Popular culture seemed more in tune with Wasserstein's interests than did academia. *Thelma and Louise*, the 1991 film about women rebelling against sexism, resonated with American women's experience. It was also the year that Tony Kushner's *Angels in America: A Gay Fantasia on National Themes* changed Broadway with its innovative style and hard look at gay culture and American politics. Terrence McNally's *Lips Together, Teeth Apart* dramatized the humorous side of gay life. On the other hand, Neil Simon's *Lost in Yonkers* was the counterpart to *The Sisters Rosensweig* in its nostalgic presentation of an American Jewish family lost in the Bronx, told from a male perspective.

Rather than structure the play with events from the women's movement of the time, however, Wasserstein chose the dismantling of the Russian republic, which, Clive Barnes noted, "created an atmosphere in real and stage life for ethnic reassessment. Certainly a time to think about anti-Semitism and what it has meant to the makeup of the world still at large." Gail Ciociola calls the play's Jewish concern "an accessory to [Wasserstein's] feminist objectives," but Jewish identity is at the heart of *The Sisters Rosensweig*. Tess listens to the recordings of her mother's Radcliffe choral group singing "Shine On Harvest Moon," and Sara believes that Tess's "thesis is to prove that my early years have no bearing on my present life." But the play proves just the opposite, despite Sara's efforts to efface her Jewish roots. Merv, a Jewish guy from Brooklyn, understands Sara's need to "assimilate beyond her wildest dreams." As Russell Shorto has noted, "America is pluralistic but its founding was an English affair." Merv tells Sara, "You mean [Gorgeous and I are] both a little . . . too Jewish. That's what we have in common. Sara, you remind me of my classmates from DeWitt Clinton High School in the Bronx who now pretend as if DeWitt Clinton was a prep school down the Connecticut River right around the bend from Groton or St. Paul's."

Sociologist Samuel C. Heilman describes exactly this tension in *Portrait of American Jews* by using Max Ferguson's double portrait called *Ralph Lauren's Worst Nightmare*. The portrait represents two alternative representations of a Jew: the clean-shaven, assimilated American Jew wearing fashions designed by Ralph Lifshitz (Ralph Lauren) from the Bronx, who set the standard for American fashion. The other panel shows the same figure, but this time, bearded, wearing a fedora, wrapped in a tallis—Ralph Lauren's worst nightmare. According to artist, sociologist, and playwright, the assimilated Jew has fooled himself into thinking that he has successfully escaped who he is. Reading from left to right, the viewer moves from the Orthodox-looking Jew to the assimilated one, while reading from right to left (Hebrew), one begins with the assimilated American and ends with a bearded Jew. In Heilman's view, the double portrait captures the two faces of American Jewry during the second half of the twentieth century. Ralph Lauren's signature style also represents this conflict. New England refinement, old money accented with Englishness, adventure in the Wild West, and Native American culture define his thoroughly American look, which belong more to country clubs, prep schools, and polo grounds than to synagogues, shtetls, or his Russian-Jewish working-class background. Accordingly, Merv describes a Jewish desire to enter traditionally WASP schools, and recounts his own efforts to assimilate by changing his name from Kantlowitz to Kant and sending his daughter to prep school at St. Paul's.

Similarly, in *Gender and Assimilation in Modern Jewish History,* Paula Hyman documents that for some Jewish immigrants from Eastern Europe,

> Americanization necessitated Anglo-conformity, the abandonment of immigrant mores in favor of far-reaching assimilation to an American culture defined by its English roots. For others, who preferred the image of the "melting pot," Americanization

demanded assimilation, but American society and culture themselves would be transformed through . . . immigrant groups.

Sara's expatriating to London exemplifies the former kind of assimilation. Moreover, the urge to assimilate runs deep in the Rosensweig family;
Sara's grandfather called her "Sadie," because he thought "Sara was too
biblical." In fact, no one has called her "Sara Rosensweig" in thirty years.

Given that Jews as a whole were historically discriminated against,
Jewish women had a double battle to fight. Not only were they not Christian or English, but they also had to fight traditional Jewish values and
East European values that subordinated women "in favor of an American aesthetic." They compensated through education. Sociologists
determined that even in the 1920s, immigrant Jewish daughters were
more likely to attend high school and college than the daughters of other
ethnic groups. By 1934 more than fifty percent of female college
students in New York were Jewish. It is also significant that when
Wasserstein was a freshman at Mount Holyoke in 1968, only 10 percent
of the students were Jewish.

Sara Rosensweig's Radcliffe education presents the conflict between
being Jewish and being American when she listens to a recording of her
1959 choral group singing an a cappella version of "McNamara's Band"
in act two, scene one. The stage directions read, "Suddenly she begins
to sing a different verse softly":

> Oh my name is Moishe Pupick
> And I come from Palestine,
> I live on bread and honey
> And on Manischewitz wine.
> Oh my mother makes the best
> Gefilte fish in all the land . . .
> > *Her voice cracks.*
> And I'm the only Yiddish girl
> In McNamara's Band.

Not only do the lyrics point to the historic territorial conflict between Palestine and Israel, which makes Jewish identity especially
precarious, but also Sara's voice cracks when she comes to the line
about being the only Jew in an Irish band. Both the alternate lyrics and
the stage directions identify the Jew as outsider. This history of marginalization seems to be the reason that Sara wants to assimilate. As

Wasserstein puts it, Sara is "WASPier than a WASP." She even likes the "openly repressed" nature of English society.

The conflict between Jewish and Anglo culture is everywhere in the play. Pfeni tells Sara that when she was still living in Flatbush with her parents, a nice Jewish man named Harry Rose, who was head salesman at their grandfather's Kiddie Tog factory, called their house every morning. When Tess asks whether Harry Rose was "New York," Sara, scoffing at Rose's Jewish accent, responds, "New York in a way that has very little to do with us. . . . Pfeni's the one who's romanticized a world we never belonged to." Once again, for Sara, being Jewish is undesirable. Pfeni retorts, "I was mistaken. . . . It was Louis Auchincloss," not Harry Rose, who called the house each day. She pretends to humor Sara by replacing the Jewish businessman with the WASP writer/lawyer who was a leading voice of America's WASP elite in the last half of the twentieth century.

In contrast, Merv's background is stereotypically Jewish: summers at the Brighton Beach Baths, college at Columbia University, and traditional Jewish food. He tells Sara that he "shtupped" her classmate Sonia Kirschenblatt the summer before she went to Bryn Mawr College. Loyal to his Jewish roots, he has visited Budapest with the American Jewish Congress and is having brunch with the Rabbi of Dublin. Both Merv and Sara's families are from Poland, and Sara reminds him of the faces of his mother's family, most of whom were lost in the Holocaust. Merv's memory of his family makes him feel close to Sara:

> My mother's family had a villa in a spa resort in Poland called Ciechocinek. And the pictures we had were of the family gathered at a picnic. The men waving at the camera or smiling, holding up a cantaloupe! They were sweet, these men, some even handsome, but they couldn't hold a candle to the women. The women in their too-large dresses with their arms folded all had your brilliant eyes—they sparkled even from those curled and faded photographs. Unfortunately, most of them and their families didn't survive. But Sara, when I look into your eyes, I see those women's strength and their intelligence.

The strength Merv attaches to Jewish women seems to come from the Holocaust experience. As much as Sara wants to escape her past and relationships altogether, their common Polish-Jewish experience brings them together romantically. Even though they tell each other that they are not each other's type, by act two, scene three, Sara confesses to Merv, "I can't seem to come up with a good enough answer for what's wrong with you. I like you." She gives Merv the Shiva statue "to ward off evil," to bring "hope and rebirth," and "to stir up [his] life a little." Reversing traditional gender roles, Sara asks Merv if he wants to "shtup" her tonight. After Merv kisses her, she tells him, "I'm old enough and kind enough not to let you love me. But . . . just for one night I could be Sonia Kirschenblatt at the Brighton Beach Baths and you a Columbia sophomore."

Given this unconventionally unromantic one-night affair between Merv and Sara, it seems ironic that the play begins and ends with "Shine On Harvest Moon." This 1908 Tin Pan Alley moon song was a pop standard by Jack Norworth and Nora Bayes. The Boswell Sisters, Jimmy Dorsey, Rosemary Clooney, Artie Shaw, Laurel and Hardy, Jerry Gray, and Nat King Cole all recorded it. The lyrics introduce a couple beneath a willow tree at night and tell how the girl departs, afraid of the moonless dark. In a solo, the boy pleads with the moon to shine so that his girl will come back. (When Clooney sings it, she sings from the female perspective—"for me and my guy.") When the boy longs for a full, September moon, the speaker responds, "All he has to say is: 'Won't you be my bride' . . . / Harvest moon will smile, / Shine on all the while, / If the little girl should answer 'yes.'" The female has the power over the moonlight and therefore the power to make or break the relationship. And so it is with Sara and Merv. More specifically, a harvest moon is the full moon nearest the time of the September equinox, when the sun crosses the equator, and day and night are equal in length. This balance of light and dark, comedy and tragedy, is just what the play achieves as it presents serious matters comically. (Jerome Lawrence addressed this issue in a letter to Wasserstein, closing with "You do what Lawrence and Lee try to do in all your plays: make all your serious plays funny and all your funny plays serious.") Moreover, the brassy, improvisational sound of the big bands that played the tune is full of American optimism, as is Sara and Merv's night together, but the relationship falls short of any kind of permanent commitment. As Wasserstein told me, "They won't marry, but they'll see each other."

Sara's relationship with Merv also indicates that intimacy can only come with accepting one's identity. When Merv asks whether she wants to "connect to another person," Sara responds, "Yes, I'm lonely, but I don't want to come home." Merv sums up Sara's confused identity:

"You're an American, Jewish woman, living in London, working for a Chinese, Hong Kong Bank, and taking weekends at a Polish resort with a daughter who is running off to Lithuania." Sara responds, "I'm a cold, bitter woman who's turned her back on her family, her religion, and her country! And I held so much in. I harbored so much guilt that it made me ill and capsized my ovaries. . . . Isn't that the way the old assimilated story goes?" Sociologists have noted that "speedy Americanization was essential for subverting the growing association in popular opinion of 'Jew' with 'foreigner.'" Sara is not just leaving Judaism behind; she has even left New York for London. Only after she connects with Merv can she answer her daughter's interview questions and say, "My name is Sara Rosensweig. I am the daughter of Rita and Maury Rosensweig. I was born in Brooklyn, New York, August 23, 1937. . . . I first sang at the Hanukah Festival at East Midwood Jewish Center." Earlier, Sara refused to sing for Merv when he asked her, but once she acknowledges her heritage, she can sing for her daughter. As feminist critic Carolyn Heilbrun writes, "women transform themselves only after an awakening."

Sara's attempt at assimilation leaves her daughter confused about her identity. In order to attach herself to a cause, Tess plans to join the Lithuanian resistance with her working-class boyfriend, Tom. Wasserstein was drawing on the pro-independence movement in Lithuania, established on June 3, 1988, and galvanized by Gorbachev's January 1990 visit to Vilnius, which provoked a pro-independence rally of around 250,000 people. On March 11, 1990, Lithuania declared independence, but the Soviet army suppressed the movement "to secure the rights of ethnic Russians." Tess may not be aware of it, but Lithuania is also historically important to her Jewish heritage. For many centuries, Lithuania was one of the great centers of Jewish theology, philosophy, and learning, and Vilnius, according to Pfeni, "was once the Jerusalem of Lithuania."

Detached from both her Jewish roots and Lithuanian's independence movement, Sara cannot understand how "a nice Jewish girl from Connecticut" can possibly find her calling in the Lithuanian resistance. Tess replies, "But I'm not a nice Jewish girl from Connecticut. I'm an expatriate American who's lived in London for five years and the daughter of an atheist." Tess feels as disconnected from her identity, and later from the Lithuanian resistance, as Heidi felt from the women's movement in *The Heidi Chronicles*. She asks her Aunt Pfeni, "Are we people who will always be watching and never belong?" Removed both from her ancestry and from America, she feels like an outsider. Wasserstein voices this concern in nearly every play. Therefore, Tess wants to know, "If I've never really been Jewish, and I'm not actually American anymore, and I'm not English or European, then who am I?" She would like to leave London and go home to school, but her mother wants to stay in London. Sara reaches back to her own mother's survival of persecution to provide Tess with assurance: "If Rita could make the Cossacks run away, then you are smart enough, and brave enough, and certainly beautiful enough to find your place in the world."

The haunting presence of the past is especially important to Jewish-American writers living in the shadow of the Holocaust, but Wasserstein does not go to those ravaged Eastern European cities in this play. Instead, she chooses Queen Anne's Gate, located in central Westminster, with its historic buildings and government agencies. According to legend, the street, named after Queen Anne, is haunted by the queen's ghost, which walks three times around the street on the night of July 31, the anniversary of her death. Whether or not Wasserstein was aware of the legend, it resonates with the play's concern about the past.

Sara finds herself haunted by the specter of Brooklyn in the fifties. She tells Merv, "The home you're talking about is the Bronx, the Brooklyn, the America of forty years ago. It doesn't even exist anymore." Merv responds, "If it doesn't exist, why are you working so hard to make it go away?"

Memoirs of Brooklyn in 1951 reveal neighborhoods that were "rigidly sex segregated": "Women played mah-jongg and canasta, while the men played pinochle, casino, and gin rummy, and bet on ball games and horses." Communities of Jews congregated on their front stoops and at candy shops; drank egg creams; ate pickles, smoked fish, chopped liver and halvah; awaited the seltzer man: "The vitality of street life remained the neighborhood's defining characteristic." Many Brooklyn Jews spent summers at the Brighton Beach Baths and on the Coney Island boardwalk. While they rooted for the Dodgers, they also danced to "Hava Nagila." Most went to synagogue only on the High Holy Days and sent their kids to Hebrew school so they could be bar mitzvahed, not so they could become religious Jews. The Brooklyn of forty years ago was both Jewish and American as Mickey Mantle and Willie Mays, Frank Sinatra, the Everly Brothers, Fats Domino, Elvis Presley, Little Richard, Chuck Berry, the Platters and the Drifters, the Lindy Hop, the fox trot, and the cha-cha infiltrated Brooklyn's neighborhoods. Two cultures define Sara and Merv's backstory.

There seems to be an important connection between Sara's rejection of Judaism and her feminism. Because her father taught his daughters that "girls weren't supposed to know about money," and "no one ever called [her] 'Gorgeous,'" Sara becomes "the first woman to run a Hong Kong bank." Sociologists note that Eastern European Jewish immigrants and their children "contest[ed] the boundaries between domestic and public life that characterized middle-class gender norms." Sara Rosensweig, born in 1937 and coming of age in the fifties, before the women's movement, challenges male hegemony by entering a male-dominated profession and gaining the reputation of having "the biggest balls at the Hong-Kong/Shanghai Bank world-wide." In doing so, she also participates in the colonialism that the play finds problematic. (Hong Kong was a dependent territory of the United Kingdom from 1842 until the transfer of its sovereignty to the People's Republic of China in 1997.) Sara's career choice defies the expectations of the women of her time and place. Carole Bell Ford documents the female experience of growing up Jewish in the fifties in Brooklyn in "Nice Jewish Girls": "women played a traditional, separate, and . . . unequal role to the men: a role transported from the shtetlach, the small towns and villages of Eastern Europe." Subordination at home also defined female marginalization at shul; women sat in the balconies or "behind the mehitzah, the formal partition that separated the women's from the men's section." Sara's appearance on the cover of *Fortune* magazine shatters the glass ceiling inherent in traditional Judaism.

Sara's generation of women also experienced a difficult transition in mainstream American culture. In her interviews with women of the fifties, historian Ruth Rosen documents: "None of us wanted to do any of the things our mothers did—nor the way they did it—during the postwar years." The play tracks three generations of this mother-daughter conflict. Sara says that Tess is "determined to make her life the opposite of mine," and Pfeni responds, "That's exactly what we set out to do because of our mother." Similarly, Rosen writes,

With one foot firmly planted in the world of their mothers, daughters of the fifties viscerally feared the constraints experienced by the adult women around them. . . . Fear of becoming an "ordinary housewife" . . . fueled the female generation gap. Could a woman in her twenties mate and bear children without turning into a domestic drudge? They didn't know. As they rejected the world of their mothers—but not necessarily their mothers' secret dreams—daughters searched for an identity based on something besides marriage and motherhood. And for that, there were precious few role models.

Born in 1937, Sara Rosensweig would have gone to high school from 1951 to '54, and college from 1955 to '59. During this time, experts warned that education "reduced the probability of a woman marrying," and critics suggested that "women should not receive the same training as men. . . . It is more important that they put a good dinner on the table than that they talk Greek." In fact, in 1950, Lynn White, president of Mills College and author of *Educating Our Daughters*, announced that education actually "frustrated" women. The president of Radcliffe College suggested that the college alter its regular curriculum because it only served to "equip and encourage women to compete with men." Moreover, in a 1955 commencement address at Smith College, even the liberal Democrat and presidential candidate Adlai Stevenson explained how much young women could accomplish during this "historical crisis"—the Cold War—"by assuming 'the humble role of housewife,' which is what most of you are going to be whether you like the idea or not just now—and you'll like it!" Furthermore, in 1956, *Life* magazine acknowledged that [women] "have minds and should use them . . . so long as their primary interest is the home." No wonder Mr. Rosensweig never felt the need to discuss money with his daughters.

Merv's wife exemplified "the feminine mystique" of the fifties against which Sara and Pfeni rebelled. He tells Sara, "She thought she could have been a contender if it wasn't for me. She put me through school, she brought up the children, and finally she got to take art classes . . . before she died. Is that fair to a talented, intelligent woman? Sadie, I've already done having someone take care of me." Still, Sara tells Merv that he deserves someone who knows how to "throw a good Shabbes" and create "a warm and happy home." She even momentarily questions her career when she confesses to Pfeni, "Maybe Gorgeous is the smartest. Maybe if I were 'settled' my daughter wouldn't be on the road to being a new-age Emma Goldman" (the Lithuanian-born anarchist). But Merv's daughter proves the contrary; she rebels against her traditional mother by joining the Israeli army.

Banker, journalist, and radio personality were far from representative of American women in the early nineties, who, Gloria Steinem reported, were "like a third-world country—low on capital, low on technology, and labor-intensive." At the time, women were trying to create "an economic base of jobs" from which they could not be fired. Most were just trying to survive economically. Newspapers reported that "women hold few top posts at banks"; "men dominate the hierarchy" and "promotions are slow." There was a two-tier class structure in which women and minority groups—the majority of the labor force—occupied the lowest positions. But Sara Rosensweig is an exception; with her "double 800's on [her] College Boards," she "thinks Harvard and Yale are second-rate" and "knew what the teacher was going to ask before she asked it," "knew what was going to become of every girl in [her] class," and "knew for some reason, I was different from them." Merv tells Sara, "You weren't a nice Jewish girl," meaning a conventional one. Wasserstein continued to be interested in a very elite sector of American women.

In contrast to Sara and Pfeni, Gorgeous embraces Judaism. At sundown, she keeps the Sabbath with the ritual of a Hebrew prayer over candles, wearing "a tichkel for [her] head." The Jewish prayer, which Sara calls "an ancient tribal ritual" and Tom calls "a séance," praises God for the wonders of the world. Sara, however, tells Pfeni to "blow out the goddamned candles," echoing a scene from *The Glass Menagerie*. The scene dramatizes the conflict between traditional female roles that are "entangled with the theological positions that legitimate them" and Sara's feminist, secular values. In other words, the most conventional sister is the most religious. Fifties conservatism has shaped Gorgeous more profoundly than her sisters. Behind the new Jewish feminism that had started in America, Annette Zilversmit points out, "there were more conventional Jewish and American gender scripts" that represented "the anxiety of autonomy." As the Newton, Massachusetts housewife, with her lawyer husband and four children, Gorgeous represents "the sister who did everything right," according to Merv. She tells Sara and Pfeni, "You're threatened by my husband, my family, and my accomplishments. Both of you wish you were me." Of the three sisters, Gorgeous was most in step with Barbara Bush and Marilyn Quayle's promotion of family values at the Republican National Convention in 1988. She remembers the limitations experienced by the women of her era: "I knew girls who were just like Tessie in high school—beautiful, talented, bright—who have had such difficult times in later life. . . . Tessie, carpe diem; now's the time to enjoy." Tess jokes that she will study hairdressing so that she can "make her way in the world." But even Gorgeous has become "a real middle-aged success story" with her radio career, which added the "little sparkle" she needed in her life "to make it all perfect." Wasserstein's plays repeatedly ask whether women can "have it all," and Gorgeous exemplifies one version of combining homemaking with a career.

While some critics felt that the play finally presented a positive portrait of independent, Jewish career women, others pointed to Wasserstein's representation of the "high cost of autonomy." Sara's two divorces, however, convey that the cost of marriage to the wrong person is higher. Nonetheless, feminists felt that Wasserstein was indicting the women's movement. Was the play claiming that being a successful woman leads to loneliness? Despite their apparent success, the sisters seem lonely, yearning, and melancholy. Linda Winer wrote that *Sisters* "hardly seems like the direction some of us desired for the woman who broke barriers with *Heidi*." It is true that Sara's exchange with her daughter suggests that she is still unsure of her identity, despite her extraordinary professional achievements. When Tess tells her mother that she decided not to join the Lithuanian resistance for herself, *not for her mother*, because "You have to have your own life," Sara asks, "I can't have yours?" Other critics argued that all three sisters revert to images of earlier Jewish female role models they had rejected, identities less threatening to society than their former choices. On the contrary, each sister makes more daring and less conventional choices by the play's end: Sara falls in love but does not marry; Pfeni leaves travel writing for political writing; and Gorgeous ends up supporting her husband.

Confusion about female identity derives in large part from the ambiguous values that Rita Rosensweig transmitted to her daughters. While she pressured Sara to succeed, and Sara says, "Mother and I had a Female Trouble conflict," Sara never defines the conflict. Instead, she tells Gorgeous, "We are happy. . . . It's just not our mother's kind of happiness." For their mother and Gorgeous, that means marriage. Upon meeting Merv for the first time, Gorgeous tells him, "Maybe you should marry her [Sara]. Some people know at first sight." In contrast, Sara tells Merv, "I don't think about us getting married." She explains, "I didn't have you a 'you' in my life at sixteen. I'm certainly not going to have a 'you' in my life now." Sara believes it is too late for love, and in this way she represents the decreasing rate of marriage at the time. By 1990, 61.9 percent of Americans were married, compared to 65.5 percent in 1980 and 71.7 percent in 1970. According to Gorgeous, Sara has simply "become a hard woman," who, her media colleague Rabbi Pearlstein says, needs a man to make her soft again. Sara, however, looks forward to

Madeline Kahn, Jane Alexander, and Christine Estabrook as the Rosensweig sisters Gorgeous, Sara, and Pfeni in the original Broadway production of *The Sisters Rosensweig*. (Photofest)

growing old together with Pfeni, like two old maid spinsters in a Muriel Spark novel (the British novelist of manners), growing "more and more eccentric . . . meaner and crabbier." Still, traditional values die hard. Sara tells Merv, "If my sisters or I had any sense, we would all have married you." Sara also advises Pfeni "during her peripatetic life" to "have at least one child." Sociologist Carole Bell Ford recalls, "As a girl . . . my parents expected me . . . to marry Jewish, teach my children to carry on the traditions." Like Merv's former wife, good Jewish women were expected to perform the traditional "supporting role—enabling their husbands to study and work, transmitting Yiddishkeit to their children, helping their children . . . rise to an even higher station in life than they expected to achieve." Nevertheless, Wasserstein has said that the two men in *Sisters* are "much nicer" and "more catalysts for the action" than are the men in *Isn't It Romantic*. In all of Wasserstein's plays, women have few successful relationships, either because "a good man is hard to find," or because they are unwilling to compromise their ideals and/or careers.

Being Jewish not only shapes the sisters' upbringing with regard to gender roles, but it also defines them through the Holocaust and anti-Semitism. He tells Nick Pym, whom Tess calls racist, sexist, and anti-Semitic, that anti-Semitism "is the true concert of Europe, but in England it's all handled a little more politely." When Nick alludes to the "Technicolor" garb of "Jewish-American professionals," Merv snaps back with a reference to usury—the lending of money at a high rate, prohibited for Christians (but not for Jews, who were banned from most other professions so often worked as moneylenders) in old European societies—and to *The Merchant of* Venice's Jewish usurer, Shylock: "It's a money-lending uniform. They're so well designed, you'd never know it costs a pound of flesh to get them." In addition, when Pfeni asks Geoffrey whether he is "part of some antifeminist, anti-Semitic plot," he jokes, "You expect me to like women *and* Jews?" Even Gorgeous's Chanel suit signifies anti-Semitism; Coco Chanel, who created the Parisian fashion house specializing in haute couture, was accused of being a Nazi sympathizer and arrested immediately after the liberation of France.

Fifty years after the Holocaust, Ciechocinek (a spa town for curing diseases, what Merv calls "the Palm Springs of Poland") is asking for a loan to begin its free-market economy, and as head of the Hong Kong/Shanghai Bank, Sara finds herself in an ironic situation: her bank loans for renovating heating and redistricting agricultural cooperatives are helping to feed those who drove her grandparents away. "Capitalism," after all, "is expensive." But Sara embraces the irony:

> I couldn't help but see it all as a minor triumph for the women with those same sparkling eyes in my mother's faded photographs. Fifty years after the lucky few had escaped with false passports, Esther Malchah's granddaughter Sara was deciding how to put bread on the tables of those who had so blithely driven them all away.

Historically persecuted, the Jew—now a woman—wields the power to transform a city. Nick Pym says that "Jews have been at the financial core of England for generations." In an 1898 pamphlet called *Concerning the Jews,* Mark Twain addressed the connection between Jews, finance, and discrimination. He concluded that the persecution of the Jews had nothing to do with religion, but rather with "the average Christian's inability to compete successfully with the average Jew in business."

Economics, he saw, took precedence over religion: "[The Jew] was at it in Egypt thirty-six centuries ago; he was at it in Rome when that Christian got persecuted by mistake for him; he has been at it ever since. . . . his success has made the whole human race his enemy—but it has paid, for it has brought him envy, and that is the only thing which men will sell both soul and body to get." In the play, when Pfeni asks Geoffrey whether their kids would be Jewish, he jokes, "They'll have to be, if they're going to run MGM." Shaping the popular imagination of America through film and theater (Sara knows the Broadway show tunes of the fifties by heart), and then exporting it abroad, has also been a significant source of power for Jewish Americans.

If Sara is the self-loathing Jew, Pfeni is the wandering one, first as anthropological writer and then as travel journalist. By definition, diaspora is the settling of scattered colonies of Jews outside Palestine after the Babylonian exile, or Jews living outside Palestine or modern Israel. This dispersion or displacement has characterized the Jewish experience from the beginning, but the Rosensweig sisters wander by choice. Tess tells Pfeni, "My mother . . . says you compulsively travel because you have a fear of commitment, and when you do stay in one place, you become emotional and defensive just like me." Whether or not Pfeni fears commitment, she is part of group of young, contemporary Jewish American female protagonists growing up in Brooklyn, rejecting marriage, and committing themselves to becoming writers. Although "the autonomous, at least not traditionally married with children Jewish American woman writer has precedent in American fiction as early as the middle nineteenth century with Emma Lazarus, and in the 1920s and '30s with Anzia Yezierska, Edna Ferber, and Gertrude Stein," in the early nineties, depictions of many single, usually intellectual or artistic heroines end in suicide, death, severe depression, or repression. The unmarried men suffer no such fates. Although Pfeni does not quite fall into those categories, she struggles with finding a career with moral significance. Critic Howard Kissel felt that Pfeni had "secularized her Jewish idealism in radical journalism," but Pfeni feels that eagerly listening to ravaged Afghan women tell their stories is exploitative, not transformative: "Somewhere I need the hardship of the Afghan women and the Kurdish suffering to fill up my life for me. And if I'm that empty, then I might as well continue to wander to the best hotels, restaurants, and poori stands." She's decided she should give up what seems to be meaningful work because she doesn't want to be doing it for the wrong reasons—appearing good while actually being selfish. Perhaps the question is whether she, as Sara suggests, "care[s] too much and [is] trying to find excuses not to." Additionally, according to Geoffrey, other women make Pfeni feel "competitive and insecure." So, she feels disconnected both from her peers and her subjects.

Pfeni is especially alien to Gorgeous, who cannot understand why Pfeni chooses to lead such an unconventional life at forty:

> Men, desirable men of any age, aren't interested in eccentric women in their forties. Eccentric women in their twenties is maybe interesting. . . . Eccentric in their thirties is all right only if you're super thin and arty successful. But wandering around the world alone at forty, Pfeni, you're wandering yourself right out of the marketplace. And don't tell me you have Geoffrey. I know you can't judge a book by its cover, but sweetsie, you're in the wrong library altogether. Don't you want what any normal woman wants?

Calling attention to prejudice against middle-aged women, the play redefines "normal woman" through Pfeni and Sara. In conversation, Wasserstein has expressed disapproval of our society's double standard that makes older men desirable and older women undesirable. Gorgeous also wants to see Sara settled "with a nice man," but Sara says she *is* settled. In addition, the radio-sex-therapist sister has bought into what Naomi Wolf calls "the beauty myth," which derives from men's institutions and power . . . and drives women to seek outside approval by getting "rejuvenation treatments" and taking "collagen shots." According to Gorgeous, "Sara never had a sense of style," so Gorgeous taught her "how to dress for success" by accessorizing. When Gorgeous tries on her Chanel suit and 7AA shoes, she "feels like Audrey Hepburn."

Wasserstein has always been interested in how Americans display status and wealth, and her choice of Chanel symbolizes an affluence that is out of reach for most people. During the American recession of the early nineties, in fact, the cost of living, led by the soaring cost of gasoline and food, exceeded many American paychecks. Gorgeous represents the fact that even the middle class is being pushed into the margins of society. Her husband has not worked in two years, because his law partnership dissolved. Gorgeous says that he thinks he "could've been Dashiell Hammett if hadn't been brought up in Scarsdale." Even in America, where social class is supposed to be fluid, the play suggests that birth still shapes fate. As Sara says, New York is becoming as "class-driven" as London. She does not want Tess to return to American schools because of America's "growing disenfranchised class, decaying inner cities, a bankrupt educational system." Sara's class-consciousness convinces Merv that Sara is "a hot-shot Jewish lady banker who's secretly a Marxist." The crown jewels that are part of Gorgeous's tour of London signify power conferred at birth. Class becomes an issue again when Tess objects to her mother's bourgeois dinner party "with capitalists like Nicholas Pym" when "there are homeless people living in boxes under Charing Cross Station" (a cross that marks the center of London, put there by Edward I as a memorial to his wife, Eleanor). Class distinctions pervade the play in humorous and serious ways. Tess's working-class boyfriend, Tom, calls cassoulet "stew," does not know what goat cheese is, and claims he only eats "primary color food." In contrast, Tess's favorite food has been sushi since nursery school, and Sara's "help is on vacation." Gorgeous wears "fake Ungaro cocktail wear with accessories" and a fake Chanel suit, and her imitation Louis Vuitton luggage inspires pity in the ladies from Temple Beth El. Moreover, Sara does not want her daughter dating a working-class boy whose father owns a radio supply store in Liverpool: "I just don't know what you have in common with someone who dreams of selling radio parts."

The play suggests that nationalism and colonialism create economic inequality. Tess is concerned about the cost of the environmental damage that fifty years of Soviet occupation has inflicted on Lithuania—the result of colonialism. She also understands the problem of nationalism: "If Western culture is to survive. . . one must look beyond the United States, England, France, or Germany." Tess feels "irrelevant" coming of age as a white, European female, but recognizes that it would be even "worse" if she were "a white European male." In other words, male hegemony is part of colonialism, which is connected to the dissolution of the Soviet Union that frames the play. Tess also reminds everyone that "the Concert of Europe," Metternich's plan to reestablish stability in Europe after Napoleon in 1815, had as its goal "nationalism." According to Merv, anti-Semitism goes "hand in hand with European nationalism." Tom reminds Nick Pym that "Lithuania has a culture and people independent from the Soviets." In this way, the play calls for destabilizing existing paradigms in order to allow individual voices to be heard. Colonialism also appears in the small details at the edges of the play; Pfeni's cab driver is a "Sikh" who drove her all around Bombay. Geoffrey is convinced that "American Jewish girls" are "well versed in British colonial history."

While Tess and Pfeni find out who they are by identifying with political causes, and Sara comes to terms with herself by accepting her Jewish identity, Geoffrey, the gay director, finds out who he is by directing plays. Having lost too many friends to AIDS, changing his address book three times as a result, he concludes that life is random, and there "cannot be a just or loving god." Upheaval such as this was common enough at the time that articles carried headlines such as "How AIDS Is Changing . . . Everything." HIV had become a global crisis that was afflicting men and women alike. Geoffrey copes through love and work. He tells Pfeni, "People like you and me have to work even harder to create the best art, the best theatre, the best bloody book about gender and class in Tajikistan that we possibly can. And the rest, the children, the country kitchen, the domestic bliss, we leave to others who will have different regrets."

Recognizing that every choice is imperfect, he advises Pfeni to devote her life to her journalism, rather than to raising a family. Although Geoffrey says that "the only time I have a real sense of who I am and where I'm going is when I'm in a darkened theatre and we're making it all up," in the same breath he says he's realized he also wants a real life outside the theater—and for him this means leaving Pfeni and returning to men. At the time, he would have faced particular adversity, as the gay community at the time was experiencing some setbacks. Colorado and Oregon passed antigay ordinances that were not overthrown by the Supreme Court until 1996. America was pushing gays into the closet. Interestingly, the musical that Geoffrey is directing, *The Scarlet Pimpernel,* is about a leader of a secret society of English aristocrats whose identity is concealed. In contrast to Geoffrey and Pfeni, the couple is happily reconciled.

Within the context of the collapse of the Soviet Union, *The Sisters Rosensweig* explores the conflict between being Jewish and American, female and male, gay and straight, poor and rich, colonized and colonizer, single and married. Each sister gains some self-knowledge, acceptance, and empowerment. As poet Deena Metzger says, "The second half of a woman's life provides the opportunity for transformations." Scholar Robert Gross, however, points out that "Wasserstein's postmodern characters are obsessed with self, yet incapable of overcoming a sense of loneliness and fragmentation." The two states are not contradictory. Not being at home in the world propels the sisters' journeys of self-exploration, just as the Soviet republics needed to experience the disorientation of independence in order to find their autonomy. In this way, the play is not just about personal possibilities, but also about national and international ones. As a nation, we were also entering an era of greater liberalism in 1991 as we moved into the Clinton administration of 1992. Pfeni, who at first abandons political writing for leisure writing, echoes an America that had moved away from progressive politics and needed to return to a national program that would help those in need. Clinton promised to be a new kind of moderate Democrat who would cut the defense budget, provide tax relief for the middle class, and offer massive economic aid to the republics of the former Soviet Union—all issues mentioned by the characters in the play. By fusing personal issues of identity with political ones, within a tradition of a comedy of manners, *Sisters* captured the end of another era in 1991. With the thawing of the Cold War, newly democratic nations needed to find their identities, just as three Jewish, American sisters needed to discover theirs within the context of an evolving women's movement.

TIME

CLINTON'S FIRST BLUNDER

How a popular outcry caught the Washington elite by surprise

Zoë Baird

Zoe Baird on the cover of the February 1, 1993, *Time* magazine for "Nannygate," the inspiration for *An American Daughter*. (Reprinted through the courtesy of the editors of *Time* magazine © 2009 Time Inc.)

5

An American Daughter (1997)

Double Standards for Women Prevail

What happens to women, sometimes, I think is blatantly unfair.

—Wendy Wasserstein

Tucked into Wasserstein's archives on *An American Daughter* are two 1993 articles—one from the *New Yorker*, by Sidney Blumenthal, called "Letter from Washington—Adventures in Babysitting," and another from the *American Lawyer*, entitled "Inside the Whirlwind," by Stuart Taylor. Both recount the story of Zoe Baird, a corporate lawyer for Aetna, nominated to be attorney general, who was forced to withdraw on January 22, 1993, because she and her husband had hired illegal aliens from Peru, the Corderos, as domestic help and failed to pay their Social Security taxes because the Corderos had no Social Security numbers. *The New York Times* ran a six-page story on Baird's "Nannygate," and the story made the cover of *Time* magazine. The *Chicago Sun-Times* headline read, "Say It Ain't Zoe, Baird Moralists." The inside article revealed that women were questioned about child care rather than about their qualifications. With her eye always fixed on the news, in particular on the status of professional American women, Wasserstein saw the built-in conflict of Baird's story: a woman was being disqualified from office for being unable to find a full-time American babysitter. It was the perfect metaphor for sexism at a time when women seemed to be contenders for powerful positions; after all, Hillary Clinton was reforming health care.

In order to distinguish her play from Baird's story, Wasserstein replaced Nannygate with Jurygate and changed the protagonist's nomination from attorney general to surgeon general, "the physician to the nation." The change reflected the crisis that she saw in women's health care and also the need for a woman to heal the wounds of America. Wasserstein's protagonist Lyssa Dent Hughes wants to educate the public about women's health care, and she advocates reproductive rights. Both Baird and Hughes were public figures destroyed by the media. The journalist Taylor attributed the Baird debacle in part to "the cold, capricious cruelty of fate," but also declared that Baird and her husband were being demonized by a political-journalistic-populist culture addicted to symbolic blood sport. Ironically, Taylor pointed out, the whole scandal would never have happened if Baird had not been honest, as other politicians had not been. The case asked whether honesty is in fact the best policy. Moreover, in 1997, when the play is set (as opposed to when Nannygate happened) Kenneth Starr was trying to bring down the Clinton presidency with an investigation into Clinton's affair with White House intern Monica Lewinsky.

An American Daughter takes place at the Georgetown home of Lyssa Dent Hughes, the great-granddaughter of Ulysses S. Grant, and an idealistic, liberal doctor in her early forties who has just been nominated as surgeon general by a Democratic president. With references to the Lincoln Bedroom scandal, First Lady Hillary Clinton's defense of her decision not to "stay home and bake cookies," her book *It Takes a Village*, the women of Sarajevo, and the Gulf War, the play is pointedly set during the Clinton administration. Lyssa seems to have it all—a medical career in which she runs a major hospital, a prominent sociologist husband, a Georgetown home, and two children. Her best friend, Dr. Judith Kaufman, an African-American, Jewish professor of oncology at Georgetown Medical and senior physician at its breast care unit, is desperately trying to conceive a child. Depressed about not having children and being unable to stop death, she tries to drown herself in the Potomac. She is divorced from a gay Jewish psychiatrist whose new partner is a florist/opera singer. But Lyssa's life does not turn out much better. In an early draft, her gay, politically conservative friend, Morrow, reveals to the media that she failed to respond to a jury notice; in the published version, her husband reveals it, and thereby destroys her prospect for becoming surgeon general. Timber Tucker, a journalist whose name echoes that of real-life reporter Forrest Sawyer, interviews Lyssa so ruthlessly that she feels compelled to withdraw her candidacy. Not even the spin doctor Billy Robbins, who is called in to coach Lyssa on how to present herself before the media, can salvage her career.

In addition, Lyssa's husband, author of an influential book on liberalism called *Towards a Lesser Elite*, cheats on her with his former student and superficial feminist, Quincy Quince, who has written a best seller, *A Prisoner of Gender.* Lyssa's father, the pro-life, Republican senator from Indiana, Alan Hughes, based on Senator Alan Simpson, is on his fourth marriage and just back from his honeymoon with Charlotte "Chubby" Hughes. He wishes that he could have prevented his daughter from withdrawing her nomination, but she decides without him. In the end, both Lyssa Dent Hughes and Judith Kaufman have failed to achieve their aspirations. But Lyssa refuses to accept defeat. As she walks up the stairs to see her children, she quotes her great-grandfather Ulysses S. Grant: "Our task is to rise and continue." To tell this story, critics noted that Wasserstein was combining several genres—"drawing-room comedy, comedy of manners, political satire, social problem play, and a domestic infidelity drama."

In the play, the public assaults Lyssa for being elitist, but she does not exploit her privilege when she has the opportunity. Director Dan Sullivan recalled the isolation that Wasserstein felt politically in New York City, where her friends would make presumptions about peoples' affinities and judge them accordingly. Therefore, in *An American Daughter,* she challenges political stereotypes—which she would do even more forcefully in her last play, *Third.* According to Sullivan, Wasserstein longed for the liberalism of "militant New York liberals, like Bella Abzug from the seventies and eighties." Here liberalism turns on itself.

While missing jury duty isn't considered specifically a women's issue, Lyssa misses it because she has too many commitments, dramatized in the first scene when she is pulled between professional and domestic duties. Wasserstein's plot choice of Jurygate, however, was not exactly analogous to Nannygate, where the double standard was glaring. As director Dan Sullivan remarked, "Nobody would look at [Senator] Charles Schumer's choices of domestic help." More recently, the press revealed that Secretary of the Treasury Timothy Geithner had employed a housekeeper with expired immigration papers but still assumed the cabinet position once the housekeeper had obtained a work permit. In 1997 it was a man's world that made it difficult for women to succeed, and so it is in 2009. Furthermore, Wasserstein's sympathy for Lyssa echoed her "feelings about Hillary Clinton's victimization, especially after Monica Lewinsky."

Zoe Baird also represented the superwoman that the playwright had always found compelling. Like Lyssa Dent Hughes in the play, Baird had a "'beyond meteoric career' at age forty. Her colleagues likened her to Bill Clinton because of her liberal instincts and her practicality." "A superb networker," she "gained the confidence of important older men from Warren Christopher to Vernon Jordan to Bill Clinton." As one friend put it, "she gives good daughter." Wasserstein underlined the last statement in her file, which influenced her title and had a loaded connotation: the paternal relationship between powerful men and their female colleagues. In other words, patriarchy dies hard, and Wasserstein wanted to tell the story of the forces that bring down extraordinarily successful women. Without national child care or equally shared domestic duties, women could not compete with men professionally. As Gloria Steinem put it, "Until men are fully equal inside the home, women will never be really equal outside." In the play, the twenty-seven-year-old feminist and author of *Prisoner of Gender* Quincy Quince, in miniskirt and leather bomber jacket, claims that "the Nannygate incident was an outgrowth of the seventies having-it-all mythology." Women who were trying to have both careers and families did whatever it took to maintain both. While feminists wanted to dispel the notion that biology was destiny, the Zoe Baird case proved otherwise. Yet Baird's accomplishments proved that she was more than capable of being attorney general.

To Wasserstein, this excuse for denial of high office insulted all women of ambition and reminded her that "ingrained prejudices about women's roles die hard." Even women were not supporting Baird, because they believed "this protégé of men like Christopher and Cutler had not paid her feminist dues." Therefore, "feminists turned their backs on her" when she was being attacked "over an issue of special concern to working women." In the play, Quincy Quince represents this lack of female solidarity. Clinton's next choice for attorney general, Kimba Wood, also withdrew her name from consideration, saying her babysitter had been an illegal alien for seven years. Later, Lani Guinier, Kimba Wood, Hillary Clinton, and Secretary of State Madeleine Albright experienced similar conflicts. Nannygate was proving to be a cultural trend. In addition, Wasserstein was troubled that women only held about ten percent of the seats in Congress, and that politicians and journalists viewed issues like child care and sexual harassment as "women's issues" rather than everyone's concern: "There's a danger in that kind of thinking." She continued to insist that women's issues were everyone's.

Wasserstein based key scenes on the public's actual response to the media frenzy. People flooded the congressional switchboards with calls demanding that the nomination be rejected. The callers did not like Baird's breaking the law, her hiring aliens, legal or otherwise, her not paying her taxes. And they didn't like her cool composure when she took responsibility. "Above all, perhaps, they didn't like her making $507,000 a year. They especially didn't like that in a forty-year-old woman with a small child at home." Television crews staked out her home in New Haven, just as they do to Lyssa Dent Hughes's in Georgetown. "Baird became a symbol of lots of things that grate on this nation's frustrated middle class." This reaction propelled Wasserstein to examine "liberal elitism" in *An American Daughter.*

Senator Joe Biden told Baird that her situation smacked of elitism because Baird and her husband were wealthy: "I'm a middle-class guy, and you need to understand that to people like me, you look like you think you're better than us, and the rules don't apply to you, and you don't have to pay your taxes like the rest of us." On the other hand, most Washingtonians were initially undisturbed, since they themselves had either employed illegal domestics or knew people who had. Biden, however, continued with comments that influenced the conflict in the play:

> A significant portion of the population . . . finds your action . . . inconsistent with the responsibilities that you will have as attorney general of the United States to enforce the very laws you knowingly violated. . . . Millions of Americans out there . . . have trouble taking care of their children . . . with one-fiftieth the income that you and your husband have, and they do not violate the law.

Accordingly, Zoe Baird came "to personify the selfish yuppie of our time." However, unlike the great-granddaughter of Ulysses S. Grant, Baird came from a working-class family.

Wasserstein had long wanted to compose a play about the liberal establishment, and with President Clinton in office, the moment seemed right. She turned to her friend and former editor of the *New Republic,* Michael Kinsley, for the facts. The play asks whether liberalism—the idea that government would protect the people from "the darkest chasms of fate and corporate greed"—had collapsed. Sociologist Paul Starr defines liberalism as follows:

> Liberalism wagers that a state . . . can be strong but con-
> strained—strong because constrained. . . . Rights to education
> and other requirements for human development and security
> aim to advance equal opportunity and personal dignity and to
> promote a creative and productive society. To guarantee those
> rights, liberals have supported a wider social and economic role
> for the state, counterbalanced by more robust guarantees of civil
> liberties and a wider social system of checks and balances
> anchored in an independent press and pluralistic society.

Wasserstein was noticing a collapse of liberal ideals in America. As Lyssa's husband says, "Make the world a better place? . . . They'll never let you get away with it. Look what happened to national health insurance." Despite the presence of a Democrat in the White House in 1997, Peter Beinart noted, "Even in big cities, old-fashioned liberalism is out of fashion." New York's mayoral race proved that Giuliani's fiscal conservatism had replaced upper-middle-class liberalism, which had been represented by Ruth Messinger. In the congressional elections of 1994, fifty-four percent of white women and fifty-two percent of married women voted Republican. In the play, Lyssa's failure to respond to her jury notice resulted from the "bad juggling of a working mother." For some, however, her oversight represents the liberal problem of entitlement, the notion that "because your heart is in the right place, you can ignore ordinary responsibilities."

Everyone at the "Renaissance Weekend" conference Quincy attends considers Walter's book, *Towards a Lesser Elite,* "a blueprint for deconstructing liberalism." Lyssa tells him, "Liberalism will live or die without you." And Quincy, who is Walter's student, believes that Walter is "the only academic who can reshape liberalism into an active stance instead of a do-gooder whine"; Walter is the only man who "gets it." In contrast, Lyssa represents an older brand of liberalism. According to Walter, Lyssa is "stuck in the past," "as rooted as any ardent right winger." He prefers Quincy and Morrow's focus on the future, believing that liberalism must be re-examined and reconstructed.

Timber, the journalist, also asks Walter whether Lyssa's "embattled nomination is indicative of the conflict inherent in liberalism and your 'greening of America' generation." Charles Reich's best-selling 1970 book, *The Greening of America,* praised the counterculture of the sixties and its values of personal freedom and egalitarianism. Like the youth of

2008, the "greening of America" generation rebelled against a government that had lost touch with its people and was causing war and poverty. The play registers the lost altruism of Lyssa's youth, which her father feels as well: "There's some idea of America out there right now that I just can't grab onto. I know I'm supposed to have opinions based on the latest polls, and not personal convictions or civil debate. . . . it's certainly not our most illuminating or honest hour. . . . I'd rather shoot cattle than run for Congress." America seemed to have lost its moral compass.

In addition, Morrow has converted to the far right "because of the inconsistency of the left." He is convinced that the "left-wing rage for selective privilege" is far more insidious than his new political identification. He attributes Lyssa's neglect of her jury notice to her liberal sense of entitlement; she was too busy with her professional duties to fulfill her civic ones. Morrow is "a Log Cabin Republican," whose mission is to work within the Republican Party to advocate equal rights for all Americans, including gays and lesbians, along with limited government, individual liberty, individual responsibility, free markets, and a strong national defense. Moreover, according to director Dan Sullivan, Morrow loosely resembles Andrew Sullivan, journalist and former editor of the *New Republic,* a classical libertarian conservative from England, whose friendship with liberal political thinkers interested Wasserstein.

Paul Krugman's *The Conscience of a Liberal* (2008) addresses a similar concern about America's lost liberalism as does *An American Daughter.* Krugman, coming of age at the same time as Wasserstein and Lyssa Dent Hughes, laments the loss of protest against social injustice that characterized the sixties. While Krugman's study revolves around the politics and economics of inequality in general, Wasserstein's focuses on gender inequality in particular. Both see a problem with concentrated wealth and power and the collapse of the middle class between 1979 and 2005. Both call for universal health care as the centerpiece of a *new* New Deal, but the play wants, most of all, a New Deal for Women.

As the great-granddaughter of Ulysses S. Grant, Lyssa Dent Hughes inherits the dilemmas of liberalism—"the rise of a powerful centralized government and the balance of military and civilian power" and "the dilemmas of American history—the legacy of slavery, secession and war." Presiding during a time when the nation's social fabric was torn over race, Grant represented reconciliation, reconstruction, and civil rights. For Wasserstein, the nineties presented a similar conflict for women, even though our racial problem was far from over. Through Judith—the black, Jewish oncologist—the play wants to redefine "American," so that the power structure is no longer only white, male, or WASP. Judith says, "Diversity is the succor of the nineties." As Walter, the sociologist, says, "The future vitality of this country is not coming from traditional sources, but from a diverse multicultural wellspring." The straight white guy was becoming the minority. Yet, while Judith is the first African-American Jew to receive a scholarship at Miss Porter's School, at the time Wasserstein was writing in 1997, the Bakke case at the University of Michigan was questioning affirmative action in college admissions. The nation was torn over how to deal with our legacy of racism.

Lyssa points out the paradox of conservatism when she demands of her right-to-life father, "How can you be adamant about individual rights and deny the most personal right—when and if to have a child?" Conservatives wanted to minimize government involvement in economic matters but to intervene in social ones, jeopardizing equality for women and the poor. While Grant refused to surrender, his great-granddaughter is forced to do so. The cases of Zoe Baird, Lani Guinier, Kimba Wood, and Lyssa Dent Hughes proved Gloria Steinem's assertion about "how much of female experience is political, not inevitable." As a descendant of Ulysses S. Grant, Lyssa is from a family that is, in Grant's own words, "American in all its branches, direct and collateral," but *An American Daughter* questions whether Lyssa has inherited the right to life, liberty, and the pursuit of happiness and concludes that she is "a prisoner of gender." In different contexts, then, Lyssa Dent Hughes and Ulysses S. Grant want to heal the nation in terms of gender and race.

Sexism flashes across the television screen when the news anchor announces that Lyssa Dent Hughes has been nominated because of the death of the previous surgeon general and the defeated nomination of Dr. Charles McDermott. He never mentions Dr. Hughes's "brilliant record as health care administrator" or her conviction that "public health is good government." Women's health, in particular, is at stake. Lyssa points out that "doctors are twice as likely to refer men to medical specialists while women of the same age and symptoms are referred to psychotherapists." In addition, Judith points out that while she has donated money to the fight against AIDS, she is "still waiting for one gay man voluntarily to come to my hospital and say, 'I'm concerned about

Excerpt from Ulysses S. Grant's June 4, 1864, letter to his eight-year-old daughter, Nellie, in which he tells her, "study your lessons and you will be contented and happy." (Chicago Historical Society, Rare Book Room)

a disease that's decimating my mother, my aunts, and my sisters.'" Although Judith may be "the jewel in the crown of the great society" (President Johnson's set of domestic programs that aimed to eliminate poverty and racial injustice in the mid-sixties), women's health care is still marginalized. Of course, women's lives were more limited when President Grant wrote his daughter, Ellen Wrenshall Grant (or "Nelly"), from Cold Harbor, Virginia, in 1864: "Be a good little girl as you have always been, study your lessons, and you will be contented and happy." The letter conveys the conflict that defines all of Wasserstein's plays;

diligent studying had not provided solace for many accomplished women. On the contrary, Lyssa reveals that Nelly's life was a disaster; her parents married her off to a philandering Brit, and she was divorced with four children. Lyssa's father tries to do better. When he teaches his daughter how to shake hands, he explains, "Firm, not like a lady, not like a man. Just shoot from the hip." He encourages an androgynous confidence.

The year 1997, however, did evidence some progress for women. For the first time in history, older women could have children using frozen eggs and DNA transplants, making motherhood an option for women who had devoted their twenties, thirties, and forties to their careers. Also in 1997, with *Planned Parenthood v. Casey,* the Supreme Court reaffirmed a woman's right to abortion under *Roe v. Wade*, challenging Pennsylvania's 1989 Abortion Control Act. In addition, the Violence Against Women Act tightened federal penalties for sex offenders and funded services for victims of rape and domestic violence. Still, the old problem of men carrying less domestic weight than women meant that men and women were not competing on an equal playing field.

In this context, the play asks why "The best intentions in females often become the seeds of their own destruction." Feminism had created a natural peripety—or reversal of intention—for playwrights. With so many professional and domestic commitments, Lyssa was too busy for jury duty. Her husband explains to the journalist, who is trying to undermine her: "My wife is a mother of two small children. She is a professor of public health at Georgetown and ran a major public hospital. Not to mention a nationally known lecturer." Walter believes her job is "making her a little nutso," and Quincy feels that Lyssa has lost her soul.

Wasserstein said that she wanted "to create a fractured fairy tale depicting both a social and political dilemma for contemporary women." In other words, she was continuing her project of exposing the problems that accompany being a successful, intelligent, powerful woman. This time, however, her protagonist was in the public arena, making her more vulnerable to the forces that infiltrate the gate of her Georgetown townhouse. Having been exposed for missing jury duty, Lyssa says, "I've probably just set back the case for every cause I believe in, cast a dark shadow on women in government, put the final lid on national health insurance." Urging Lyssa to "shut that gate," Dr. Judith Kaufman is convinced that "a woman's life is all about boundaries," and she affirms that if Lyssa were a man, her failure to do jury duty would be a non-issue, an oversight. And so it was in 2009 when Timothy Geithner was confirmed as Secretary of the Treasury despite his failure to pay his nanny's taxes. In 1997, Walter muses on whether feminism "should cease in the twentieth century, like Soviet communism or the rotary dial." Wasserstein's question was one year ahead of the *Time* magazine 1998 cover story "Is Feminism Dead?" featuring the heads of Susan B. Anthony, Betty Friedan, Gloria Steinem, and Ally McBeal. Trying to advance women in politics resulted in a backlash against them.

In 1997, family therapists Betty Carter and Joan Peters were examining gender expectations within marriages in their new book *Love, Honor and Negotiate.* They observed couple after couple "gripped in an unforgiving vise, caught between traditional role models and a changing world—particularly once they have children." After being in the media spotlight, Lyssa tells her husband, "I never meant for our lives to be about me." Even a woman at the top of her game felt she should be in her husband's shadow. Carter and Peters concluded, "Most American couples backslide into traditional sex roles as soon as their children are born." Traditional family therapy theory did not respond to the problems of gender, and so Carter and Peters founded the Women's Project in Family Therapy. Just as family systems therapy dispelled the classic Freudian approach that treated the individual apart from the family, the Women's Project analyzed marriages as "families enmeshed in cultural structures—structures that often exert unbearable pressures on families, making spouses blame each other for what are really social problems." It was the conflict in *An American Daughter.*

Lyssa's media coach tells her that feminism is too radical for many Midwestern women. Therefore, he advises her to emphasize family values and humility, instead of her liberal, eastern, elitist political views in her television interview. She should not "play up Miss Porter's boarding school" (an exclusive all-girl's prep school in Farmington, Connecticut). Getting elected, he explains, is just a question of "knowing what people want, giving it to them, and then getting on with it." Politics is performance. Accordingly, for her interview, he advises her to wear "feminine attire . . . a bow or headband," and to talk about how much she misses her mother, who was attractive and churchgoing: "Women respond to that." Here, again, the play echoes the headline news of its time. After her assertion that "she didn't want to stay at home and bake cookies" caused an uproar, Hillary Clinton had made her next public appearance wearing a headband, holding her husband's hand.

Lyssa Dent Hughes (Christine Lahti) in front of a podium in the June 5, 2000, Lifetime TV movie of *An American Daughter.* (Lifetime/Photofest © Lifetime Television)

Lyssa's coach also advises her to focus on "Grant the General and not Grant the President," because of the whiskey scandal during Grant's presidency. (Grant's internal revenue supervisor, John A. McDonald, let whiskey distillers cheat the government in return for political contributions, costing the U.S. Treasury a million dollars a year.) Grant's public life was not always within legal limits. Senator Hughes explains, "He made bad investments, he drank, and some say he even screwed up Reconstruction." Others believed that the race problem would have progressed more quickly if the Grant Administration had been more efficient—yet without Grant, there might have been no Reconstruction at all. The senator says, "A great American hero, he was imperfect like us all."

Lyssa's interview also reveals conflicting values about perfection for women across generations. When Lyssa describes her mother as an "ordinary Indiana housewife" who "took pride in her icebox cakes and cheese pimiento canapés," she goes from being "a compromise candidate to the . . . soccer mom's anti-Christ." Housewives feel diminished, causing female public opinion to run against Lyssa Dent Hughes four to one. *New York Post* headlines read, "Dr. Icebox Shops." Timber Tucker reminds her, "You have been for the past ten years on the *Ladies Home Journal* list of American Women Role Models. Is that what makes women envious of you? Are you too perfect?" According to *Time Zone* polls, American women find her "condescending and elitist," and her failure to respond to jury duty makes "many women feel that [Lyssa's] private life disqualifies [her] from such an important humanitarian position." It mirrors the case against Zoe Baird.

Morrow also equates liberalism with elitism. With Lyssa's nomination he believes "another political dynasty like the Roosevelts or the Kennedys is being established. Americans always enshrine their elite." Graduating from Bryn Mawr with the president's wife, Lyssa is not just elite, but also the metaphorical classmate of Hillary Clinton, who also went to a Seven Sisters school, Wellesley. By linking liberalism with elitism, *An American Daughter* examines class in America. Lyssa's spin doctor feels that Lyssa's ancestry breeds liberal entitlement: "Simple people who aren't great-granddaughters of presidents and PhDs in public health serve on a jury when they receive an official notice." But Lyssa tells Tucker, "My greatest privilege is my family." As a senator's daughter and the great-granddaughter of Ulysses S. Grant, Lyssa "can put [her headband] on and take it off," play the conventional woman when needed and then discard the role. Still, Timber tells Lyssa he should call her segment "An American Snob"—that the "Dunkin' Donut twins in Eugene" and "the cashier at the Shreveport airport" are "America to me. Ba-da-bing, ba-da-boom. She gets you a beer and turns into a sandwich." Lyssa is supposed to appeal to this Midwestern populism in her interview. Her spin doctor coaches her as follows:

> You may be a privileged person but you're also a working mom, you love your husband, you love your kids, you've got great family values, and on Sunday you go to church and enjoy hiking. . . . No sarcasm admitted. Nothing East Coast, Ivy League, smarty-pants, no women's lib, no highfalutin charm. Remember, you're from Indiana.

Indiana represents conservative values, but Lyssa has moved east— geographically and culturally. In 1997, however, Americans began leaving cities and moving to small towns, which have traditionally been more conservative than urban centers. The references in *An American Daughter* reveal an America in conflict: divided between "red" and "blue" values, Republican father and bleeding-heart liberal daughter, Speedways in Indianapolis and Dean & De Lucas in New York, icebox moms in Indiana and pro-choice soccer moms in Washington, D.C., cashiers and surgeon generals, Dinah Shore in 1956 and female doctors in 1997, the Romneys and the Clintons.

In 1997, Wasserstein felt conservatism in the air, even though we had a liberal president. Lyssa's son yells, "Mom! Someone in Alaska hates you! Mom, they think you're what's wrong with America." Wasserstein could not have known that John McCain would choose Alaska governor Sarah Palin for his running mate in 2008, and that Alaska—the outer edges of America—would become a metaphor for an America out of step with feminism. But her words were prescient. *An American Daughter* says that feminism needed to be not just about a woman running for office, but also about a woman with progressive values being considered by an electorate who did not feel threatened by her.

Although Lyssa is "a bleeding heart liberal" and her father is a conservative senator from Indiana, the play wants to make political distinctions ambiguous. In his interview with Lyssa, Timber asks, "Who are the good guys and who are the bad guys?" Lyssa responds, "I don't look at things in black and white. It's not even really good medicine." Accordingly, Morrow, who betrays her, is a gay Republican, as opposed to the typically liberal gay character. In addition, calling Timber "Timber Canoe and Tyler too," Lyssa alludes to the popular 1840 Log Cabin Campaign song that praised Whig candidates William Henry Harrison (the "hero of Tippecanoe"—the 1811 battle between United States forces and the American Indian confederation) and John Tyler, while denigrating incumbent Democrat Martin Van Buren. Thus Lyssa invokes the dichotomy between elitism and populism, cowboys and Indians, Whigs and Democrats. But the victors are not really the good guys, and so it is with Timber and Lyssa.

In the original draft for Lincoln Center rehearsals, Lyssa's coach advises her to help bridge this gap by revealing her husband's affair with Quincy: "Americans will forgive a wife who with the help of her loving family overcomes a personal deficiency." After all, Lyssa remains faithful to her husband: "I'll be here when you get home." But Lyssa refuses to be "hung out to dry, even if [she has] to wear a headband, bake cookies, or sing lullabies." Clarifying Hillary Clinton's 1992 comment about choosing to fulfill her profession, rather than staying home to bake cookies, Jackie Judd of ABC News pointed out that "Clinton went on to say feminism means the right to choose work, or home, or both; but the damage had been done. She'd been tagged an elitist and an ultra-feminist." Quincy concludes that Lyssa is "being repositioned by the media as a victim feminist," and Walter is convinced that "the women of America . . . are furious with you. You're pretty, have two great kids, are successful, admired, thin, have a great soul. In the heartland that means you're one privileged, ungrateful to her mother, conniving bitch." Lyssa's failure to do jury duty, however, results more from overcommitment than from elitism.

Similarly, during the 1996 presidential campaign, American feminists felt they were watching a scripted act. According to Marcia Gillespie, editor-in-chief of *Ms.*, both parties had a "1950s recipe" for women:

> Go for warm and fuzzy on prime time, and feature tearjerker issues, the more hankie appeal the better. (But whatever you do, stay away from controversial issues like abortion, affirmative action, and lesbian and gay rights—and steer way clear of poverty.) . . . Focus on family values, talk a lot about how much you love children, how committed you are to protecting and caring for them and to supporting the family. Oh, and if possible, be sure to have the candidates reveal some personally traumatic incident that transformed their political views. . . . The generic Woman's vote that the politicos salivated for is from the group they categorized as "Soccer Moms." To qualify you had to be white, married with kids, suburban, middle-class, and mainstream. Otherwise, you were simply odd woman out.

Reducing women's issues exclusively to children and family when "every issue is a woman's issue," this script mirrored Timber Tucker's appeal to "icebox moms" and Chubby's advice to Lyssa to protect her family at all costs. On the editor's page of *Ms.*, Gillespie concluded, "This . . . patriarchal-think . . . seeks to keep the race/class hierarchy firmly in place . . . and denies . . . that women's concerns extend far beyond our homes."

Timber's interview questions about Lyssa's mother open up the tension between two kinds of women. Lyssa describes her mother as a conventional fifties housewife, but Senator Hughes remembers his former wife as "a bright, complicated person. . . . If she were an ordinary Indiana housewife, she might have been in a lot less pain." According to the senator, his wife "wanted to see the U.S.A. in a Chevrolet," but Lyssa does not remember her mother having "any sense of adventure at all." In fact, the year that Dinah Shore became the voice for Chevrolet in America—1956—was not a time of great adventure for women. It was, of course, before the women's movement, and Mamie Eisenhower was First Lady. With her love of feminine clothes and jewelry, her pride in

TIMBER

They are convinced, at least according to our latest *Time Zone* poll, that you are both condescending and elitist.

LYSSA

The women of America should concern themselves with the fact that breast cancer, ovarian cancer, and uterine cancer research is grossly underfunded compared to prostate cancer. The women of America should concern themselves with the possibility of their reproductive rights being taken away from them. The women of America should concern themselves that their children are increasingly smoking, falling prey to drug addiction and to the rapid growth of teenage pregnancy. The women of America should not concern themselves with my father's wives, my cooking, or my mother.

INT. Control Room'd. Billy Robbens is standing. Boy leaning forward,

TIMBER

So you're emotional on this subject.

LYSSA

Yes, I'm emotional. I share that with the women of America.

WALTER

My wife is a very committed doctor.

CUT TO Time zone set
INT

LYSSA

Would you like to know, Timber, why I have avoided public life until this nomination? Because I know I can make a difference in the world without going through any of this. I know if I raise money for a walk-in clinic where there never has been one it'll make a difference. I know if the chemotherapy room at my hospital has decent telephones and fresh wallpaper it'll make a difference. I know I can take a splinter out of my son's hand and make a difference. The people I work with look at life and death every day. Sometimes we manage to save life and sometimes we don't. But it has nothing to do with whether we did or didn't like our mothers. It has to do with service.

TIMBER

Dr. Hughes, are you saying you're not fit for public life?

A page from the script of *An American Daughter* with production notes by Wasserstein. (Courtesy of the Wendy Wasserstein estate)

her home, and her focus on her husband, a West Point graduate, Mamie represented the feminine mystique. It was the era to which Lyssa's mother belonged, and Timber, the journalist, uses it to undermine Lyssa: "Did you feel her horizons were limited?" When Lyssa challenges the questions bearing on her confirmation, Timber responds, "Many women in America feel your attitude towards your mother is your attitude towards them." He then asks if her father's political career caused her mother to suffer by "sacrificing for his career" and if Lyssa likes her father's fourth wife. Angry about the irrelevance of the questions to her qualifications for surgeon general, she highlights significantly neglected issues in women's health: "American women should instead concern themselves with retaining their reproductive rights, with the fact that breast cancer, ovarian cancer, and uterine cancer research are grossly underfunded compared to prostate cancer," and with teenage drug addiction and pregnancy.

Outside the play, feminists were arguing that women's issues should include all forms of social injustice: war and nuclear armaments, poverty, ageism, racism, classism, education, immigrant rights, and the civil rights of lesbians and gay men. The culture, however, seemed conservative. Lyssa's political coach tells her to "soft-pedal" her position on abortion in order to appease her father. She knows that she has to play the role that the public wants, but she also wants to maintain her integrity: "I'm a senator's daughter. So I can put [the headband] on or take it off." When Lyssa finally takes off her headband, she is refusing to be someone else, which prevents her from becoming surgeon general. As director Dan Sullivan says, "The question that Lyssa confronts turns 1960s idealism on its head: can an ethical, progressive person enter public life without having to betray her values? . . . to be a politician, everyone has to turn into someone else. From a feminist point of view, however, the play is about women as outsiders." Lyssa feels betrayed, telling her father, "You never told me it was going to be this hard." He responds, "You never asked." Women were not prepared for the assaults they would face.

In the mid-nineties, popular culture addressed the longing for a woman who could vanquish patriarchy and injustice with a TV series called *Xena: Warrior Princess.* She was a mortal woman, six feet tall, dressed like a warrior, who could defeat anyone. This superwoman certainly did not exist in real life, or in *An American Daughter.* Defeated, Lyssa longs for the simplicity of her childhood, telling her father, "I'd give anything for you to show up and say, 'Everything's going to be fine." For women in public service, there seemed no refuge or consolation. Still, Lyssa takes full responsibility, telling her interviewer, "If there's any fault, it's mine."

Lyssa (Christine Lahti) and Walter (Tom Skerritt) in an interview scene from Lifetime's TV movie of *An American Daughter.* (Lifetime/Photofest © Lifetime Television)

Timber accuses Lyssa of thinking herself "too good for public life," but Lyssa sees prejudice against women in his comment:

There's nothing quite so satisfying as erasing the professional competency of a woman, is there? Especially when there's such an attractive personal little hook to hang it on. . . . She must be a bad, cold person. That's why she achieved so much! And anyway it would be all right if she were a man and cold. That man would be tough . . . . But a woman? A woman from good schools and a good family? That kind of woman should be perfect! And if she manages to be perfect, then there is something distorted and condescending about her. That kind of hard-working woman deserves to be hung out to dry. That's a parable the Indiana housewives can tell their daughters with pride. They can say for those of you girls who thought the Lyssa Dent Hughes generation made any impact, you're wrong! Statistically they may have made an impact but they're still twisting in the wind just like the rest of us.

Women, she believes, are held to different standards than men; their professional competence is questioned in a way that men's is not. Coldness in men is considered toughness, but not so for women. Perfection and diligence in women mean condescension. Not so for men. So, while Lyssa's generation seems to have made progress, they are emotionally in turmoil. Coming of age in the seventies, Lyssa Dent Hughes is Heidi Holland in 1997. Both feel stranded.

Or was the woman's problem part of a larger moral problem, unrelated to gender? Lyssa's stepmother tells her:

> There are plenty of not-nice people in the world. They'll tear you apart just because they're jealous or disappointed or, even worse, because they have nothing better to do. Then, after it's all over, after all the damage and hurt is done, you come back to yourself. So you can ruin your life by being valiant and impressive or find the most idiotic means to gracefully move forward.

Chubby advises Lyssa to move forward by protecting her family at all costs. According to her, Lyssa's antagonist is not gender, but betrayal by other jealous, disappointed, or bored people. In an earlier draft, Morrow, a close family friend, turns out to be one such person. He zeroes in on Lyssa's failure to do jury duty for the benefit of the reporter and later claims, "I forgot they were people I know and like." In fact, in the mid-1990s, articles were appearing about "a rapid rise of mean-spiritedness, fed by radio and television. . . . The mood of the country was depressed, angry, overwhelmed, feeling isolated and cut off, mistrustful, mean, hurt, fearful people." Walter asks Morrow, "Do you hate us all because we're straight?" Timber asks Morrow, "Is there anything people like you really believe in?" Relationships in *An American Daughter* are tenuous. Morrow says he represents "a persecuted minority" and "objects to the current left-wing rage for selective privilege or self-righteous entitlement." Judith claims that Morrow and "the brightest minds" misguidedly believe that "sexual preference is the reason for all personal and societal happiness." Gay awareness, she believes, will not solve all social problems. "There won't be a national health insurance or decent schools because of where you choose to place your penis." Moreover, she complains that AIDS receives more attention than women's cancers. Representing those gay Americans who moved to the far right "because of the inconsistency of the left," Morrow tries to compensate for his betrayal of Lyssa by offering to donate sperm to Dr. Kaufman's cause (in an earlier version of the script, he offers to donate sperm because she wants to have a child). Judith "refuse[s] to be used as [Morrow's] easy way out."

Lyssa's withdrawal from her nomination as surgeon general became Wasserstein's metaphor for inequality for women. Lyssa tells Timber, "I really wanted that job. I would have been good." In the end, a leather goods company asks Lyssa to do an ad on horseback: "Ulysses S. Grant's fifth-generation granddaughter charges into battle with a Doone & Burkey purse." It seemed that in 1997 feminism had become image and status, rather than real progress. Judith also sees the incident in a larger context: "I believe by denying Lyssa Hughes this post, we will be denying the country the talents of a remarkably concerned and inventive public servant, but also denying the girls of America someone who they could, with pride, imagine themselves growing up to be." The play asks, who are the role models for American women? Senator Hughes considers his daughter's "tremendous reserves of strength and compassion as close to a female role model as we get." He jokes that in light of Jurygate, Amy Fisher and Arianna Huffington should have been Lyssa's role models instead of Eleanor Roosevelt and Florence Nightingale. Eleanor Roosevelt represents everything that Lyssa would admire in an earlier American woman: a participant in the American Red Cross, the League of Women Voters, the Women's Trade Union League, the Women's Division of the New York State Democratic Committee, and international relief projects; a teacher of young women; and an advocate of the rights and needs of the poor, of minorities, and of the disadvantaged. Lyssa's admiration for Florence Nightingale is especially appropriate, as a doctor and prospective surgeon general facing obstacles. Nightingale became a nurse in spite of the restrictive societal code for affluent young English women, who were expected to become wives and mothers. Like Eleanor Roosevelt, she cared for the poor. "The Lady with the Lamp" made her solitary rounds late at night during the Crimean War. She was also a pioneer in her understanding of hygiene and of the mind-body connection. A nineteenth-century feminist, she believed that marriage would interfere with practicing medicine and therefore rejected two marriage proposals. Moreover, like Wasserstein's characters, her affluent background enabled her to do her work. But Lyssa's father believes Arianna Huffington is a more reasonable heroine. Author and founder of the *Huffington Post,* a liberal online news and commentary Web site, Huffington was a conservative while married to oil millionaire Michael Huffington. Senator Hughes's reference to Amy Fisher, however, is highly ironic. Called the "Long Island Lolita" by the press, Fisher was convicted in the 1992 shooting of the wife of her lover Joey Buttafuoco. Born in 1974, Fisher represents a younger generation of women gone wrong, like Quincy Quince.

For Quincy, the Lyssa Dent Hughes story becomes just another occasion for competition between talk shows. Quincy says, "Barbara and Diane can't believe Tucker nabbed you from under them. The Lyssa Hughes interview is a real get." She never mentions the significance of two female journalists losing to a man or that the interview undermines and objectifies Lyssa; even before the hazing questions, one of the crew asks, "Where do you want to put her?" The rivalry between Lyssa and Quincy, two generations of feminists, is also fierce. Lyssa feels "bitterness" and "envy" toward Quincy for having "baited" her husband. Yet Quincy believes that she is "the one who can advance [Lyssa's] cause." Nothing could be further from the truth, and yet *Time* magazine touts Quincy as "bringing feminism into the twenty-first century," creating its "rebirth." Walter also believes that his student is "committed to making a tired ideology new." Quincy's "new" feminism includes her belief that "sweet women are trapped by their own hostility," and she sums up her book, *The Prisoner of Gender,* as "sexism made simple." She is convinced that Dr. Hughes is a prisoner of her gender, "a disempowered victim," and that she has "disenfranchised her femininity." On the other hand, as a nineties feminist, she feels more liberated. With Walter as her academic mentor, she says, "We're at a place now where we can look beyond gender for mentors." Her next book will be about fathers and daughters; in other words, she believes that she has transcended patriarchy and paternalism.

Yet Quincy, too, is a victim of sexism. When *Time Zone* expresses interest in hiring her full-time, Timber assumes she'll be doing "women's issues" and "personal profiles." More condescending, the offer is for "an exclusive on the fanatic at Legal Seafood." The scene conveys that women were slotted to cover either "women's issues" or more sensational stories. Sexism, however, was simpler in the twenties and thirties when, Quincy points out, women "were only able to excel in show business, cosmetology, and aviation."

Part of being "a prisoner of their gender" means being acquisitive and competitive, as it did in *The Heidi Chronicles.* Lyssa lists—

humorously—her goals as follows: "to make heaps of money, get our children into Harvard, and have upper arms that don't jiggle." Walter thinks that she is "slightly hysterical" because she is "overcommitted and determined to do everything well." When Timber asks him whether his wife is "one of those remarkable young women who does everything right," Walter confirms that Lyssa "[will] give up her own sleep before she'll ever give up our family time." Moreover, whenever Lyssa was called for jury duty, she "had to be out of town lecturing . . . or at a world conference for gonorrhea." Accordingly, in the Lincoln Center draft, Lyssa's stepmother says, "You think a woman of my generation could handle your life?" Walter affirms, "Most women I know are booked solid from morning till night." In fact, Lyssa's final jury notice arrived when both boys had chicken pox, there was a crisis at her hospital requiring her presence, and "the nanny disappeared . . . with the neighborhood drug-dealing security guard." In 1997, psychologists began insisting, "We have to give up the myths that women can't have it all except by doing it all and that men don't have to do it all but can have it all." Even Lyssa attributes Walter's affair with Quincy to "the frigid, overextended no-fun narcissists of [her] generation." As a result of Lyssa's quest for success, Quincy finds Lyssa soulless and unhappy. Quincy wants to believe women's lives have no boundaries, but Lyssa exemplifies that women were bumping up against limitations.

Quincy also wants it all: to start her family before she focuses on her public life, and then to restore women's sexual identity with a book called *Venus Raging*: "Sex for Lyssa's generation became just something else to be good at. . . . My generation wants to do it all, but we want to have some fun, too." Only concerned with her fame, and lacking ethics, she has an affair with Lyssa's husband, her former professor. Referring to Grant's letter from Vicksburg, she tells Lyssa, "I can't imagine what it is to literally fight for one's principles." Moreover, when Lyssa withdraws her nomination, Quincy regards it in terms of publicity: "She's still gotten a lot of heat out of it." Quincy expects to sell a lot of her books as a result: "They'll be taking *Prisoner of Gender* across America." Quincy's exploitative nature as well as Lyssa and Judith's situations exemplify that American women had become prisoners of gender.

In contrast to Quincy, whose mother taught her "a woman's life can have no boundaries," Dr. Judith Kaufman believes "a woman's life is all about boundaries." The African-American, Jewish oncologist regrets that she can neither "make life nor stop death." She describes herself as having "the career of a fifty-five-year old man, the infertile reproductive cycle of a forty-two-year-old woman, and the emotional stability of a fifteen-year-old girl." Having spent her life trying to relieve other people's pain and sorrow, she now wants a home with a family, leading her to take "mega-doses of insane fertility drugs." When Lyssa tells her to "just grow up and make [a home]," Judith says that she cannot make one just for herself. She is determined to have a family, having been taught that "if I was a good girl and worked hard, I could achieve anything." Although she prefers "the reliable variables of science" to the precariousness of public life, she finds herself as stranded as Lyssa. Lyssa tells her, "All lives don't have to be about children," but she cannot convince Judith. Judith's failed quest for fertility coincides with Lyssa's withdrawal from her nomination; the play registers political and personal defeat for women and is appropriately set during the festival of regrets, the Holy Taschlich.

As an African-American Jew, Judith represents the intersection of two kinds of racism, and Quincy calls her a "walking Crown Heights." For her role models, Judith looks to Lena Horne, the iconic American singer and actress descended from a mixture of African-American, Native American, and Caucasian ancestors, whom W. E. B. DuBois classed among "the talented tenth," the upper stratum of the American black population. In other words, something like herself. While Horne was a progressive role model, Judith wanted to be a scientist, so only Marie Curie came close to her aspirations—and she was white. "So I had to make up for myself who I was going to be." The American story of self-invention finally applied to people who had been historically discriminated against.

Set against the backdrop of the Clinton administration, Sarajevo, and the Gulf War, with references to Jefferson and de Tocqueville, Jesse Helms and Strom Thurmond, *An American Daughter* explores the conflict between liberal and conservative values, as well as the conflict within the liberal establishment. In doing so, it raises important questions: Had liberals in fact become too elitist in the late nineties, or was Lyssa Dent Hughes a victim of sexism? Or both? Could one be both liberal and elitist? Why had the liberal gay population moved to the right? Had political categories become entirely blurred? How were we to define life, liberty, and the pursuit of happiness for professional women when the need for child care collided with their work? Was it wrong to employ illegal immigrants, who otherwise would have no income? Had feminism become as obsolete as the rotary phone? Did high-powered career women feel stranded by having exchanged careers for children? Was gender or jealousy the biggest obstacle for women? In *An American Daughter* anyone could turn on you—liberal or conservative.

Wasserstein says her play is about "the sadness of a generation" in a personal and a political sense. If America is the patient, and Lyssa has been nominated surgeon general to heal its wounds, the treatment never happens, because she must withdraw her nomination. When Lyssa speaks on television in the opening scene about the importance of education to good health care, she stumbles on the word "health," instead saying, "heal," as if to say that the nation needs to be healed before it can become healthy. For Wasserstein this healing needed to happen for women and for liberalism in general. *An American Daughter* wanted to usher in a new era of equality for women, but in Wasserstein's view, women still faced their Robert E. Lee and had yet to achieve their Appomattox, even though Janet Reno had become attorney general in 1993. The playwright diagnoses the problem of a double standard for women—without providing a prescription. By 1997, the microchip was empowering individuals by giving them more access to information than ever before, but we were still working out our social structure.

A photograph of Easter Sunday in old New York, on Fifth Avenue and West 48th Street, circa 1917–19. (Museum of the City of NY/Photofest; © Museum of the City of New York)

6

Old Money (2000)

A New Gilded Age

Cash has merged with class.

—Wendy Wasserstein

In order to understand America, Wasserstein knew she had to explore not only gender, but also money and class. New York society especially fascinated her, and the impetus for writing *Old Money* came in 1996 when she was "seated at a most fashionably attired table" on the Upper East Side that reminded her of a scene from Edith Wharton's *The Age of Innocence*. Wharton's social tragedy exposed the contrast between the polished outward manners and the less benevolent human nature beneath them at the turn of the twentieth century. Wasserstein, however, was more interested in the way the opulence of the Gilded Age at the end of the nineteenth century echoed the end of the twentieth:

> There was a bowl of three dozen roses bunched so closely in a ponytail that each petal skimmed another; amusing jelly beans in silver thimbles; and pomegranates worthy of a Dutch still life masterfully dotting the tablecloth, as if after the meal we could all play croquet. The table, so thoughtfully conceived, seemed to contain all the trappings of a new gilded age.

Coined by Mark Twain and Charles Dudley Warner in their 1873 novel called *The Gilded Age: A Tale of Today,* the Gilded Age referred to extravagant displays of excessive wealth by America's upper class during the post–Civil War and post-Reconstruction era (1877–1890) that ended with

Cornelius Vanderbilt IV with his fiancée, Rachel Littleton, circa 1920. (Photofest)

the Panic of 1893. Industrialists and financiers like Cornelius Vanderbilt, John D. Rockefeller, Andrew Carnegie, and J. P. Morgan accrued great wealth. The Rockefellers made their money in oil, the Du Ponts by selling gunpowder, the Vanderbilts through railroads. These "high society" families could live off income from their inheritances rather than from salaries, creating multiple generations of wealth. At the time, there was no income tax to curtail the enormous fortunes in America's growing industries, and so the Rockefellers, Morgans, and Carnegies built their opulent mansions along New York's Fifth Avenue.

In their discussions of social class, historians refer to Charles Darwin and Herbert Spencer's idea of natural selection and "the survival of the fittest" that justified the stratification of the wealthy and poor. Drawing on Darwin and Spencer, Yale economist William Sumner argued in *What Social Classes Owe to Each Other* that assistance to the poor weakens their ability to survive in society. In opposition to the social Darwinists, a movement arose to help the poor, including attorney Clarence Darrow, who argued that poverty, not biology, created crime. Moreover, economist Thorstein Veblen described economic behavior as socially rather than individually determined, maintaining that "conspicuous consumption and conspicuous leisure" of the wealthy defined social status in America. Similarly, *Old Money* attempts to understand economics in terms of social and cultural change. While Veblen saw a conflict between old and new values, Wasserstein's play dramatizes both the continuity and the differences between the two centuries. According to Lewis Lapham, "The play of wealth, energy and untutored liberty" that characterized the late nineteenth century re-emerged in the late twentieth century. Both eras, he observed, had a "half merry, half desperate air." Henry James also observed "youth on the run . . . with the prize of the race in sight." Moreover, in their extravagance, both Gilded Ages resembled a Gatsby party with "floating rounds of cocktails," "cars from New York . . . parked five deep in the drive," "halls and salons and verandas . . . gaudy with primary colors," and orchestras "playing yellow cocktail music." Both Wasserstein and Fitzgerald were fascinated by old and new money and the way it shaped the American character. In the twenties, Fitzgerald cautioned that the American pursuit of happiness had become the pursuit of wealth. Similarly, in the late nineties, Wasserstein observed that "cash" had replaced "class."

Old money was never just about money; it was about an aristocratic way of being—knowing how to dress, speak, socialize, attend the right cultural events, read the right books, go to the right schools. Edith Wharton defined American social aristocracy in her 1934 memoir, *A Backward Glance,* as "long established standards of honour and conduct, of education and manners." In 1776, however, Adam Smith had not imagined such social stratification, writing that "no oppressive aristocracy has ever prevailed in the colonies." After all, the American experiment was supposed to be democratic and classless, unlike Europe. As social historian Eric Homberger explains, "Aristocracy in America was not an established position in a comprehensible social hierarchy, as in Britain. Rather, it was a meaning attached to certain individuals, families, and locations by themselves and others."

The Articles of Confederation and the Constitution of 1787 prohibited titles of nobility in the United States of America, and after the American Revolution, primogeniture, which in Europe assured the transmission of wealth and property to a single heir, was abolished. Yet, for three generations following the death of John Jacob Astor in 1848, the Astors, who personified New York society, continued the rule of primogeniture, and some Americans continued to be enthralled by class distinctions. Ward McAllister, self-appointed arbiter of New York society from the 1860s to the early 1890s, coined the term "the Four Hundred" to refer to "the number of people in New York who really mattered"—the people who felt at ease in the ballrooms of high society. Some thought the number referred to the capacity of Mrs. William Backhouse Astor Jr.'s ballroom. In reaction to McAllister's elitism, O. Henry wrote a collection of stories in 1903 called *The Four Million* to insist that every human being in New York was worthy of notice. At the time, institutions like the Patriarchs and the Social Register held the keys to an exclusive club that had always fascinated Wasserstein.

The playwright noted an important distinction between old and new money; in Wharton's Old New York, "men and women are desperate to buy their way into society, but the gates are open only to those who are from approved backgrounds and have good taste." New York aristocrats were "self-defined" and felt "entitled" to their position in society. Like contemporary celebrities, the aristocrats of New York's Gilded Age knew their lives were on display. Homberger documents that "From Henry Brevoort's dress ball at his home on lower Fifth Avenue in 1840, until the death of Mrs. Astor at her home on Fifth Avenue in 1908, New York experienced an age of aristocracy." Manhattan, in particular, was where everything was happening. Nineteenth-century writer Louis Simonin observed: "All American society is modeled on that of New York. . . . No American City can dispute with New York in . . . magnificence, nor contest with her in the amount of business transactions, the riches, the elegance, the luxury, and splendor of the fetes and receptions." *Old Money* reflects this exuberant New York at the end of the nineteenth and twentieth centuries, resulting in a comparison between old and new money. Wasserstein writes, "During an earlier New York gilded age a man's worth might be based on his money, but the money would never be mentioned in public. Furthermore, despite a man's fortune, proper society would always judge him by his 'manners,' his breeding and bloodline." Her observation echoes Wharton's, but her view of new money reflects John Adams's statement in 1808: "We do possess one material which actually constitutes an aristocracy that governs the nation. That material is wealth. Talents, birth, virtues, services, sacrifices are of little consideration with us." Accordingly, in 2000, the party publicist in *Old Money*, Flinty McGee, says, ". . . society has merged with celebrity. Cash frankly has superseded class. We live in an asset-based meritocracy. There are sixty-four new millionaires a day in Silicon Valley, and no one cares where they come from. So everything's much more democratic."

In contrast to new money, the Old New York that Wasserstein was writing about echoed Henry James's 1905 essay "New York Revisited."

The Waldorf Astoria Hotel circa 1900. (Photofest)

James called New York City "the huge American rattle of gold," "expensively provisional," "forbidden the pleasures of art or the comforts of history, oddly uncertain of itself despite the bluster of its immense wealth and sham refinement, willing to sell last week's truth or yesterday's celebrity." New Yorkers worshipped money, which manifested itself through its architecture and its social structures. Industrialists and financiers "staged costume balls, bought diamond collars for their dogs, feasted on oysters in golden bowls." The rich were eating at Sherry's and Delmonico's and sleeping at the Waldorf Astoria. The "vulgar splendor of the Waldorf" appalled James—with its "huge-hatted ladies, bad violin music, and marble fountains."

Wasserstein combined her study of the nineteenth-century Gilded Age with her experience at the "new gilded" table around which were seated "certified members of the Hollywood and Wall Street A-lists," who "travel[ed] by private plane." She recalls, "Toward dessert the discussion came around to how much a very successful producer [perhaps Jeffrey Katzenberg] was worth." The host of the dinner party in *Old Money* and restorer of the Upper East Side mansion where it is set is a legendary high-risk arbitrageur, Jeffrey Bernstein, born on Coney Island Avenue in Brooklyn, a graduate of Yale Law School, formerly a civil liberties lawyer but now, at age forty-eight, "at the pinnacle of New Money society." His son, Ovid Walpole Bernstein, is a senior at Manhattan's Trinity School. The guests at his party (in addition to many unseen luminaries) include seventy-five-year-old Vivian Pfeiffer, noted architectural historian and Columbia professor, grandson of the robber baron Tobias Vivian Pfeiffer, who commissioned the mansion; forty-year-old Hollywood producer Sid Nercessian; his eighteen-year-old daughter, Caroline, and his beautiful, Asian second wife, Penny ("the world's leading online panty manufacturer"); Flinty McGee, thirty-five, a party publicist and "arbiter of the new A-list"); and Saulina Webb, fifty-four, a noted sculptor and sister of Jeffrey's first wife.

Each actor also plays a character at another party in the Pfeiffer mansion eighty years before: Schuyler Lynch, sixty-two, the architect of the Pfeiffer mansion; the house's owner, fifty-year-old Tobias Vivian Pfeiffer, a coal miner who busted unions and built railroads across America; his mistress, thirty-five-year-old Florence DeRoot; his son, Tobias Vivian Pfeiffer Jr., a student at St. Paul's School who wants to defy his father's plans for him to go into business; Arnold Strauss, forty-eight, a first-generation American Jew who made a fortune in the department store business; Sally Webster, forty-eight, an artist, diarist, and traveler living in Greenwich Village on her trust fund; Betina Brevoort, seventy, the eldest member of turn-of-the-century New York society; and Mary Gallagher, a seventeen-year-old Irish maid who wants a better life. Both gilded ages consist of social climbers and opportunists, and also some dreamers and artists.

Old Money belongs to a tradition of American comedies of manners about the rich—from Philip Barry (*Philadelphia Story, Holiday, Paris*

Bound) and Edna Ferber (*Giant, Saratoga Trunk, Ice Palace*) to John Guare (*House of Blue Leaves, Six Degrees of Separation*) and Douglas Carter Beane (*As Bees in Honey Drown*). Anna Cora Mowatt's 1845 play, *Fashion; or Life in New York*—the first American satire about high society in nineteenth-century New York—especially influenced *Old Money.* Wasserstein, however, wanted to highlight "the changes in values between the past two turns of centuries . . . by traveling back and forth in time." Accordingly, by the end of the play, the Bernstein mansion has become "a museum of the digital revolution with relics of the late twentieth century, like laptops, cellular phones, and paper money."

In order to document money and class around 1900 and 2000, the playwright needed a setting that would resonate with both eras. Therefore, set designer Thomas Lynch created an Upper East Side mansion with a "gauzelike quality through which time and fashion can move easily." Wasserstein had long been an admirer of architects Charles McKim (1847–1909), William Rutherford Mead (1846–1928), and Stanford White (1853–1906), who founded the most prestigious architectural firm in the United States in 1879. They were part of the City Beautiful and Beaux Arts movements, an architectural style that combined classical Greek and Roman architecture with Renaissance ideas adopted for grand public buildings and opulent mansions. The style provided order and formality to American cities during the Gilded Age. Stanford White designed the summer homes of the Astors and the Vanderbilts, as well as the Washington Square Arch, Madison Square Garden, and the New York Herald Building. To capture McKim, Mead, and White's turn-of-the-century Manhattan, Wasserstein conceived of Schuyler Lynch, an architect who would be a contemporary of Charles McKim "but considered a renegade for his ornamental style." Lynch builds an Upper East Side mansion to rival Henry Frick's and Felix Warburg's. Built in 1908 at the northeast corner of Fifth Avenue and Ninety-second Street, the Warburg mansion became the Jewish Museum in 1991. (Warburg joined the investment bank Kuhn, Loeb & Co., financing America's expanding railways and growth companies, including Western Union and Westinghouse.) In the play, Betina Brevoort reports, "I went to the Kuhn Loeb wedding last week. They're creating a financial dynasty."

Money buys real estate, and Wasserstein was writing about both. At the beginning of the twentieth century there was a construction boom. Henry James observed, "New office buildings, new town houses, new hotels jostled with one another for a place." By the autumn of 1905, the

New York Times building appeared on West Forty-third Street; Longacre Square became Times Square; 1,250 square feet of ground at No. 1 Wall Street sold for $700,000—the highest price ever paid for any piece of real estate anywhere in America; and the Hotel Astor opened.

Also important to the play's setting is the fact that the highest concentration of wealthy people in New York City has always lived along Fifth, Park, and Madison avenues. In the play, Saulina refers to her late sister's apartment on Sixty-third and Park, and to their parents' apartment on Seventy-fifth and Madison. Wasserstein watched the price of New York real estate soar along with the salaries of a small group of people. Accordingly, the play explores the connections between real estate, money, and power. As a high-risk arbitrageur, Bernstein buys the stock of a company being acquired in a merger, while selling short the stock of the acquirer. Arbitrageurs, then, make a profit from the difference between market prices. With these profits, Bernstein can afford the old Pfeiffer mansion, and he wants the power that it confers. His son points out that at an earlier time his father "would never have been invited [to his own party]. And my dad would hate that. This way he controls it. He can go in and out." Ovid says his father believes that the world is divided into three groups: "the players, those who wish they were players, and those who have no idea who the players are. He says life is intolerable only in the middle category. My dad also says the lesson of Tobias Pfeiffer is you become a player by making up your own rules." In other words, those who are far removed from power are less frustrated than members of the middle class, who are close to but not part of the superstructure. Being a player also means having your party on "Page Six of the *Chronicle*," being invited to the party, or having "a write-up" about your house "in the Home section." Bernstein again links money to power when he says, "There's no glory in not having it. I want to be in the game because it's a very dull and inequitable world when you're not. You're forced to trust the system and at the mercy of mediocre bureaucrats. But if I'm rich, people want to know my opinion about newspapers, movie studios, and the Democratic Party."

On the other hand, "Money insulates people," and education often reflects that class division. Bernstein went to Yale, while Flinty went to North Central Kansas State. Northeast elitism stands in contrast to Midwestern populism, as it does in *An American Daughter*. Flinty hopes to gain entrance into Bernstein's world: "I'm putting my dibs in early. You're already number fourteen on the *Chronicle*'s list of New York's most eligible bachelors." "The Most Eligible" list is a favorite of Wasserstein's; she both mocks it and is attracted to it. Jeffrey claims "there's a waiting list" to date him. Moreover, the wealth of this world is excessive: Sid and Penny just bought the two properties adjoining their summer home in Nantucket and are awaiting town board approval before building a thirty-six-room house there. Being Jewish and Asian, however, they will change Nantucket's "too white," "too Republican" composition. The son of new money, Ovid socializes with the super-rich: "One of my friends' dad is buying the Museum of Natural History, but they're having a hard time finding a housekeeper."

Jeffrey and his guests are, of course, new money, which the play distinguishes from old money when the two worlds meet. Pfeiffer wants to know if Bernstein has his kind of power and influence. Bernstein claims that as "a master at high-risk arbitrage," he can "make [Pfeiffer's] entire fortune in just an hour." Pfeiffer, however, knows

> you could lose it too. . . . it doesn't add up to a load of beans. Except money. In my day we were building a nation with steel, coal, and even . . . Standard Oil. We were laying down railroads, inventing automobiles. You just move numbers.

According to Pfeiffer, old money was about building a country, while new money is about accruing money. Pfeiffer challenges Bernstein to name the legacy he's creating with his fortune, and Bernstein dodges the question by claiming moral superiority, saying he "never abused the working man or attempted to bust a union." "Well, at least not directly," Pfeiffer retorts.

Being connected with the rich, powerful, and famous defines new money. At Bernstein's party, Henry Kravis (an American business financier and investor, worth $5.5 billion, who heads a private equity firm, Kohlberg Kravis Roberts & Co.) and Charlie Rose (interviewer of the movers and shakers of American culture) are "schvitzing in the garden." So is Alan Greenspan. Saulina gives her sculpture to Martha Stewart. Being connected also means hiring the right people. Penny wants to hire Asa Kent, who designed the Pfeiffer garden and "just did Vera [Wang's] in Southampton. . . . He's first on everyone's list." Trends matter; Penny "promised [their feng shui master] we'd commit to purity in all aspects of our life." And Sid predicts that Saulina, the sculptor, is "due for a comeback," because "Jane Fonda collected you." Popular culture carries greater weight than academia. When the party publicist remarks that the dean of the Yale School of Art thinks Saulina's "feminist art [is] dated and retro," Sid replies, "Academics! What the fuck do they know?"

If you are not an insider, then you are an outsider, like Flinty from Independence, Kansas. Flinty wonders "what it's like to be them. . . . It must be so wonderful when no one can ever say no to you." Vivian suggests, "Maybe the trick is not to care," but as a party publicist, Flinty must care: "It's my entire life." Bernstein has already hinted to Flinty, "Maybe all our lives aren't what you crack them up to be," but Flinty thinks otherwise: "Yours most certainly is. . . . Rhodes scholar, you started the *Yale Human Rights Law Journal,* worked as a teacher in a Head Start program in Tuscaloosa for two years. And now you're living in a house the *Times* called 'the perfect evocation of a new gilded age.'" From working-class roots, Flinty thinks Bernstein displays the perfect blend of intellect, populism, and wealth.

Vivian sees that Flinty's admiration comes from being an outsider, telling her, "Only someone who wasn't from this world would become so enamored of it." Flinty realizes, though, that entrance into the world of money and power requires some ruthlessness: "Bernstein has a reputation for being a prickly guy. . . . Gotta be a little prickly to be at the head of the pack." According to Bernstein's sister-in-law Saulina, the sculptor, he is "a master at playing the world to his advantage." *Old Money*, then, is an anthropological study of the personalities that acquire money and its power. Hollywood producer Sid also wants to be a player. Flinty reveals to Jeffrey that "Sid is showing up here tonight [because he] reveres real money. He's desperate to be put on that museum board, and you control it. He would sell his mother to be considered legit. He'd even offer you to produce a picture with him." For Sid, art is a means to power, and his money enables him to purchase Rauschenbergs and Schnabels. Similarly, in 1917, Arnold Strauss, the department store owner and "climber," attends Pfeiffer's dinner in order "to get on the museum board," and Florence (Old Man Pfeiffer's mistress) reminds Pfeiffer that "we worked very hard to get you" the position of head of the museum nominating committee. But when Strauss fails to identify Botticelli's *Last Communion of Saint Jerome*, his nomination is denied. Connections facilitate nominations, but membership requires knowledge. Toby, the son of old money, ironically feels Strauss's rejection is "unfair." Thus the play suggests that old money, or the old boys' network, is obsolete. Symbolically, at the end of the play, the Older Ovid/Vivian tells his grandson that he can gain admission into the secret passage-way of the house with the quarter that he hands him: "Some people used to think this would open any door. All problems solved. If anybody stops you, just show this to them and say, 'I am entitled to certain rights and privileges. This, my good man, is old money.'" Old money used to buy access to opportunity, but it definitely did not solve all problems. And the next generation was not always interested in buying their grandparents' values anyway. In any case, the scene demonstrates that a sense of entitlement comes with money. Historian Eric Homberger documents such entitlement in *Mrs. Astor's New York*:

> Late nineteenth-century New York aristocracy, under the lead-ership of Ward McAllister and Mrs. Astor, consisted of 400 individuals marked by wealth, refinement, and family standing. The "Four Hundred" coined by McAllister is perhaps the great-est single American contribution to the idea of aristocracy. The label reflected a self-awareness among aristocrats that they constituted a narrowly defined, highly select inner circle of New York upper class.

In the 1917 scene, however, the grand dame of New York society, Betina Brevoort (based on the actual old money family), says, "I take our mu-seum very seriously, Tobias. I heard about Mr. Strauss's donation. We mustn't encourage newcomers to believe the world is open to them just because they can pay for it. Fortunes come and go, but it's quality and history that matter." The play conveys that money buys things, but not the things that matter. Vivian humorously reminds her that her ances-tors were "Dutch pirates," deflating both her history and her money. In the present, Caroline claims that her father is Penny's "ticket to Breast Express and the panty business." Sid is offended, but Penny says, "I al-ways tell Sid life can be wonderful. You just have to figure out a way to pay for it." Marrying for money is as much a part of new money as it was with the arrivistes of old money. Sid says Penny puts up with him "be-cause when you have perfect taste, you need to acquire a lifestyle to practice it."

Sid also wants his daughter to make a connection with the editor of the *Times* at the party. She calls him a hypocrite for showing up at a for-mal dinner in a T-shirt and jacket "just to show how . . . above it all you are, but the truth is, you take it all much more seriously than anybody else." In fact, everyone on the board of the Met is there by connection. Saulina's sister, Jessica (Bernstein's first wife), was on the board, which led to Bernstein's involvement. The sisters are from "a distinguished New York family." Saulina wants Sid to know that Jeffrey is "in a position to bring his name up because of [Jessica]." Connections make Caroline feel like a "fake." "Awards are all fakes," she says.

This conflict between authenticity and fraudulence becomes part of the conversation about old and new money. Flinty questions whether Pfeiffer is really old money: "Bernstein, I recognize class. He's sweet, but this is a man without a trust fund." Flinty is mistaken, because Pfeiffer is old money, unlike Bernstein. Thus the scene raises the question of whether it is still old money when it is all gone. Bernstein's restoration of the Pfeiffer mansion becomes a metaphor for the fundamental difference between an imitation and an original. In this way, Bernstein's Upper East Side restoration echoes Gatsby's Long Island mansion, which "was a factual imitation of some Hotel de Ville in Normandy, with a tower on one side, spanking new under a thin beard of raw ivy. . . . " Wasserstein, like Fitzgerald, was interested in how Americans used new money to make it seem old. Saulina, the artist, also confronts Jeffrey about the façade of money: "You're hiding behind this party, this house, these people!" Jeffrey responds, "What's the matter with these people? Everyone in America wants to be with these people. I want to be with these people. You're out of touch, Saulina, and that's the problem with both you and your art. You're living in the past. Think about the future." America, of course, has always been about the future, rather than the past. But Saulina cares about the people she used to know and love, not about following trends: "I watched Jessica fade, and somehow you managed to vanish too. Where have you gone, Jeffrey?" Jeffrey cannot understand Saulina's point of view: "The man in front of you is who I always wished I could be. If I wasn't who I am now, I'd waste my life envying this man's every waking breath." Bernstein's comments resonate with Lewis Lapham's observation that

> In the equations of American failure and success, the values assigned to the words "money" and "class" shift. . . . Sometimes they serve as synonyms for freedom or beauty or truth, sometimes as surrogates for God. The multiple meanings are peculiarly American. For Europeans "money" and "class" refer to a store of wealth or an accident of birth. But . . . Americans impart spiritual connotations to . . . money.

Sally Webb (Mary Beth Hurt) dancing to "Hello My Baby" with Schuyler Lynch (John Cullum) at Bernstein's Upper East Side mansion. At right is Mark Harelik as Jeffrey Bernstein, arbitrageur. (Sara Krulwich/The New York Times/Redux)

Bernstein believes that "Money can buy you happiness" and "only losers have time" to question that assertion. When his son does so anyway, Jeffrey replies, "It takes care of most things very nicely." Bernstein cannot imagine who would not be happy living in his house, but Saulina is uncomfortable with its opulence.

In a play that explores truth and pretense, Sid appropriately wants to shoot an updated version of Sheridan's *The Rivals* in the Pfeiffer mansion. The eighteenth-century Restoration comedy of manners satirizes sentimentalism and pretensions. With the exception of Julia, each of the characters in *The Rivals* lies to get what he or she wants from the other characters. Sid sees *The Rivals* as a reflection of contemporary values gone bad, suggesting that the eighteenth century was yet another Gilded Age. Moreover, Hollywood, where names and status get pictures made, seems to be the most gilded institution. Sid boasts about the project:

Kenny Branagh wants to do it. And we'll put in Buffy the Vampire Slayer as Lydia Whatshername, and it'll be cutting and edgy and I think have something to really say about all our fucked-up values today. A sort of American Beauty meets Shakespeare in Love with a touch of Sense and Sensitivity.

Caroline reveals the rosebud tattoo she got when her father made "that update of *Citizen Kane* with Matt Damon." No one is sure about the significance of "rosebud" in Orson Welles' film, but Caroline drops the allusion to it and to Matt Damon to impress Ovid. Similarly, Flinty plans the Costume Institute Gala not because she cares whether "Audrey Hepburn's Givenchy wardrobe is preserved," but because "everybody you ever read about was there. All of the 'it' girls are swapping baby pictures while Puff Daddy is off whispering to Henry Kissinger. And of course Robert's flowers to die for. I just feel so lucky to be right in the middle of it. I love my life. And you should too." In the world of old and new money, mingling with celebrities and even buying the right flowers makes someone an insider.

While Jews are insiders in the twentieth century, they were usually not part of the old money that inhabited a mansion like Pfeiffer's. During World War I, America often shut its doors on Eastern European Jews. Flinty says, "I don't think Jews lived in these houses," but Sid can imagine Jeffrey Katzenberg growing up in one. Anti-Semitism also appears when Pfeiffer asks Vivian/Schuyler, "My house was bought by a Jewish boy?" In addition, when Pfeiffer wants his painting back from the Metropolitan Museum of Art, his comments are racist, classist, and selfish. The architect reminds him that the painting now belongs to the people of New York City, but Pfeiffer retorts: "The hell with the people of the city of New York! The problem with you, Schuyler, is that you were entirely too well-bred! But I won't be told by a Jew Boy peddler . . . what happens to my painting!" J. P. Morgan, after all, did not lend money to Jews. The play's reference to the Felix Warburg mansion is doubly significant—both as an emblem of the Gilded Age and of Jewish success in the financial industry. The discussion about Jews turns to "how much Katzenberg is worth." Flinty guesses five hundred, while Sid comes in "under four," concluding "Katzenberg's not real money. He couldn't afford this house." Sid defines wealth by whether or not someone needs to work: "Katzenberg still has to work for a living. Even with the Disney settlement. He doesn't have enough fuck-you money to stop. Katzenberg's poor. Bill

J. P. Morgan in Monte Carlo in the early twentieth century. (Photofest)

Gates, even when they split him in half, makes a decent living."

Flinty assumes that Bernstein has old money etiquette: "I bet Bernstein's mother taught him never to talk about money in public." Bernstein, however, says, "You can never be too rich or too thin," while old money Pfeiffer says, "That's just the sort of thing we could never say out loud in my day." Old money connotes reserved behavior, while new money is brash and flashy. According to Pfeiffer, "It's all about his money. Mr. Bernstein is cultivating a style, not a character." Even Bernstein thinks that being a businessman means lacking cultivation when he tells Flinty, "You're the expert on society. I'm just a small businessman." Advising his son Ovid, who has a passion for New York history, he says, "Don't become the kind of dilettante intellectual who wastes his life dwelling on the past. It's great that you read, but read for a purpose." He is anti-intellectual and pragmatic. Lewis Lapham has observed that American "distrust of the contemplative temperament comes from a suspicion of anything that cannot be counted, stuffed, or framed." Wasserstein chose to throw a history professor from old money into the mix of new monied guests, because America has a reputation for looking forward rather than backward; as a commercial culture, we prioritize the concrete over the intangible. When Ovid asks, "How important is money?" Bernstein replies with irony that it's "the road to liberation. . . . Just ask any revolutionary." In contrast, Saulina reveals to her nephew that when she and Jeffrey were in college, "this house would have been the last place he'd imagine himself living in. It was his idea for us to teach together in that Head Start program. In those days your dad would have ripped this party to shreds." The idealists of the sixties became the materialists of the nineties; it was the story Wasserstein kept writing. Ovid tells Saulina, "My father's life is stuck somewhere between Cesar Chavez [the American farm worker, labor leader, and civil rights activist] and Baron Rothschild," son of the prominent banking family.

Bernstein bought the Pfeiffer mansion in 1998, one year after the *Wall Street Journal* reported that he "pioneered a fixed-income arbitrage bank into the largest trading desk [where transactions for buying and selling securities occur] in the world." The American economy was thriving, dot-coms were booming, and unemployment had dropped to below five percent. In this opulent time, Bernstein throws parties in a robber baron's mansion and buys "Beaux Arts painting, Gulfstream jets, and Victorian lacquer lamps and furniture," and Penny Nercessian hires "Breast Express," allowing her mobility. "Penny pumps the milk, and the Wells Fargo wagon is right there waiting." Sid calls Breast Express "the best fucking thing since Mallomars." The driver, trainer, and nurse technician are "a bargain at five thousand a week." In this way, money enables women's liberation; Breast Express, a nanny, and a night nurse "saved [Penny's] life. It's the only way I've been able to work and still cope." In the 1917 scene, Florence DeRoot, Pfeiffer's mistress, also links money and freedom. She tells Pfeiffer, "Money means I won't have to base my life on a man whom I have no remote interest in." For 1917, it was a radical thought. In the present, however, Sid still views women as sexual objects, encouraging Bernstein to have an affair with the publicist. To Bernstein's son, entering a moment later, his remark about a new film project takes on a double meaning: "What's the point of being rich, Ovid, unless it gives you the ability to play?"

For the men in the play, money has not necessarily been liberating. Bernstein can buy anything, but his marriage fell apart, as did the marriages of five of his managing partners. He did not even know how ill his wife was before she died. Significantly, she died while watching *Pride and Prejudice* with Saulina. Austen's novel of manners anticipates the play's suggestion that social standing and wealth are not necessarily advantages. Money can bring materialism, divorce, and insecurity. Caroline tells Ovid, "Since my dad left, my mother has had her eyes, her nose, and her throat done. [She] has thirty million from her divorce and no confidence at all." Her mother's example leads Caroline to confess, "Sometimes I think it makes more sense to end it all now instead of wasting more of my time and my parents' money. Like, last year I tried to kill myself three times, once with pills, once with Drano, and the last time with a Swiss Army knife. . . . My mother would have more time for her masseuses and her yoga trainer." Caroline chooses topless dancing over going to Brown, because she tells Ovid, "I want to never be really frightened" like her mother, who is "terrified of everything." Ovid and Caroline bond over their parents' broken marriages.

The Pfeiffer mansion can be read as a metaphor for the emergence of two opposing forces in America—money and social justice. Caroline Nercessian, daughter of the Hollywood producer, studied the Pfeiffer house in Advanced Placement History, and her senior paper was entitled "Seeds of Revolution: From Robber Barons to Emma Goldman." "Robber barons" were businessmen and bankers who amassed huge personal fortunes, often from pursuing anti-competitive or unfair business practices. On the other hand, anarchist-writer Emma Goldman fought for freedom from tyranny. With Alexander Berkman, she planned to assassinate Henry Clay Frick, who embodied corporate America by turning coal into coke for use in steel manufacturing, creating the Frick Coke Company. Frick later partnered with the Carnegie Steel Company, which would become United States Steel. Goldman's writing and lectures addressed atheism, freedom of speech, militarism, capitalism, marriage, free love, and homosexuality. Ironically, anarchism and capitalism both advocated "deregulation," but anarchists wanted freedom for everyone, while robber barons wanted wealth for themselves.

In the play, Pfeiffer exemplifies the robber barons' ruthless business tactics. He tells his son, "When you go into business, you'll realize a time comes in every deal when you push your opponent to the edge, and, inevitably, if they're even slightly shaky, they'll drop like flies." He agrees to testify in Congress at an antitrust hearing in exchange for a presidential disqualification of his son from the army, but he believes that "trusts were the best thing that ever happened to this country!" Business trusts enabled monopolies in order to restrain trade or to fix prices. Vivian Pfeiffer's father felt some guilt about his family money and turned his father's wealth into philanthropy: "In every town that my grandfather busted a union, my father built Pfeiffer libraries and Pfeiffer hospitals. He gave his entire fortune away." On the other hand, Flinty feels that Pfeiffer's grandfather's decision to leave money to civic causes is "the sickest thing I've ever heard." Yet she idolizes Mrs. Astor's contributions to the New York Public Library. The play documents the benefits and detriments of money—both old and new.

Old Money also asks whether inheritances and legacies hinder freedom. In the flashback, Pfeiffer the philanthropist tells his son the professor, "I freed you of a legacy. . . . I gave you a chance to find some independent energy." But his son claims, "You denied me a legacy." According to his father, however, "You just politely stepped aside to make room for someone who wanted it more. Like the man who lives here now." In other words, new money is hungrier than old. In this way, the play is about the conflict between generations. Vivian believes that his father let his grandfather destroy his life and was detached from his son's [i.e., Vivian's] life. While the coal miner's son believes that he will "go down as one of the most generous men in history," his own son feels, "You gave away what cost you the least." In other words, inheritance comes free—without sacrifice or work. Old money made Vivian uncomfortable, and so as a boy he would hide inside the hidden passageway behind the sculpture, "the only place I felt safe." Old money has gone bad. Betina Brevoort, celebrated for having a perfect sense of taste and propriety, has a great-granddaughter who "was recently arrested for dealing cocaine out of the Groton School basement."

At the end of the play, halfway through the twenty-first century, Ovid's grandson rebels against inheritance when he says, "One day I want a house like this. But I'm going to build it. I want the world to know I'm here." He suggests that inheritance does not allow an individual to forge a unique identity. Statistics show that old money earns more wealth through accumulated interest from generation to generation than most Americans earn by working. British economist and political scientist Stephen Haseler maintains that inheritance makes up six percent of our GDP each year and that "America is becoming an inheritance culture where much of one's economic opportunity is from family inheritance, not personal achievement." In the play, however, Flinty presents an argument for inheritance: "People with real money owe it to society to keep themselves and their children thoroughly enjoying it. Because if the rich aren't happy, then who the hell will be? You set the standard."

In 1917, Toby wants to defy his father's plans for him to go to Princeton, then into his business, eventually taking over the family home. "I can see the life my father has mapped out for me, and I want no part of it," he says. "I want to do work that means something to me." He aspires to write and direct musicals, because in show business "no one cares what your real name is." Inheritance rests on passing assets from generation to generation. In contrast, Toby imagines that he is the son of an Italian immigrant who got kicked out of Italy and decided to go to America to write songs on Tin Pan Alley for the Ziegfeld girls to dance to and George Cohan to sing. His father, however, does not understand the leap of faith required by an artist: "Can you tell me right now for certain your music will be as popular as 'On the Sidewalks of New York'?" Toby's uncertainty leads Pfeiffer to affirm, "Then you're wasting your time. . . . You'll always be a pawn and second-rate. And I haven't built a fortune to have it whittled away by a second-rater. In a gilded age, Toby, it's only a foolish man who doesn't take advantage." Pfeiffer does not realize that artists, like financiers, can only be successful by taking risks. Alan Greenspan's 1998 speech about the American economy also addressed the importance of risk to a successful economy: "No matter how regulated and supervised, throughout our history many of the benefits banks provide modern societies derive from their willingness to take risks. . . ." The same can be said for art. Toby later recognizes that accepting the family estate is easier than creating art: "The truth was, as an independent man I was fairly mediocre. As the keeper of a legacy I was far superior." In the end, Vivian feels left behind. He tells his father, "I have a recurrent dream that the rest of the world is dancing forward while I make my final exit through the secret passageway." Therefore, Vivian encourages Ovid to "do whatever it is for yourself. My father wanted to write music and never did." Vivian believes his father was "too scared" to pursue his dream just as he has been: "I spent my entire life writing to get back here. I never escaped." In the same spirit of courage, when Caroline tries to slit her wrists in rebellion against her father, Saulina tells her, "If you and I try very hard, then they don't have to win. But if you give up, you'll never know how strong you could be."

Toby also rebels against class distinctions when he dances with the maid, Mary. When she says, "It's not my place. You should be at your father's table," Toby insists, " From now on, I'll be making my own decisions for what I should be doing. I'm my own man now. . . ." Toby imagines a century of innovation and a socialist utopia when he tells Mary, "People, not just social-register people, will have decent houses with good schools and theaters in every town. Nothing will be the same! Not in painting, not in marriage, not in war! This will be the century of

American ingenuity!" They choose to dance to the 1890s Tin Pan Alley hit song about disappointed love, "After the Ball." Toby's son Vivian also breaks class lines when he dances and falls in love with Saulina Webb. Jeffrey Bernstein marries into the Old New York Rhinelander family and becomes an ambassador to Switzerland. Class distinctions dissolve.

Even within their own circle, the rich have not found love. Vivian Pfeiffer, who grew up in the mansion, tells Saulina, "I've lived most of my life alone. Over the years I've had a variety of unavailable crushes." He cautions her, "Don't make the same mistake I did. Fall in love, Saulina. Don't waste your life alone." For Vivian, the independent female artist is not a positive option, but neither is being a bachelor. Saulina remarries at fifty-two, the year before she dies, and offers the same advice to Ovid: "Fall in love, Ovid. Don't waste your life alone." In the past, Sally Webster, the forty-five-year-old diarist, decides to remain single because she has a wonderful house on Bank Street, a family farm in Rhinebeck, and vacations in Europe. She humorously calls herself "a utopian Marxist Colony Club libertarian." The Colony Club is the city's most exclusive private women's social club; of course, exclusivity and egalitarianism do not go hand in hand. Here, the single woman seems to have it all.

This play about money also explores the relationship between money and art. Toby admires the architect's ability to design buildings, but the architect Schuyler Lynch notes that the building is named after the person who financed it, Tobias Pfeiffer. Toby explains: "My father wants to see his name on your building, because somewhere he knows it's the one thing he can't do." Money and art need each other. Aunt Saulina encourages Ovid to follow his artistic dream rather than his father's commercial one: "I wish I could release you from pleasing all of us." Saulina retrieves her artwork from Bernstein's house, because she is convinced that someday he will "start a newspaper, a bank, a preschool. I won't have my work lost in his shuffle." Art is sacred for Saulina.

Saulina's removal of her art from the Bernstein mansion raises the question of how to live life. Vivian Pfeiffer, who is dying of cancer, believes that Saulina is "much too cynical," while Saulina feels that Vivian is "much too forgiving." Pfeiffer does not want to die "a bitter man." The two discuss how people organize their lives; Vivian admires structure, "solid beginnings, middles, and ends," while Saulina is "a big fan of chaos. Maybe that's why my life has made no sense." Vivian is sure that "most lives make no sense. Some are just better orchestrated." Saulina interprets "better orchestrated" to mean reverting to traditional female roles. Recalling the benefit dinners to which she escorted her late sister, she notes the women around those tables for whom "life seemed to make utter and complete sense. In the mornings they lifted weights and at night they lifted their ten-ton Harry Winston diamond brooches. I advised my daughter to strive to become one of them." Even in 2000, some of Wasserstein's women long for the feminine mystique.

Saulina is concerned that her daughter is teaching English in a rain forest without an area code or e-mail. As an artist, Saulina feels especially vulnerable—overlooked by Sid and counting on him for recognition, she says angrily, "But it's all right, because he has plans to make me important again." Sid claims that Saulina's art is dated, overshadowed by "the next wave, the cutting edge." "She was interesting maybe fifteen years ago. Now she's a bitter, angry, mediocre cow. That's just the truth." Saulina asks herself why she bothers to continue sculpting. "I can't bear to be judged anymore." So the play examines the fragility of the artist as much as it does the entrapments of money. When Saulina begins to cry after Vivian asks her to dance the gavotte, Vivian encourages her to cry for everyone. Saulina used to tell her daughter that tears wash away sadness and bring renewal. But Vivian adds, "Until it all comes back again. And the true pattern of life emerges." Saulina conveys that sadness brings clarity, while Vivian suggests that life's true pattern is sadness. It is unclear whether the play is making a connection between Vivian's darker view of the world and the fact that he is from old money, and Saulina's more affirmative view and her new money.

Wasserstein's representation of money—both old and new—reflects the ambivalence that has characterized the American attitude towards money from the beginning. As Lewis Lapham observes, on the one hand the American colonies saw money as "just a commodity," because "the real American experiment was about the discovery of a moral commonwealth, a nation governed for the common good." On the other hand, Americans have equally regarded money as "a sacrament"; "America was about the miracle of self-enrichment." In the latter sense, "visible signs of wealth testify to an inward state of grace." For Americans, money has been both a virtue and a sin—the means to access and power but also a burden. It could buy goods, services, and contacts but not love. For all of their wealth, the characters of *Old Money* have holes in their hearts.

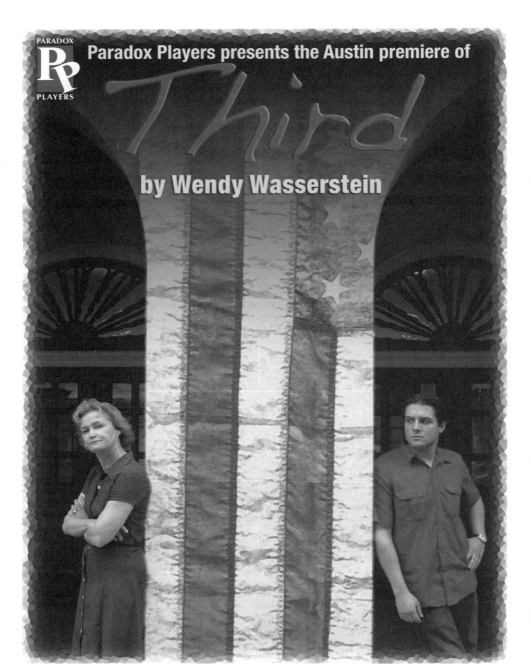

A promotional image for the Paradox Players, Austin, Texas, production of
Third in September–October 2008. Design by Melinda Barker; pictured are
Bobbie Oliver and Mason Stewart. (Courtesy of Paradox Players)

7

Third (2005)

Problems with Liberalism

You decided he plagiarized because you needed that to be true. Just like they decided there were weapons of mass destruction because they needed that to be true.

—Emily Jameson

Set on the brink of the Iraq War in 2002–3 in a small New England college town, *Third* takes an even harder look at the problems of liberal ideals than did *The Heidi Chronicles* and *An American Daughter*. Attractive, fifty-four-year-old Laurie Jameson is the first female professor to earn tenure in the English department of a top-ten liberal arts college. She accuses her student Woodson Bull III, called "Third," of plagiarizing his essay on *King Lear* and files a complaint with the college's Committee of Academic Standards. Third is not guilty of plagiarism and wants to take his professor to the American Civil Liberties Union. Jameson's colleague Nancy Gordon, who sits on the committee, sides with the student. So does Jameson's twenty-year old daughter, Emily, who meets Third in a bar on the night the United States invades Baghdad. Although the committee of Academic Standards votes in favor of Third, the charges of plagiarism result in his academic probation, the suspension of his wrestling scholarship, and his father's depression. His limited family income forces him to transfer with a scholarship to Ohio State because he is unable to afford his acceptance to Stanford. In the background of the academic drama, Jameson's father dies from Alzheimer's, and Nancy Gordon undergoes cancer treatments.

Jameson comes to realize that Third did in fact write his "psycho-sexual interpretation" of *King Lear*. She apologizes, and he forgives. Despite their disagreement, Nancy Gordon applauds Jameson's diehard belief in the liberal ideals that led her to question Third's academic integrity. At the same time, the play questions liberal self-righteousness; defending the marginalized sometimes results in victimizing others. The play conveys that a liberal arts education, freedom of thought, and therefore democracy were on the line. If imposed wrongly, liberal ideas could become fascistic.

Professor Jameson spouts politically correct ideas to her class about *King Lear*. She instructs her students to "look with fresh eyes at these established works of western literature," to "eliminate heterosexist, racist, or classist barriers." She encourages them not to be "reverential" or "afraid to contradict me or challenge the norms of the dominant culture." Since the eighties, literature departments have been dedicated to reading literature from a variety of critical approaches that broaden interpretations to include discussions of race, class, and gender. By asking questions that engaged society, Marxist, feminist, and race criticism challenge the New Criticism of the fifties that examined a literary work in isolation from its context, focusing on form, structure, and theme. In her "revisionist view of *King Lear*," Professor Jameson views Goneril and Regan as "good guys," Lear as "narcissistic," and Cordelia as "masochistic." In other words, she challenges the conventional reading of Lear as hero and the two evil daughters as antagonists. According to director Dan Sullivan, "The idea of making Goneril and Regan heroes is outrageous, but within the power structure, they have been forced into doing what they're doing; it's a way to get the kids to think about role playing." In terms of Jameson's personal life, though she mocks Cordelia, she behaves in this loving way with her own father by keeping him with her. In addition, Jameson's feminist approach to literature informs her new book, humorously entitled *Girls Will Be Boys: The Demasculinization of Tropes in Western Literature*. With terms like "the girlification of Cordelia," Wasserstein was having fun mocking feminist academic trends, which did not always agree with creative work about women.

Third understands what it means to challenge hegemony from the perspective of an athlete who wants to become a sports agent. He explains to his professor, "In sports, the really powerful guys are all African-American. They're busting up myths about American power and class a lot more than anyone reading gay fiction in this little college town." Jameson believes Third is just "some preppy, privileged wrestler," "a walking red state" who "fits right in with the power elite, with the white men still running this government, this country, the world." The play, however, cautions against labeling people, says Dan Sullivan. Twenty years earlier, Third would have been representative of the students at an elite eastern liberal arts college, but by 2002, he was a minority. In preparing to direct the play, Sullivan said that he studied an "amazing collection of culturally and racially mixed students from the late nineties at Bennington College in which Third would not fit." While Wasserstein was not specifically writing about Bennington, it was a good model for the director. "Now it would be like Middlebury or Williams . . . not a sports school, which is why [the college in the play] has a wrestling program."

Third calls Professor Jameson "ma'am," instead of "professor." Used as a form of polite address for a woman, "ma'am" conveys that Third comes from a culture that distinguishes between professional men and women, and it also can have a military connotation. While Third's manners seem conservative, he embraces liberal ideas, telling Jameson, "You're the gender bender. You're the man!" Jameson responds with humor, "I'm the woman," and so the conflict seems semantic. Third views her no differently than he views his male professors, while Jameson wants to be regarded as a woman equal to a man without *being* a man.

As in *Old Money*, *Third* calls attention to an America driven by money and power. But Third does not come from money, and he reads Lear from a Marxist perspective. "If Lear strips Cordelia of her dowry, her suitors will reject her." His financial analysis leads him to a psychoanalytic conclusion: "Lear's wrath is the outcome of his sublimated desire" for Cordelia. Father wants daughter.

Not only does Professor Jameson not accept Third's interpretation, but she also cannot believe he wrote it. Her resistance conflicts with her pledge to keep a thoroughly democratic classroom, and she realizes that it is misplaced. "If I can't bang the president on the head, I want to bang Third on the head." During the hearing, Jameson vents her frustration in a "fantasy interlude" as she sweats through her hot flashes: "If we permit this kind of unethical behavior within these gates, then . . . it will proliferate outside them. And this man's type of easygoing insidious charm and amoral intelligence will continue to be rewarded with the most powerful positions in this country. That's why I need to be vigilant." She projects her frustration with American politics onto her student. Her colleague tells her that accusing Third of plagiarism is not about her or the country: "It's about one kid with a good mind that you were determined to close down." Accordingly, Third asks, "Why waste your time on me? Pick on someone powerful. Go destroy corporate America or stop the war in Iraq."

When the play opens in 2002, Professor Jameson is watching President Bush proclaim on television that because Saddam Hussein "has weapons of mass destruction," his "regime is a grave and gathering danger." At the time, Congress was voting on whether to authorize the use of force in Iraq, based on the idea that Saddam "threatened democracy." Jameson later listens to the TV newscaster announce that "the House of Representatives passed the president's resolution to use force if necessary in Iraq." In fact, in 2003 the Bush and Blair administrations decided to invade Iraq in order to disarm it of weapons of mass destruction, to end Saddam Hussein's support for terrorism, and to free the Iraqi people. Jameson's frustration with the war reflects a worldwide disapproval at the time. Between January 3 and April 12, 2003, thirty-six million people across the globe took part in almost 3,000 protests against the Iraq war. Jameson's older daughter Zooey and her girlfriend, a Guggenheim poet, attend a candlelight vigil to protest the war, but her younger daughter is not out organizing with her friends, which perplexes Jameson. The 9/11 Commission and former CIA director George Tenet later concluded that no weapons of mass destruction had been found, that there was no evidence of ties between Saddam Hussein and al-Qaeda, and that Bush was intentionally building a case for war with Iraq without factual evidence. Professor Jameson feels a disconnect between this "dangerously regressive climate" and the *New York Times* including same-sex commitment ceremonies in its marriage listings. Wasserstein chronicled this dissonance in nearly every play; America's rhetoric did not match its actions.

While Jameson is outraged by the injustice of American foreign policy, Third wants to protect his own rights. "It's unfair and I want to beat it," he tells Nancy Gordon. His personal opinions become political toward the end of the play when he takes the open microphone in his dorm dining hall to confront his politically correct classmates, who are protesting for nude dorms and against the Patriot Act. He links the discrimination against student athletes to a national backlash:

I hear you guys saying . . . you don't understand what's going on west of here . . . in those states that show up red on Election Day in the heartland. Well, I can tell you that when someone like me, a Midwesterner, and athlete, on the fence politically, comes looking to you for answers, I am dismissed, even before I ask the goddamn question. And from my point of view, that's how you lost this country.

Addressing Third's feeling of isolation, director Dan Sullivan commented,

Before Obama, who is more centrist, there was a tendency of liberals to polarize. . . . Wendy felt politically isolated in New York, where friends would make presumptions about peoples' affinities and judge them accordingly. It stems from her humanism, which she took on full force in Third.

Everyone in the play feels robbed of something—Third of his civil liberties, Jack Jameson of his memory, Laurie of her childbearing years, her husband of academic prestige, Nancy of her health, Emily of the freedom to date working-class guys. And so, when Jack, finding he cannot count backwards, yells, "The goddamn bastards took it from me," he seems to speak for everyone.

Jameson believes that Third's desire to become a sports agent is as exploitative as America's foreign policy. She tells her analyst:

He is interested in transacting deals, which is exactly why, frankly, I believe this country is interested in the Middle East. . . . What we want ultimately is to make their transactions, to metaphorically be their sports agent. We'll just take ten percent of their gross and their oil. We want peace so we can sell more sporting events on international cable television and Woodson Bull the Third, the graduate of this elite American college, can be our agent.

In comparing the problem of American colonialism to agents exploiting their clients' talents for money, Wasserstein points up what Dan Sullivan says is "a necessary evil in all professions." In another way, *New Republic* editor Peter Beinart explains the changed relationship between American democracy and our sense of manifest destiny in his 2008 book *The Good Fight:*

By championing freedom overseas, America itself could become more free. That liberal spirit won America's trust at the dawn of the cold war. Then it collapsed in the wake of Vietnam. Now, after 9/11, and the failed presidency of George W. Bush, America needs it back. . . . [but] American leadership is not American empire.

Both Beinart and the play call for liberalism without imperialism.

Professor Jameson feels that greed defines American foreign policy: "I hate the times we're living in." Moreover, when Jameson's daughter meets Third at a bar where he is working over spring break, she tells him, "Most people feel pretty untethered now 'cause the world is in such an unpredictable place. So, you can either buy into it all . . . and live under the illusion that there's still such a thing as security, or you can become a cynic and just let it rip." This insecurity comes not just from terrorism, but also from being a victim of political correctness. Emily explains to her mother, "You decided he plagiarized because you needed that to be true. Just like they decided there were weapons of mass destruction because they needed *that* to be true." People create the realities they want to justify their values and agendas. Still, terrorism is real, and fear of it pervades the play. Dan Sullivan reflects, "After 9/11 we are vulnerable. Terrorists could someday be in control of nuclear weapons, so the odds are not in our favor."

Third feels targeted by "socio-economic profiling," because Professor Jameson believes that "no one with [his] verbal facility and interests would write this. . . . it's the work of an advanced scholar, not a wrestler, even from Groton" (a private boarding school in Massachusetts founded in 1884). She assumes that a jock is incapable of intellect and that Third is "a living dead white man." Third tells Emily the truth: "She said I plagiarized my paper . . . because I'm a wrestler." He confronts Jameson about her prejudice: "You have a problem with me because I'm happy. I'm straight. I'm white. I'm male. And I happen to like America." Although he seems to be a "privileged, preppy, frat boy," Third is the son of a small-claims lawyer in Ohio and does not vote the Republican ticket. Like America's invasion of Iraq, the professor's assumptions about Third are based on misconceptions. Emily tells her mother, "You categorized him and you got it totally wrong. . . . for all your endless babbling about open perspective, you're the most limited person I know." Some political analysts similarly see the problem of polarizing the Right and the Left:

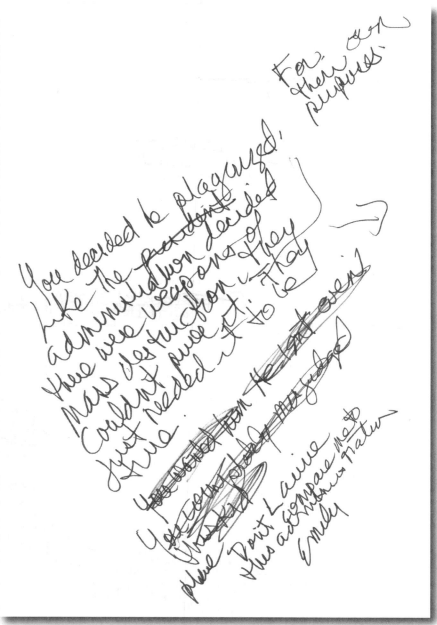

Notebook page with Wasserstein's notes on *Third*. (Courtesy of the Wendy Wasserstein estate)

"Liberalism cannot merely define itself against the right but must fervently oppose the totalitarianism that blighted Europe a half century ago, and which stalks the Islamic world today." *Third* demands the same objective for liberalism: to promote freedom, not just as an end but also as a means.

Third's case also conveys that social class is bound up with the accusation of plagiarism. If you look conservative, a liberal might target you. On the other hand, Third's Republican girlfriend sees him "as a bad risk" because he is not a Republican. A classmate from Groton and a squash player at Yale, she "already has the house in Greenwich picked out after she gets her joint law and business degrees from Harvard and makes partner at Goldman Sachs." Not staying within class lines also causes conflict between Jameson and her daughter, Emily. A student at Swarthmore, Emily dates a bank teller in Philadelphia who dropped out of Trenton State. "I've sort of had it with smart people," Emily says. Her mother advises her, "If it's money you're after, find some senior partner at Morgan Stanley." Emily rejects her mother's world, which is supposed to be liberal but is actually elitist: "I want out of your world, Mother. I don't want to judge people on their schools, their influence, or the success of their latest essay in the *New York Review of Books*." She believes that her mother resents her father "because he's not a star." Moreover, she tells Third that going to Swarthmore excludes her from being "a real person." Status and its symbols continue to be both problematic and compelling for Wasserstein.

In examining liberalism, the play takes a hard look at a liberal arts education. Referring to faculty, Emily tells Third, "They're not supposed to ruin it for you. They're supposed to make you understand why you like it." When Third appeals to Jameson's colleague Nancy Gordon, she sympathizes with Third. She knows that students use their education for personal gain. "If you stole intellectual property . . . given the world we're living in, if you could cultivate this art, you could become the CEO of a major corporation." But Third has not stolen, so perhaps he would not survive in unethical corporate America.

In the end, Professor Jameson feels remorseful about misjudging Third's ability. She tells him, "Maybe I'm the one who doesn't belong here. Most of my ideas were crystallized in 1969." In other words, the sixties—the Cold War, the end of Camelot, the Vietnam War protests and Johnson's Great Society, civil rights, women's rights, and the counterculture—shaped Laurie Jameson's ideas. In particular, 1969 represented both conservative and liberal forces: the election of Richard Nixon on the one hand, and the Women Strike for Peace demonstration in Washington, D.C.; Woodstock; and the largest antiwar demonstration in American history on the other. Attaching herself to liberal ideals, Jameson "thought [she] could change the world." Her colleague explains to Third, "Jameson is still holding the torch. To her it still matters." Jameson also reminds her junior colleague Nancy Gordon, "When I first came here, this college was dominated by Woodson Bulls. And I decided I would give everything I've got to change this place and open the door for women like you." Jameson's accusation of Third, however, reflects a perversion of the original goals of feminism.

Jameson longs for a simpler time, reflected in the 1959 Frankie Avalon song, "Venus," that she listens to after the conflict with Third. The song's lyrics detail a man's plea to Venus, the Roman goddess of love and beauty, to send him a girl to love and one who will love him as well. They recall a time when Jameson's husband, a political science professor, admired her for her "liveliness of mind," a reference to Jane Austen's protagonist Elizabeth Bennett in *Pride and Prejudice*. Jameson's lively mind of the sixties has become more defined by "pride" and "prejudice" in the twenty-first century. In contrast, Third understands the need to evolve and to adapt to change when he tells Jameson:

> It's like wrestling. If you always stay in the same category, you never grow. Personally, I know I'd be much more at home at a big state school. Here I'm considered practically a retro-heterosexual sociopath. But at least it's a challenge for me. That's why I came to this college. Every other day someone here is coming out of the closet as a vegan anti-globalization bisexual who is currently experimenting with the opposite sex. This place has the first transgender dorm in America.

Third wants to stretch his comfort zone, but Jameson, like many of Wasserstein's protagonists, resists change. She says, "I keep thinking about a James Taylor song [from] college. . . . about that country road and I don't know where the hell it goes." She is also uncomfortable with cultural shifts—that popular culture of the sixties has become high culture on public television in 2002. The intangibility of her existential angst bothers her more than concrete causes of anxiety—like cancer and menopause. When Third tells her, "At least you're protected by this institution," Jameson responds, "Woody, sometimes your protection can become your own confinement." Recognizing her earlier misjudgment, she puts her academic hood over his shoulders and confers on him an honorary degree.

Third is surprisingly forgiving of the professor who wronged him. But he sees that in Jameson's eyes, he was unique:

> I've always thought I was a regular guy, but in your eyes I was 'Pinky, the Aborigine lesbian.' I hated you for it, but I knew for once I was actually interesting. I'll never be that intellectually mesmerizing to anyone again.

Yet Jameson never considered Third an intellectual. He even tells his friend to take Jameson's course, but this appreciation feels unearned. Without bitterness, Third tells her, "Stick with the hope."

Nancy Gordon also forgives Jameson. Having always envied Jameson's optimism, she says, "You're the one who always had faith in the future and the work we had to do." Gordon believes that Jameson's heart was in the right place and that she is "a solid, good woman" and "one of the great teachers here." Once she overcame her "anger and humiliation" at Jameson's going behind her back to monitor the progress of her cancer, she "thought it remarkable how much you cared." The paradox is striking. In Third's case, Jameson's caring has resulted in damaging a student's academic career. Gordon's forgiveness seems tied to having survived cancer. She wants "to live the last third of [her] life without hating everything." Therefore, *Third* is about new beginnings; Nancy Gordon falls in love with a reconstructionist rabbi "on a drip" for cancer treatment. Jameson decides to take a leave of absence from academia and go west to attend her colleague's wedding.

Third seems to be a play about a collapsing liberalism that Wasserstein began writing in *The Heidi Chronicles and An American Daughter.* Director Dan Sullivan, however, understands the play as "a reassessment of liberal values and of the stereotyping of conservatives and liberals; the polarization gets wider on a yearly basis. . . . We tend not to see the people through the polemic on both sides." Conservatives often charge liberals with being "soft on inflation, labor militancy, and Communism," while liberals view conservatives as overly involved in people's personal lives and too little involved in their economic well-being. The gap between the two needed to be bridged.

Third says that democracy is fragile—even on a college campus. The attempt to enforce academic integrity raises questions about the integrity of democracy, not just at a small New England college, but in America at large. New England as setting and home of Emersonian individualism makes Third's thwarted civil liberty especially ironic. When Tocqueville visited America in 1831–32, however, he concluded, "I know of no country in which there is so little independence of mind and real freedom of discussion as in America." He saw that democracy did not go hand in hand with equality, that individuality conflicted with sameness: "Every citizen being assimilated to all the rest, is lost in the crowd, and nothing stands conspicuous but the great and imposing image of the people at large." The professor wants her students to "assimilate" to her point of view. But when an open-minded, white, Midwestern jock writes what he thinks about *King Lear*, he finds himself caught in a liberal undertow.

Wasserstein in front of a *Heidi Chronicles* marquee on Broadway, 1989.
(Courtesy of the Wasserstein family)

Conclusion

Throughout her career, Wasserstein wrote about the traps of being an educated woman, and also about Jewish-American identity and social class in America. As C. W. E. Bigsby puts it, "The theatre is an arena in which societies debate with themselves. It is where that delicate negotiation between the individual and the group finds its natural context. Its very form and circumstance is an exploration of that relationship." Written with a dark-edged comedy, Wasserstein's plays capture the zeitgeist of their moment. In this way, the playwright carries on a dramatic tradition advocated by anarchist Emma Goldman, writing in 1914 on the significance of modern drama: the artist was or should be what August Strindberg called a "lay preacher, popularizing the pressing questions of his time."

Like Lillian Hellman and Lorraine Hansberry before her, Wasserstein wrote in the mode of realism, because she was more interested in her subject than in formal experimentation. Hansberry's 1979 comment from an interview with Studs Terkel can equally be applied to Wasserstein: "The realistic playwright states not only what is, but what can and should be." In the early part of the twentieth century in America, Rachel Crothers' *A Man's World*, Susan Glaspell's *The Verge*, Zona Gale's *Miss Lulu Bett*, Georgia Douglas Johnson's *Plumes*, and Sophie Treadwell's *Machinal* were dramatizing the predicaments of being female in a male world. Mid century, Clare Boothe's *The Women*, Lillian Hellman's *The Little Foxes*, Shirley Graham's *It's Morning*, Gertrude Stein's *The Mother of Us All*, Fay Kanin's *Goodbye, My Fancy*, Jane Bowles's *In the Summer House*, Alice Childress's *Trouble in Mind*, and Hallie Flanagan and Margaret Ellen Clifford's *Can You Hear Their Voices?* continued the project.

There is an angry side to Wasserstein's comedy, but her plays are never as dark as those of some contemporary American women playwrights: Emily Mann's exploration of the Holocaust in *Annulla*; Anna Deavere-Smith's play about the Crown Heights riots, *Fires in the Mirror*; Suzan-Lori Parks's depiction of African-American culture in *Top Dog/Underdog*; Lynn Nottage's play about the plight of women in the civil war—torn Democratic Republic of Congo, *Ruined*; or Paula Vogel's absurdist dramas about prostitutes and pornographers. Wasserstein, perhaps, has most in common with Theresa Rebeck, who satirizes celebrity culture.

A social observer, she never ventured into absurdist modes, because she wanted to give audiences a photographic representation of the way we were. New York City was often her touchstone—the other character in her plays—and it shaped her intrigue with social class. As one scholar of New York culture puts it, "When you grow up Jewish and middle-class in Flatbush, the dream is of one day reaching the heights, which is New York City."

Most importantly, Wasserstein's plays explore the pressing issues for women in the latter part of the twentieth century and into the twenty-first: the transition between the feminine mystique and feminism in *Uncommon Women*, the confusion of the single woman during and after the women's movement in *Isn't It Romantic*, the dissolution of the feminist movement in *The Heidi Chronicles*, the Jewish identity of middle-aged women in *The Sisters Rosensweig*, the double standards faced by women in politics and the conflict between liberal and conservative values in *An American Daughter*, money and class in *Old Money*, and a reassessment of liberal values in *Third*. Senator Alan Hughes in *An American Daughter* speaks for Wasserstein, it seems, when he tells his daughter, "There's some idea of America out there right now that I just can't grab onto." The playwright felt that the moral core that had defined the sixties for the nation had somehow disappeared.

Each play longs for an idyllic time, represented by the liberal values of the sixties. In a Chekhovian moment, Gorgeous tells her sisters in *The Sisters Rosensweig*, "I wish that on one of our birthdays, when all the children and men have gone upstairs to sleep . . . each of us can say at some point that we had a moment of pure, unadulterated happiness! Do you think that's possible?" Sara responds, "Brief. But a moment or two."

Wasserstein's female characters seek to define life, liberty, and happiness within an American context that spans the 1968 Eugene

McCarthy Rally, the 1980 assassination of John Lennon, the 1991 collapse of the Soviet Union, the 1993 Zoe Baird story and the Clinton Administration, backward to Ulysses S. Grant's Civil War, to the Gilded Age at the end of the nineteenth century, and finally to a small New England town in 2003. As Helene Keyssar suggests in *Feminist Theatre*, "Characters in feminist plays only rarely transcend their contexts." Wasserstein's characters find themselves bumping up against conventional gender roles.

While she never wanted to be labeled a "feminist playwright," Wasserstein always kept her eye fixed on women in society. As Bill Clinton acknowledged in 2008, "Gender is the defining issue of our social structure." The inordinate demands placed on women concern Wasserstein in every play. In conversation she told me, "The pressure is still on the woman to somehow make it all work." Recent headlines in the Sunday *New York Times* echo her concern ten years later: "For Girls, It's Be Yourself, and Be Perfect, Too." Parents fear that competition, consumerism, and the obsession with achievement among competitive high schools may cause "anorexia of the soul." This concern led Wasserstein to write *The Heidi Chronicles* in the eighties. Accordingly, nearly all of the plays ask whether women can have it all, and they answer, for their time, "no."

Critics assaulted *The Heidi Chronicles*: Alison Solomon, in the *Village Voice*, said, "It assures us that [intelligent, educated women] are funny for the same traditional reasons women have always been funny. They hate their bodies, can't find a man, and don't believe in themselves." Laurie Stone attacked Wasserstein on National Public Radio for demeaning feminism by having Heidi prefer the word "humanist" to "feminist." Similarly, Phyllis Jane Rose in a 1989 issue of *American Theatre* accused Wasserstein's protagonist of going "to the heart of male domination . . . becoming complicit with the status quo." Therefore, a conclusion about Wasserstein's plays must remind readers that the playwright did not pour her plays through ideological molds. Instead, her dramatic conflicts derive from her observations about women wrestling with "public images" and "the private tensions which shape the individual's response to the world." If Wasserstein had wanted to promote ideology, she would have been a theorist, not a playwright. It is important to read the play in the context of the Reagan eighties and Susan Faludi's *Backlash*. Furthermore, by reaching commercial audiences with this play and others, Wasserstein opened up the conversation about female identity to many people who might not have attended more avant-garde plays tucked away in Off-Off-Broadway theatres. Winning the Pulitzer Prize places a playwright in the center of debate, making her subject to criticism that she would not otherwise encounter.

Wasserstein's plays expose the double standards experienced by women. In conversation, she asked, "Why are successful men in their forties considered desirable, while successful women in their forties are deemed threatening? Who made that up? Why are women's problems considered secondary to men's?" The problem continues to exist. Commenting on the 2008 vice-presidential campaign, political commentator Cokie Roberts remarked, "No one calls men 'shrill. . . .' Women still have to be careful about self-deprecating humor. . . . No one asks men who will take care of their children. . . ." Similarly, Wasserstein told me:

> I truly believe that it's just like racism or anything else. It's amazing to me that—there are limitations in life, biological ones, such as women can have babies and men can't, but probably in twenty years men will have babies—but to say that there are limitations on someone's life based on their gender is shocking to me. And it's all made up. I was talking to a man the other day, and he said, "Well, you know, a woman's window of opportunity ends at thirty-two. You really have to maximize between twenty-eight and thirty-two to marry, because women in their forties, or women with children, it's a dime a dozen." I thought, "Who the hell are you?"

Despite Wasserstein's outrage about sexism, director Dan Sullivan clarifies that the playwright writes about the present and holds out hope for the feminist ideal in the future. In any case, for Wasserstein, equality and choice were not literary matters as much as they were political rights that she wanted to address in the public venue of theaters.

The conflicts between biology and destiny are as unresolved in the plays as they are in our current culture. Caroline Kennedy, under consideration to fill a New York Senate seat in 2009, told the press that she had to "be at home, instead of in the Senate, because of very private family matters." Or was the political climate simply too hostile, echoing the predicament of Lyssa Dent Hughes in *An American Daughter*? On a recent visit to Mount Holyoke College, students disclosed to me that some of their peers post to the "Holyoke Confessional" blog "to confess to wanting to be a stay-home mom." Other classmates, they added, "would never admit it." Wasserstein, too, felt the tug of fifties conservatism when limited roles for women also meant simplicity and safety. In a 1991 essay in *Bachelor Girls,* she wrote:

> I don't want to go home to my apartment in Manhattan. I want to go home to Flatbush, Brooklyn, 1958, when all you had to do was be a nice girl and everything else would fall into place. And if you got good grades, everything would fall into place even better. I want to feel for just one moment the safety before sleep, when it seems all is right with the world. But all isn't right with the world. Of course, it wasn't in 1958, either.

America—before and after the women's movement—was fraught with conflict for women, just different kinds. Not only were women unable to erase the history of male hegemony with one movement, but they also had to contend with more complex choices than women of previous generations. In the end, all of Wasserstein's characters are trying to figure out who they are, and this journey often involves coming to terms with their Jewish identity.

Wasserstein's plays anticipated the current wave of books about affirming female independence: Betsy Israel's *Bachelor Girl: The Secret History of Single Women in the Twentieth Century* (2002), Maureen Dowd's *Are Men Necessary?* (2005), Carl Bernstein's biography of Hillary Rodham Clinton called *A Woman in Charge* (2008), and Nancy Pelosi's book, *Know Your Power: A Message to America's Daughters* (2008). Moreover, Wasserstein would be especially fascinated by First Lady Michelle Obama's efforts to bridge the personal and the political: "Women are capable of doing more than one thing well at a time," Obama said in a 2008 interview. While she has exchanged her job as an attorney for the position of "Mom in Chief," her real goal is "to help women transform their lives." Wasserstein might be bewildered, though, by the First Lady's semantic choice. In the eighties, such a claim would have been considered "retro." But in the twenty-first century, some successful women are comfortable enough with their achievements to announce that they are placing motherhood at the top of their resume.

In making the personal political, Wasserstein writes comedy. She says:

> As somebody who believes in the individual voice, I still believe in the theatre and what can happen there. I believe in comedy,

in its spirit, and in its ability to lift people off the ground. I also think there are stories to tell, and as a woman writer, I want to tell those stories, to work out those conflicts. I want to take these conflicts from the political down to the personal. And the personal level, to me, is somewhat comedic.

She wrote about the quotidian lives of middle-class characters with a Chekhovian combination of comedy and irony, seriousness and sadness. For her, comedy hides and copes with pain. Admiring Chekhov's ability to track the way time advances and damages peoples' lives, she said:

I think that the idea of finding moments in people's lives when they could turn to the right or turn to the left, or why they don't turn at all, is fascinating. . . . If you can really capture bourgeois human nature, there's something comedic there, because it has to do with surviving. Otherwise, if you really took it all seriously, ultimately there's death. (She laughs loudly.) . . . I think Sara Rosensweig is right. There are possibilities in life. There is also great sadness.

That combination of wistfulness and humor defines her plays.

Notes

Introduction

1–3 "People are products of the time . . ." "You laugh, you cry . . .": Jan Balakian, "Wendy Wasserstein," in *Speaking on Stage*, ed. Philip C. Kolin and Colby H. Kullman (Tuscaloosa: University of Alabama Press, 1997), 379–391.

3 "to promote positive social change," realism's linear form reflected male experience, "normalizes the traditionally unequal power relations": Patricia R. Schroeder, "Realism and Feminism in the Progressive Era," in *The Cambridge Companion to American Women Playwrights*, ed. Brenda Murphy (Cambridge: Cambridge University Press, 1991), 31.

3 "documentary literature . . .": Alfred Kazin, *New York Jew* (New York: Knopf, 1978).

3 "the premise that art and life were inextricably linked": Veronica Makowsky, "Susan Glaspell and Modernism," *The Cambridge Companion to American Women Playwrights*, 50.

3 Dorothy Parker: Howard Stein, "Wasserstein Reconsidered," *Theater Week*, October 31–November 6, 1994, 22–25.

4 comedies by early American women, "American identities, experiences, and perspectives," "unparalleled freedom . . . pursuit of happiness": Amelia Howe Kritzer, "Comedies by Early American Women," *The Cambridge Companion to Women Playwrights*, 3.

4 ". . . the issues of women would not be taken care of . . .": Jan Balakian, "Interviews with Wendy Wasserstein," *The Journal of American Drama and Theatre* 9, no. 2 (Spring 1997): 66.

4 "Women writers . . .": Frederick R. Karl, *American Fictions 1940–1980* (New York: Harper & Row, 1983), 47.

4 "the female hero," "Women have become . . .": Matthew Roudane, *American Drama Since 1960* (New York: Twayne, 1996), 115.

5 Academics have read . . . : Claudia Barnett, ed. *Wendy Wasserstein: A Casebook* (New York: Garland, 1999).

6 "fostering the alliance of liberal arts": *Mount Holyoke College at a Glance* (South Hadley: 2009).

6 "to marry Harvard": Wendy Wasserstein, "Hillary Clinton's Muddled Legacy," *The New York Times*, Op-Ed, August 25, 1998.

6 "Smith is to bed and Holyoke is to wed": Colleen O'Connor, "The Wendy Chronicles," *The Dallas Morning News*, February 7, 1994, C2.

6 "Women who graduated in '64 and '65": Balakian, "Interviews with Wendy Wasserstein," 67.

6 "Suburbia Screw," ". . . a vague interest in Bernini," ". . . secretly believed they were screwed too": Wendy Wasserstein, *Bachelor Girls* (New York: Vintage, 1991), 147–48.

6 "They changed the rules in the middle of the game": Wasserstein, "Hillary Clinton's Muddled Legacy."

6 "'have-it-all optimism' imploded": O'Connor, "The Wendy Chronicles."

7 "Suddenly women had the same career opportunities . . . individual destiny": Wendy Wasserstein, "Hillary Clinton's Muddled Legacy."

7 "C'mon, Campbell . . .": CNN, November 2008.

7 "If Hillary Clinton had graduated . . .": Balakian, "Wendy Wasserstein."

8 "a sense of we were going to change things . . .": O'Connor, "The Wendy Chronicles."

8 Jacqueline Onassis attended: Balakian, "Interviews with Wendy Wasserstein," 65.

8 "Things change": Wendy Wasserstein, "Miami—A Musical Comedy." Produced by Playwrights Horizons. Music by Jack Feldman, lyrics by Bruce Sussman and Jack Feldman. November 24, 1985, revised December 16, 1985. Draft #4. Unpublished ms. in Mount Holyoke College Archives and Special Collections.

8 Helen Gurley Brown . . .: Diana Maychick, "*The Heidi Chronicles* Strikes a Familiar Chord with the Playwright's Diehard Fans," *The New York Post*, March 5, 1989, 5.

10 "Tikn olam . . .": Carole Bell Ford, "Nice Jewish Girls," in *Jews of Brooklyn*, ed. Ilana Abramovitch and Seán Galvin (Lebanon, MA: Brandeis University Press, 2002), 135.

10 "In the books it's patriarchal . . . we were 'very smart'": Balakian, "Interviews with Wendy Wasserstein."

10 "I think in many ways my idea of show business . . .": Balakian, "Wendy Wasserstein."

Chapter 1. *Uncommon Women and Others*

Quotations from Wendy Wasserstein, *Uncommon Women and Others*, in *The Heidi Chronicles and Other Plays* (New York: Vintage, 1991), abbreviated "UW."

13 President Richard Glenn Gettell presided: *Mount Holyoke College Bulletin 1967–68*, Series 61, No. 2, November 1967.

13 103 female faculty . . . 95 male faculty: Nora Mariano, archives assistant, Mount Holyoke College Archives and Special Collections, e-mail to author, February 23, 2009.

13 Wasserstein was registered . . . . : Wasserstein archives at Mount Holyoke College.

15 Housemothers: "House Matrons" are listed in the first Mount Holyoke campus directory, published in 1903/04. The practice of employing such women began when separate dorms were built in 1897 to replace the Seminary Building, where students and teachers had lived from 1837 to 1896. The 1972/73 annual report for the dean of students (pp. 4–5), describes the process of replacing housemothers with graduate students, which began in the late 1960s and ended with the retirement of the last ones at the end of the 1972/73 academic year.

15 buses of boys from Yale . . . . : 1971 Mount Holyoke College freshman handbook, 15.

15 "The whole history of college dances . . .": Chris Durang, e-mail to author, June 2007.

16 CUNY's MFA program: Mount Holyoke College Archives and Special Collections.

16 "When I was a playwriting student," "I can't get into this": Wendy Wasserstein, Mount Holyoke playbill for memorial, 2006.

16 Phoenix Theatre . . . *Great Performances*, Lucille Lortel: Mount Holyoke College Archives and Special Collections.

18 Despite the 1967 . . . : Ann-Marie Imbornoni, "Women's Rights Movement in the U.S.," Timeline of Key Events in the American Women's Rights Movement (Information Please® Database, Pearson, 2006).

18 Outside the iron gates . . . Title IX: Ruth Rosen, chronology in *The World Split Open: How the Modern Women's Movement Changed America* (New York: Penguin, 2000).

19 "I just didn't know . . .": Sylviane Gold, "Wendy, the Wayward Wasserstein." *The Wall Street Journal*, February 7, 1984.

19 "Smith is to bed and Holyoke is to wed . . .": UW, 5.

19 ". . . into women's things": UW, 11.

19 "that men were more interesting": UW, 56.

19 "Wendy opened the way": Emily Mann, e-mail to author, February 18, 2009.

20 In this way: Mary McCarthy, *The Group* (New York: Signet, 1963).

20 "During rehearsals . . .": Alma Cuervo, conversation with author, February 2007.

20 "Each woman has a real-life prototype": Mary Jane Patrone, e-mail to author, 2007.

20 Betty Friedan's: Betty Friedan, *The Feminine Mystique* (New York: W. W. Norton, 1963).

20 Mabel Dodge: wikipedia.org/wiki/ Mabel_Dodge_Luhan.

21 Kate Millet's: Kate Millet, *Sexual Politics* (New York: Doubleday, 1969).

21 Germaine Greer's: Germaine Greer, *The Female Eunuch* (New York: McGraw Hill, 1970).

21 and Jacqueline Susann's: Jacqueline Susann, *Valley of the Dolls* (New York: Grove, 1966).

21 *Car 54, Where Are You?*: www.imdb.com/title/tt0054528.

22 Judy Collins, "Both Sides Now": www.judycollins.com/biography.html.

22 James Taylor's "Fire and Rain": snopes.com/music/songs/firerain.asp.

22 Leonard Cohen's "Suzanne": Suzanne Verdal McCallister interviewed by Kate Saunders, transcription by Marie Mazur, BBC Radio 4 FM, June 1998.

22 Bob Dylan, "Lay Lady Lay": wikipedia.org/wiki/Lay_Lady_Lay, accessed May 25, 2009.

22 the Dave Clark Five: The Dave Clarke Five rivaled the Beatles between 1964 and 1967, with more appearances on the Ed Sullivan show than any other band. www.daveclarkfive.com.

22 Erhard Seminar Training: skepdic.com/est.html, accessed February 23, 2009.

22 Fluffernutter: www.marshmallowfluff.com.

22 The National Student Strike: Bruce J. Schulman, *The Seventies* (New York: Da Capo Press, 2001), 14, 16, 39.

22 Earlier drafts . . . : Mount Holyoke College Archives and Special Collections.

22 "As a movie buff . . .": Durang, e-mail to author, 2007.

23 "go where no one else will go": Mary Lyon, quoted in *Mount Holyoke College Bulletin*.

24 "Since the end of World War II . . ." "the problem that has no name," "A strange stirring . . ." feeling "empty" . . . courses on marriage and the family: Friedan, *The Feminine Mystique*, 15.

25 "Well, God knows there is no security in marriage . . . ": UW, 66.

25 in college she embraces: Virginia Woolf, *A Room of One's Own* (London: Harcourt, 1929).

25 To address this problem: Susan Edmiston, "How to Write Your Own Marriage Contract," *Ms.*, December 1971, 66.

26 drinking song: Mount Holyoke College Archives and Special Collections.

26 "If we could marry any one of us . . ." ". . . picture in the Sunday *Times* . . ." ". . . Carter would *need* me": UW, 39–40.

27 "When we got to Holyoke . . .": Mary Jane Patrone, e-mail to author, 2007.

28 "Mount Holyoke ... has tried to foster . . .": President Gettell's speech, Mount Holyoke College Archives and Special Collections, 3.

29 "The heart is the capital": *Mount Holyoke College Bulletin*.

30 "The college produces . . .": UW, 7.

30 "When I get it together . . .": UW, 11.

30 "Miss Lyon's Seminary . . .": UW, 15.

30 "When I get out of here . . .": UW, 19.

30 Gracious Living: Mount Holyoke College Archives and Special Collections.

32 "I knew we had a purpose": UW, 24.

32 "Women will be part-time . . ." "By the time a class has been out ten years . . .": *Mount Holyoke College Bulletin*, 1971.

32 "I'm just a little talented at a lot of things": UW, 54.

34 "It's not difficult to catch up . . . legal professions": David Reisman, "The Dilemma of Women," Mount Holyoke College Archives and Special Collections.

34 "Mary Lyon, sending her early students out . . .": *Mount Holyoke College Bulletin*, 1969–70, p. 17.

35 Rosie the Riveter: www.rosietheriveter.org.

35 "I suppose this isn't . . .": UW, 25.

35 Rita's feelings forecast: Vivian Gornick, "Why Women Fear Success," *Ms.*, December 1971, 50–51.

36 ". . . a student should examine . . .": UW, 29.

36 "because I'm Phi Bet and you're not?" UW, 30.

36 "Sometimes when I'm in the library . . .": UW, 49.

36 "two Uncommon Women, mysterious but proud": UW, 49.

36 "anatomy is not destiny": UW, 32.

36 "This entire society . . .": UW 34.

37 "Our entire being . . .": UW, 33.

37 "should be forced to answer phones . . .": UW, 37.

37 Rita's sentiments echo: Gloria Steinem, "If Men Could Menstruate," *Ms.,* October 1978, 110.

38 "If they have it . . ." "write with their cocks . . .": UW, 58.

38 "Women have to be better . . .": Reisman in Mount Holyoke College Archives and Special Collections.

38 "If I fall in love . . .": UW, 39.

38 Published in 1952: Simone de Beauvoir, *The Second Sex*, New York: Vintage, 1989. xxxix.

38 The college "places at its center . . .": UW, 57–58.

39 "I'm having trouble . . .": UW, 62.

39 "I guess women . . .": UW, 63.

39 "He's handsome and talented . . .": UW, 27.

39 " . . . So I don't talk": UW, 53.

39 "without any embarrassment . . .": UW, 70.

39 "Jim Crow pattern," "unconscious male hegemony," "Women study as if . . ." women "have to be better . . ." "not just knowledge": Reisman in Mount Holyoke College Archives and Special Collections.

40 "learning unfamiliar techniques": UW, 50.

40 "maturing mind . . .": UW, 47.

40 "the college fosters . . . " "Robert says . . . ": UW, 54.

40 Friedan: *The Feminine Mystique*, 69 and 71.

41 "At least you made a choice": UW, 54.

41 "I don't want my life . . .": UW, 56.

41 "If I didn't fulfill obligations . . .": UW, 57.

41 Camilla Peach: Mount Holyoke College Archives and Special Collections.

41 first issue of *Ms.*: *New York Magazine*, December 20–27, 1971.

42 "I am prepared for life": UW, 48.

42 "That one gesture . . .": Christa Santangelo, "Wendy Wasserstein Writes Plays That Touch Audiences on a Personal Level," *The West Side Spirit*, March 6, 1988, 1, 5.

42 Germaine Greer's test: UW, 37.

43 "I guess it never occurred to me . . .": UW, 66.

43 "Although President Gettell announced . . .": President Gettell's, Mount Holyoke College Archives and Special Collections.

43 "Women still encounter . . .": UW, 68.

43 "I need fifty words . . .": UW, 70.

43 "June is the month," women with college degrees: *Ms.*, December 1971, 32.

43 "girl Friday for an eastern senator": UW, 64.

44 In Howard Hawks's 1940 film: Howard Hawks, *His Girl Friday*: www.imdb.com/title/tt0032599.

44 After the 1969–70 bulletin . . . : Nora Mariano, Mount Holyoke archives assistant, e-mail to author, 2007.

44 Perhaps Samantha's suggestion: Ingmar Bergman, *Cries and Whispers*: www.imdb.com/title/tt0069467.

44 "period piece": Wasserstein, Holyoke playbill for *Uncommon Women*.

44 Wasserstein reflects: Wasserstein, "Mrs. Smith Goes to Washington," *Bachelor Girls* (New York: Vintage, 1991).

45 Reisman's 1968 commencement speech at Mount Holyoke: Mount Holyoke College Archives and Special Collections, 1968.

Chapter 2. *Isn't It Romantic*

Quotations from Wendy Wasserstein, *Isn't It Romantic*, in *The Heidi Chronicles and Other Plays* (New York: Vintage, 1991), abbreviated "IR."

47 "You mean having it all?": IR, 133.

47 "the sadist vice president": IR , 116.

47 Janie's "family": IR , 107.

48 "women being told how to live their lives . . ." Sylviane Gold, "Wendy, the Wayward Wasserstein," *The Wall Street Journal*, February 7, 1984, 30.

48 earlier drafts: Mount Holyoke College Archives and Special Collections.

48 "a grown woman": IR, 147.

48 *Fiddler on the Roof*: www.musicalheaven.com.

48 *The Rockford Files*: wikipedia.org/wiki/The_Rockford_Files.

48 "practicing for the wedding": early draft, Mount Holyoke College Archives and Special Collections.

48 "You've hit on something fundamental . . .": Frank Rich letter in Mount Holyoke College Archives and Special Collections.

49 first Jewish settlers . . . Upper West Side: Jules Chametzky, John Felstiner, Hilene Flanzbaum, and Kathryn Hellerstein, introduction to *Jewish-American Literature* (New York: W. W. Norton, 2001).

50 horseradish, Schlomo: IR, 109 and 115.

50 "I scream here on Central Park South": IR, 83.

50 "Manhattan has . . . been . . .": Frank Rich, "The De Facto Capital," *The New York Times Magazine*, October 6, 2002, 68–69.

51 "Everything is awful . . .": IR, 80.

51 sociologists determined . . . .: Kate Zernike, "Why Are There So Many Single Americans?" *The New York Times*, January 21, 2007, section 4; 1, 4.

51 "I have been rejected . . .": IR, 107.

51 "1,000 men for every . . .": IR, 153.

51 "Wasserstein was registering . . .": Janet Cockrum, Priscilla White, "Influences on the Life Satisfaction of Never-Married Men and Women," *Family Relations*, 34, no. 4 (October 1985): 551–556.

51 Census Bureau . . . : Richard Stengel, "Snapshot of a Changing America," *Time*, September 2, 1985.

51 "the 'marriage gap' . . .": Kate Zernike, "Why Are There So Many Single Americans?"

52 "Monkey," "great deal of attention": IR, 120.

52 "She'll go back to work in something nice . . .": IR, 109.

52 "Don't let it take over your life . . .": IR, 129.

52 "com[ing] home to Cynthia Peterson's . . ." "All I want is a home": IR, 138.

52 "a little disorganized," "a little bit of a nudge," "trying to move forward": IR, 130

52 "get on the Belt Parkway": IR, 137.

53 "receiver off the hook": IR, 112.

53 "You have all the answers . . . I want a life too . . . not right for [her]": IR, 130.

53 Blumstein and Schwartz: Christine Doudna, "American Couples: Surprising New Finds About Sex, Money, and Work," *Ms.*, November 1983, 116–119.

53 "harder than it has to be": IR, 109.

53 ". . . steal your ideas": IR, 131.

53 ". . . see you later": IR, 128.

53 "a potential mother . . .": IR, 112.

53 "Everything is a negotiation . . ." "blocking each other's lives": IR, 113.

54 The New Right: Susan Faludi, *Backlash* (New York: Doubleday, 1991).

54 Alice Schwarzer: Ibid., 363.

54 Beneath the chauvinism: Suzanne Gordon, "The New Corporate Feminism," *The Nation*, February 5, 1983, 129, 143, 147.

55 "on the verge of breakthrough": Faludi, *Backlash*, xix.

55 Psychologist Carol Gilligan: Carol Gilligan, *In a Different Voice* (Cambridge: Harvard University Press, 1982), xiii, ix, x, xi, xvii, xix.

56 "It's all about control": early draft, Mount Holyoke College Archives and Special Collections.

56 Marty "isn't a solution": IR, 85.

56 "We can wait till it's right. . . . Maybe it's because I'm Lillian's daughter . . .": IR, 104.

56 ". . . the trick is not to get frightened": IR, 144.

56 stigma of "the spinster," Daly: Mary Helen Washington, "Working at Single Bliss," in *Women: Images and Realities*, ed. Amy Kesselman (Boston: McGraw Hill, 2003), 271–72.

56–57 "inseminate [herself] with a turkey baster": IR, 127.

57 "one of the only things that's worthwhile": IR, 132.

57 "Driving along the Long Island Expressway": IR, 124.

57 "There's nothing wrong with being alone": IR, 103.

57 "Did you teach me": IR, 120.

57 "not even on the waiting list": IR, 110.

58 "felt the tug of a conservative ending": Harry Haun, "Is It or . . . 'Isn't It Romantic,'" *Showbill*, March 1984, 5–6.

58 In the original production . . . "right for her to dance alone": Michiko Kakutani, "A Play and Its Author Mature," *The New York Times*, January 3, 1984, C9.

58 definition of "romantic": wordnet.princeton.edu/perl/webwn.

58 "much younger than Janie": IR, 88.

58 "You can have a nice life": IR, 90.

58 "Marty could make a girl": IR, 85.

58 "opposite sexes unite": Northrop Frye, "Archetypal Criticism," in *Anatomy of Criticism: Four Essays* (Princeton: Princeton University Press, 1957).

59 from one kind of society to another: C. L. Barber, *Shakespeare's Festive Comedy* (Princeton: Princeton University Press, 1963).

59 "Lib/Men, Lib/Women mixer": IR, 86.

60 "No longer for losers," "Don't be too eager to please," ". . . feminine virtues": *Ms.*, August 1983, 40–41.

60 "a little *naches*": IR, 120.

60 "the only way marriages ever took place," "settle for Mr. Alright," "with all the single people around": Diana Bletter and Lori Grinker, *The Invisible Thread* (Philadelphia: The Jewish Publication, 1989), 132.

61 Mary Wells's: Smokey Robinson and the Miracles, "My Guy": www.rockhall.com/inductee/smokey-robinson.

61 "When I'm twenty-eight," "Imagine spending your life pretending": IR, 104.

62 "I made choices . . .": IR, 143.

62 "What do you do?": IR, 144–45.

62 "I had never thought about it before": Kakutani, "A Play and Its Author Mature."

62 "It doesn't take any strength to be alone," "turn someone into an answer": IR, 145.

63 international films: Molly Haskell, "Women's Friendships," *Ms.*, December 1983, 23.

63 Helen Gurley Brown: Helen Gurley Brown, *Having It All: Love, Success, Sex, Money* (New York: Simon and Schuster), 451.

63 She drew on the ideas: Albert Ellis, *Guide to Rational Living* (Chatsworth, CA: Wilshire, 1975).

63 Janie "lives from the inside out," "Someone like Harriet . . . : Haun, "Is It or . . . 'Isn't It Romantic.'"

63 "Of course you should learn to live alone": IR, 144.

63 Some sociologists . . .: Janet Corcoran and Priscilla White, "Influences on the Life Satisfaction of Never-Married Men and Women," *Family Relations*, 34, no. 4 (October 1985), 551–556.

64 "I don't want to sneak around": IR, 137.

64 "Volare": IR, 96.

64 Between 1971 . . . Democratic National Convention . . . Take Back the Night . . . In 1983: Ruth Rosen, *The World Split Open* (New York: Penguin, 2000) and Timeline of Key Events in the American Women's Rights Movement (Information Please® Database, Pearson, 2006).

65 *Terms of Endearment*: wikipedia.org wiki/Terms_of_Endearment.

65 *The Big Chill*: en.wikipedia.org/wiki/The_Big_Chill_(film).

65 Marlo Thomas and Alan Alda introduced: Marlo Thomas and Alan Alda. *She's Nobody's Baby* (New York: Simon and Schuster, 1983).

65 "changed the way women over thirty-five . . .": Elsa Dixler, "Wanna Be a Feminist Intellectual," *Ms.*, October 1983, 82–83.

67 "Do you think it's possible . . ." "having it all is just": IR, 134.

67 "you can have a family": IR, 92.

67 "perceptions of Heidegger": Notebook page, Mount Holyoke College Archives and Special Collections.

67 "life is negotiation . . . is possible": IR, 120.

67 "You can have it all but maybe not all at once": Jeanne Athos-Adler, e-mail to author, February 2009.

68 "I'm going to try to do it: have it all": IR, 119.

68 earlier draft: Mount Holyoke College Archives and Special Collections.

68 "Harriet will find a nice boy . . .": IR, 122.

68 "Hello, Mother . . ." "to give her a little push, too": IR, 120.

68 "That's why we put out such nice products": IR, 122.

68 "If I could take her by the hand . . .": IR, 120.

68 "would love for Janie to take over": IR, 118–119

68 "Nixon did all right for himself": IR, 122.

68 "a source of women's oppression," "rooted in family life," "the women's movement was being blamed": Betty Friedan, *The Second Stage* (New York: Simon and Schuster, 1981).

69 "a true feminist position," "communal responsibility": Anne Roiphe, *Ms.*, October 1983.

69 "If I had a daughter": Irene Nathan, "Matchmaker," in *The Invisible Thread*, 130–32.

69 "Misogyny and 'separate but equal . . .'" "Once Jewish-American women realized . . ."

70 turned to Eastern religions, Mary Daly's *Beyond God the Father*: Paula E. Hyman, *Gender and Assimilation in Modern Jewish History* (Seattle: University of Washington Press, 1997), 299–300.

70 This "TV play": Erica Monk, *The Village Voice*, December 27, 1983, 109.

70 "Israel's very important to me": IR, 110.

70 historical fact: Samuel C. Heilman, *Portrait of American Jews: The Last Half of the 20th Century* (Seattle: University of Washington Press, 1995), 12.

71 "Steiff toys": IR, 121.

71 "the farther we got away . . .": Alfred Kazin, *New York Jew* (New York: Alfred A. Knopf, 1978).

71 From 1950 to 1990: Heilman, *Portrait of American Jews*, 6.

71 "where people have real values . . . Hymie's Highway Delicatessen," "Schlomo": IR, 110.

72 Notebook page: Mount Holyoke College Archives and Special Collections.

72 "elixir of life," "central switchboard," "cosmopolitan," "universal," "individualistic": *Jews of Brooklyn*, ed. Ilana Abramovitch and Seán Galvin (Waltham: Brandeis University Press, 2002), 9.

72 Brighton Beach has been a mecca . . . Ukrainian origins: Abramovitch, *Jews of Brooklyn*, 3.

72 "urban Atlantic seashore": Ibid., 125–127.

73 Brighton Beach Hotel: Ibid., 83–85.

73 the traditions of Flatbush: . . . : Ibid., 92 and 88.

73 "challah bread . . . a candle to light the way": IR, 107.

73 used to tell jokes at Grossinger's: IR, 97.

73 Grossinger's: catskillarchive.com/grossinger/index.htm.

73 borscht belt: en.wikipedia.org/wiki/Borscht_Belt.

74 "coping with the challenges . . . deflated pomposity": Sarah Blacher Cohen ed., *Jewish Wry: Essays on Jewish Humor* (Detroit: Wayne State University Press, 1987).

74 laughter can temporarily resolve: Henri Bergson, *Laughter—An Essay on the Meaning of the Comic* (New York: Macmillan, 1914).

74 forbidden actions, "stories created by Jews": Sigmund Freud, *Jokes and Their Relation to the Unconscious* (New York: W. W. Norton, 1960.)

74 Wasserstein links comedy with being Jewish: Jan Balakian, "Wendy Wasserstein," in *Speaking on Stage*, eds. Philip C. Kolin and Colby H. Kullman (Tuscaloosa: University of Mississippi Press, 1996).

74 ". . . involved in a shtetl": IR, 116.

74 "has not experienced enough pain": IR, 86.

74 "Whenever I get most depressed . . .": IR, 96.

74 "alternative, she jokes, is "dependency": IR, 82.

75 "I'm reflective and eager to please": IR, 109.

75 "It's weird going to someone's parents' house": IR, 99.

75 "And he's great in bed": IR, 103.

75 "there's something comedic . . .": Balakian, "Wendy Wasserstein," 379.

75 "an extra from Potemkin": IR, 82.

76 Saab cars, lacrosse sticks: Wendy Wasserstein, *Shiksa Goddess* (New York: Alfred A. Knopf, 2001), 6.

76 "Charlie Girl" commercial (on YouTube): IR, 81.

76 "attractive, bright, charming," "took a year off": IR, 82.

76 Popularized by sociologist: Digby Baltzell, *The Protestant Establishment* (New Haven: Yale University Press, 1987).

76 Helena Rubinstein: wikipedia.org/wiki/Helena_Rubinstein

77 "with your hair in your eyes": IR, 149.

77 "If I was thirty-six," "Everything is settled": IR, 148.

77 "Everything presses itself out," "it just isn't mine right now": IR, 151.

77 "I don't see how I can help . . . if I don't": IR, 149.

77 Like the nineteenth-century . . . : Ellen DuBois, *Eve and the New Jerusalem* (New York: Pantheon, 1983).

77 "Who's going to take care . . ." "*I* will": IR, 151.

77 "Your house isn't my home": Notebook page, Mount Holyoke College Archives and Special Collections.

77 "All you have to do is trust me": IR, 151.

78 "How does it feel to be on your own": Notebook page, Mount Holyoke College Archives and Special Collections.

78 "to find out about living": Zora Neale Hurston, *Their Eyes Were Watching God* (New York: Harper and Row, 1937, 1965, 1990).

78–79 Wasserstein wanted to reach broad audiences: Letter from Robert Shapiro Productions, Mount Holyoke College Archives and Special Collections.

79 "life is as shaky as a fiddler": Joseph Stein, Jerry Bock, Sheldon Harnick, Sholem Aleichem, *Fiddler on the Roof* (New York: Limelight, 2004).

Chapter 3. *The Heidi Chronicles*

Quotations from Wendy Wasserstein, *The Heidi Chronicles*, in *The Heidi Chronicles and Other Plays* (New York: Vintage, 1991), abbreviated "THC."

81–82 "I thought the point was . . .": THC, 232.

82 "I wrote this play because . . .": Walter Shapiro, "Chronicler of Frayed Feminism," *Time*, March 27, 1989, 90–2.

82 second wave of feminism: en.wikipedia.org/wiki/Second-wave_feminism.

82 "Clara Peeters used . . .": THC, 160.

82 "This painting has always . . .": THC, 161.

82 "The Shoop Shoop Song": wikipedia.org/wiki/The_Shoop_Shoop_Song.

83 "Don't look desperate . . . hang around with your girlfriend": THC, 163.

83 "he can twist and smoke . . .": THC, 164.

83 "The Chapel of Love": en.wikipedia.org/wiki/Chapel_of_Love.

83 protesting the United States' bombing: *Mount Holyoke College Bulletin*.

83 *Griswold v. Connecticut*: Ruth Rosen, *The World Split Open: How the Modern Women's Movement Changed America* (New York: Penguin, 2000), xix.

83 "a charismatic creep": THC, 181.

84 "being very difficult": THC, 167.

84 "the changes in this country . . .": THC, 170.

84 "really suburban": THC, 171.

84 "concerned citizens": THC, 169.

84 "tuna sandwiches": THC, 173.

84 "very smart," "what do mothers teach their sons . . .": THC, 171.

85 "Take a Piece of My Heart":
http://en.wikipedia.org/w/index.php?title=Piece_of_My_Heart.

85 New York feminists . . . Miss America protest: Rosen, 150, 159–60.

86–87 also a year of . . . liberal hope . . . ended: Gini Holland, *The 1960s* (San Diego: Lucent, 1999).

87 *"might have beens"*: *The Sixties: The Years That Shaped a Generation*, directed by Stephen Talbot. PBS, 2005.

87 "McCarthy is irrelevant . . .": THC, 168.

87 Adlai Stevenson: Stevenson served one term as governor of Illinois and ran, unsuccessfully, for president against Dwight D. Eisenhower in 1952 and 1956, later serving as ambassador to the United Nations from 1961 to 1965.

87 "You're the one whose life . . .": THC, 172.

87 "You'll be one of those true believers . . . just a phase": THC, 173.

87–88 "White Rabbit": wikipedia.org/wiki/White_Rabbit_(song).

88 Aretha Franklin's "Respect": THC, 175.

88 "I love you": THC, 178.

88 "lamb": THC, 179.

88 "work through . . .": THC, 176.

88 "Hostess cupcake": THC, 177.

88–89 "I mean . . . any sound": THC, 179.

89 "The problem isn't really him . . . unbelievably attentive": THC, 182.

89 "'Personal' means . . .": THC, 180.

89 "worthwhile": THC, 182.

90 "Every woman . . . difference": THC, 181.

90 "work within the male-establishment," "You either shave . . .": THC, 178.

90 consciousness raising groups. . . to actions: Iska Alter, "Wendy Wasserstein, *The Heidi Chronicles*, and the Evasion of History," presented at Hofstra University's Women in Theatre conference (October 6, 1994).

91 "nothing is going to change . . .": THC, 181.

91 "No more master penises!": THC, 187.

91 "our team," "our potential": THC, 188.

92 *"My* liberation . . . as yours," "I know you think . . .": THC, 189.

92 "a sadness like yours": THC, 237.

93 "We're not in Montana anymore": THC, 193.

93 "Sure, why not?" "Makes sense . . .": THC, 196.

93 "divorced Senate wives": THC, 219.

93 "I've always known . . ." "We'll see": THC, 197.

93 "I don't want to come home to an A+ . . .": THC, 201.

93 "On a scale of one to ten . . .": THC, 202.

94 "The New Girl Network": cited in *Ms.*, April 4, 1977.

93 "it's either/or . . . otherwise we'd be getting married": THC, 202.

93 *Hello New York*: THC, 215.

95 "sexy and greedy": THC, 243.

95 "People saw money . . .": Stuart A. Kallen, *A Cultural History of the United States Through the Decades: The 1980s* (San Diego: Lucent, 1999), 52.

95 $43 billion: Ibid., 18.

95 trickle down: Ibid., 60.

95 "The 1980s were a triumph . . .": Ibid., 61.

96 "There are no such things . . .": Ibid., 18.

96 "awaiting the rebirth . . .": THC, 218.

96 "the standard for success . . .": THC, 215.

96–97 "We're serious people . . .": THC, 219.

97 "An arbiter of good taste . . .": THC, 243.

97 "helped get . . . decide what it's all for": THC, 222.

97 Boomers: www.aginghipsters.com.

97 "A man for all genders": THC, 248.

97 "lemon soufflé at Lutèce": THC, 242.

98 "Do you think it's time to compromise?": THC, 217.

98 retire Superwoman: Gloria Steinem, "The Stage Is Set," *Ms.* July–August 1982, 77–78, 226.

98 "Once my career's in place . . .": THC, 211.

98 "make a pot of money": THC, 226.

98 Robert Brustein argued: Robert Brustein, "The Heidi Chronicles," *The New Republic*, April 17, 1989, 32-4.

98 "It was the whole idea of the We . . . being acquisitive . . . young forever": Jan Balakian, "Wendy Wasserstein," in *Speaking on Stage*, eds. Philip C. Kolin and Colby H. Kullman (Tuscaloosa: University of Alabama Press), 1997, 379.

100 ". . . unless [men let] her have it all": THC, 247.

100 ". . . ask men to compromise": THC, 217.

100 His idea resonates: Pete Hamill, "Great Expectations," *Ms.*, September 1986, 34.

101 "three women turning thirty . . .": THC, 225.

101 ". . . blaming everything on being a woman . . .": THC, 226.

101 "sting of the liberal backlash . . . child care": Lindsay Van Gelder, "Carol Gilligan: Leader for a Different Kind of Future," *Ms.*, January 1984, 102.

101–2 According to some journalists . . . careers at risk . . . institutional realities . . . between work and family: Ibid., 37, 38, 102.

102 "Unfulfilled, frightened of growing old alone": THC, 226.

102 At the time: Jennifer Crichton, "Who's Winding the Matrimonial Clock?" *Ms.*, July 1986, 54, 84.

103 "Every other woman . . . hormone in Brazil": THC, 223.

103 ". . . what makes you a person . . ." ". . . been so many people . . .": THC, 224.

103 Smokey Robinson: THC, 241.

103 "What's it all for?" THC, 243.

104 advances for women: Rosen and Timeline of Key Events in the American Women's Rights Movement (Information Please® Database, Pearson, 2006).

104 "brown rice and women's fiction": THC, 229.

104 ". . . all in this together": THC, 232.

104 ". . . women are big": THC, 227.

104 "Heidi plays by the rules . . .": Balakian, "Wendy Wasserstein."

104–5 "What has made women unhappy . . . greatest female adventure," The *New York Times* . . . resurgence of inequality: Faludi, x, xvii, xix.

107 Not all women: Emily Mann, e-mail to author, February 2009.

108 "unmotivated conclusion . . . manlessness": Mimi Kramer, "Portrait of a Lady," *The New Yorker*, December 26, 1988, 81–2.

108 Laurie Winer, "Christine Lahti as an Angry Heidi in 'Chronicles,'" *The New York Times,* October 9, 1989, C13+.

108 transformation of the structures: Annette Kolodny, "A Map for Rereading: Gender and the Interpretation of Literary Texts" in *The New Feminist Criticism*, ed. Elaine Showalter (New York: Pantheon, 1985), 46–60.

108 L.A. producers, "How can they say . . .": Balakian, "Wendy Wasserstein."

108 a middle-class Broadway audience . . . : Moira Hodgson, "The Heidi Chronicles," *The Nation*, May 1, 1989, 605–6.

108 evaded serious feminist issues: Corrine Robins, "Betrayals," *American Book Review*, November–December 1989, 4.

109 art historian undermined: Ibid., 10.

109 "What strikes me . . . informed spectator": THC, 206.

109 "Women have traditionally . . .": Balakian, "Wendy Wasserstein."

109 pro-choice demonstration, "right to choose . . .": Gloria Steinem, "A Basic Human Right," *Ms.*, July–August 1989, 39, 41.

109 "mommy track": Barbara Ehrenreich and Deirdre English, "Blowing the Whistle on the 'Mommy Track,'" *Ms.*, July–August 1989, 56.

110 "Hairy legs haunt . . ." nonprofessional women . . . roles at home: *Time*, December 4, 1989.

111 Betty Friedan's 1981 book: Betty Friedan, *The Second Stage* (Cambridge: Harvard University Press, 1998), 6.

111 Georgia O'Keefe retrospective: THC, 249.

111 adoption: Nancy Gibbs, "The Baby Chase," *Time*, October 9, 1989.

111 "compromised feminism": Alter, "Wendy Wasserstein, *The Heidi Chronicles*, and the Evasion of History."

Chapter 4. *The Sisters Rosensweig*

Quotations from Wendy Wasserstein, *The Sisters Rosensweig* (New York: Harcourt Brace, 1993), abbreviated "TSR."

113 "The Self-loathing . . .": interview with author.

113 "in a culture that denies it": Lynn Darling, "Wendy and Her 'Sisters,'" *Los Angeles Times*, October 18, 1992.

113 "Three middle-aged . . .": Judith Miller, "The Secret Wendy Wasserstein," *The New York Times*, Sunday Section 2, October 18, 1992, 1.

114 ". . . like British theatre . . .": Laurie Stone in Gail Ciociola, *Wendy Wasserstein* (Jefferson, NC: McFarland, 1998), 84–85.

114 Living Newspaper, Federal Theatre Project: wikipedia.org/wiki/Living_Newspaper

115 "Like Chekhov . . .": Darling, "Wendy and Her 'Sisters.'"

115 comparison between *The Three Sisters* and *The Sisters Rosensweig*: Gaylord Brewer, "Wendy Wasserstein's Three Sisters: Squandered Privilege," in *Wendy Wasserstein: A Casebook*, ed. Claudia Barnett (New York and London: Garland, 1999), 119.

115 "Pfeni has romanticized a world we never belonged to": TSR, 9.

115 ". . . my life is stuck. 'I've forgotten . . .": TSR, 17.

115 "If I could only get . . .": TSR, 68.

115 ". . . pure, unadulterated happiness": TSR, 86.

117 "The decade of the bimbo is over . . .": TSR, 32.

117 "Some critics complained . . .": Brewer, 120.

117 "these are not tragic lives": interview with author, Philip C. Kolin, *Speaking on Stage* (Tuscaloosa: University of Alabama Press, 1996).

117 George S. Kaufman, Moss Hart, and Noel Coward: Wasserstein, preface to TSR.

117 Wasserstein must have been: George S. Kaufman and Edna Ferber, *Dinner at Eight: A Play in Three Acts* (New York: Samuel French, 1935).

117 In 1939: Moss Hart and George S. Kaufman, *The Man Who Came to Dinner* (New York: Dramatists Play Service, 1998.

117 "the furrier who came to dinner": TSR, 81.

117 Hans Christian Andersen: wikipedia.org/wiki/Hans_Christian_Andersen.

117 "true female sexuality . . . Danny Kaye": TSR, 50 and wikipedia.org/wiki/Danny_Kaye.

117 Noel Coward: www.noelcoward.net.

118 Philip Barry's *Holiday*: Kenneth MacGowan, *Famous American Play of the 1920s* (New York: Dell, 1983).

118 "Well, I'm not shy . . .": TSR, 76.

118 "A good man is hard to find": TSR, 92.

118 "Tea time is over . . ." TSR, 93.

118 "When they send the tanks in . . ." "It's just like my mother . . .": TSR, 39.

118 ". . . that August weekend . . .": Clive Barnes, "Wendy's Wonderful 'Sisters' Three," *New York Post*, March 19, 1993, 72.

118 democratization of Eastern Europe and the fifteen republics: Mikhail Gorbachev, "A Call for Democracy," and Mort Rosenblum, "War and Peace After the Cold War," in *The 1990s*, ed. Stuart A. Kallen (San Diego: Greenhaven, 2000).

119 ". . . what in God's name the entire twentieth century was for": TSR, 51.

119 "glasnost for women": "1990: The Year That Was," *Ms.*, January–February 1991, 15.

119 Anita Hill . . . Susan Faludi: Ruth Rosen, *The World Split Open: How the Modern Women's Movement Changed America* (New York: Penguin, 2000) and Timeline of Key Events in the American Women's Rights Movement

(Information Please® Database, Pearson, 2006).

119 Kathleen Barry blamed the demise of feminism . . . : Kathleen Barry, "Deconstructing Deconstructionism (or, Whatever Happened to Feminist Studies)," *Ms.*, January–February 1991, 83–85.

120 "developing a uniquely female . . .": Charles Bressler, *Literary Criticism: An Introduction to Theory and Practice* (Englewood Cliffs: Prentice, 1994), 184.

120 Barnes: "Wendy's Wonderful 'Sisters' Three," 24.

120 Gail Ciociola calls: Gail Ciociola, *Wendy Wasserstein* (Jefferson and London: McFarland), 2005.

120 ". . . my early years have no bearing . . ." TSR, 13.

120–21 "assimilate beyond her wildest dreams," "you mean we're both a little . . . too Jewish . . .": TSR, 81.

121 "America is pluralistic, but . . .": Russell Shorto, "All Political Ideas Are Local," *The New York Times Magazine*, October 2, 2005, 54.

121 Sociologist Samuel: Samuel C. Heilman, *Portrait of American Jews: The Last Half of the 20th Century* (Seattle: University of Washington Press, 1995).

121–22 "Americanization necessitated Anglo-conformity . . ." "American aesthetic": Paula E. Hyman, *Gender and Assimilation in Modern Jewish History* (Seattle: University of Washington Press, 1997), 94.

122 no one has called her "Sara Rosensweig" . . . : TSR, 58.

122 more than fifty percent of female college students: Hyman, *Gender and Assimilation,* 104–05.

122 "Oh my name is Moishe Pupick . . . MacNamara's Band": TSR, 83.

123 "Sara is WASPier than a WASP": conversation with author.

123 likes the "openly repressed": TSR, 35.

123 "New York in a way that has very little to do with us . . . belonged to," ". . . Louis Auchincloss": TSR, 9.

123 "shtupped" Sonia Kirschenblatt: TSR, 55.

123 "My mother's family . . .": TSR, 79.

124 "I can't seem to come up with . . ." "to stir up [his] life a little": TSR, 104.

124 "I'm old enough and kind enough": TSR, 58.

124 "Shine On Harvest Moon": wikipedia.org/wiki/Shine_On,_Harvest_Moon.

124 "They won't marry . . .": conversation with author.

124 "connect to another person," ". . . come home": TSR, 57.

125 "I'm a cold, bitter woman . . .": TSR, 81.

125 "speedy Americanization . . .": Hyman, *Gender and Assimilation*, 96.

125 "My name is Sara Rosensweig . . .": TSR, 107.

125 "women transform themselves . . .": Carolyn Heilbrun, "Introduction," in *On Women Turning Forty*, ed. Cathleen Rountree (Freedom: Crossing Press, 1991), 2.

125 Pro-independence movement in Lithuania and "to secure the rights of ethnic Russians": www.topix.com/world/lithuania/2009/02/polish-president-leads-lithuanian-independence-day-celebrations.

125 "the Jerusalem of Lithuania": TSR, 13.

125 "a nice Jewish girl from Connecticut," ". . . the daughter of an atheist": TSR, 10.

125 ". . . will always be watching and never belong?": TSR, 100.

126 "If I've never really been Jewish . . . then who am I?" "If Rita could make the Cossacks run away . . .": TSR, 106.

126 "The home you're talking about . . ." ". . . make it go away": TSR, 82.

126 "rigidly sex segregated": Mark Naison, "Crown Heights in the 1950s," in *Jews of Brooklyn*, ed. Ilana Abramovitch and Seán Galvin (Waltham: Brandeis University Press, 2002), 151.

126 "women played . . . horses," spent summers . . . religious Jews: Ibid., 146.

126 "The vitality of street life . . .": Ibid., 144.

126 Mickey Mantle . . . infiltrated: Ibid., 151.

127 "girls weren't supposed to know . . ." "no one ever called. . ." "Hong Kong bank": TSR, 23.

127 "middle-class gender norms": Hyman, *Gender and Assimilation*, 8.

127 "the biggest balls . . .": TSR, 8.

127 Hong Kong: wikipedia.org/wiki/Hong_Kong.

127 "women played a traditional . . ." "behind the mehitzah . . .": Carole Bell Ford, "Nice Jewish Girls," in Abramovitch, *Jews of Brooklyn*, 130.

127 "None of us wanted . . .": Rosen, *The World Split Open*, 45.

127 Tess is "determined . . ." ". . . because of our mother": TSR, 11.

127–28 "With one foot . . .": Ruth Rosen, *The World Split Open*, 39.

128 education "reduced the probability of a woman marrying . . ." "women should not receive . . ." "frustrated . . . equip and encourage . . ." "humble role of housewife," ". . . is the home": Ibid., 41.

128 "She thought she could have been a contender . . ." TSR, 57–58.

128 "throw a good Shabbes": TSR, 82.

128 "Maybe Gorgeous is the smartest . . .": TSR, 77.

128–29 "like a third-world country": Gloria Steinem, *Ms.*, March, 1992, 21.

129 "women hold few top posts . . . promotions are slow": "Kansas City Star," in *Ms.*, March 1992, 23.

129 two-tier class structure: *The New York Times*, January 20, 1985.

129 "double 800s," "knew what the teacher was going to ask . . ." "You weren't a nice Jewish girl," "Harvard and Yale are second-rate": TSR, 54.

129 "a tichkel . . ." "an ancient tribal ritual," "a séance," "blow out the goddamned candles": TSR, 37–38.

129 "entangled with the theological positions that legitimate them": Abramovitch, *Jews of Brooklyn*, 134.

129 "the anxiety of autonomy": Annette Zilversmit, essay given to author, 1998, 2.

129 "the sister who did everything right": TSR, 30.

129 "Both of you wish you were me": TSR, 75.

129 "I knew girls . . .": TSR, 44.

129 "make her way in the world": TSR, 6.

129 "real middle-aged success story": TSR, 31.

129–30 "little sparkle . . . to make it all perfect": TSR, 30.

130 "high cost of autonomy": Joyce Antler in Zilversmit.

130 indicting the women's movement . . . melancholy: Ciociola, *Wendy Wasserstein*, 86.

130 "hardly seems like the direction some of us desired . . .": Linda Winer, *Newsday*, November 1, 1992.

130 "You have to have your own life," "I can't have yours?": TSR, 106.

130 "Mother and I had Female Trouble . . . " ". . . not our mother's kind of happiness": TSR, 36.

130 "I don't think about us getting married . . . in my life now": TSR, 86.

130 By 1990 . . . in 1970: www.census.gov/.

130 "become a hard woman": TSR, 38.

131 Muriel Spark: wikipedia.org/wiki/Muriel_Spark.

131 "more and more eccentric . . . meaner and crabbier": TSR, 12.

131 "If my sisters or I had any sense, we would all have married you": TSR, 53.

131 "have at least one child . . .": TSR, 4.

131 "As a girl . . . expected to achieve": Carole Bell Ford in Abramovitch, *Jews of Brooklyn*, 134.

131 "much nicer," "more catalysts for the action": Balakian interview.

131 "a good man is hard to find": TSR, 105.

132 "true concert of Europe . . .": TSR, 42.

132 "money-lending uniform . . .": TSR, 45.

132 ". . . women *and* Jews": TSR, 68.

132 "Capitalism is . . . expensive": TSR, 79.

132 "I couldn't help but see . . .": TSR, 83.

132 "Jews have been at the financial core . . .": TSR, 41.

132–33 "the average Christian's inability to compete . . . soul and body": Mark Twain, *Concerning the Jews* (New York: Harper & Brothers, 1898).

133 ". . . if they're going to run MGM": TSR, 68.

133 diaspora: wikipedia.org/wiki/Diaspora.

133 ". . . you compulsively travel . . . just like me": TSR, 7.

133 "the autonomous . . . Stein, no such fates": Annette Zilversmit, essay given to author, 1995, 1, 3.

133 Critic Howard Kissel: Howard Kissel, "Family Circus: Wasserstein Turns 'Sisters' into a Jovial Juggling Act," *Daily News*, October 23, 1992.

133 "Somewhere I need the hardship . . .": TSR, 77.

134 "care[s] too much . . ." TSR, 78.

134 "competitive and insecure": TSR, 17.

134 "Men, desirable men . . .": TSR, 72.

134 disapproval of society's double standard: Jan Balakian, "Wendy Wasserstein," in *Speaking on Stage*, eds. Philip C. Kolin and Colby H. Kullman (Tuscaloosa: University of Mississippi Press, 1996).

134 "the beauty myth . . . collagen shots": Naomi Wolf, "The Beauty

Myth" in *Women: Images and Realities, a Multicultural Anthology*, ed. Amy Kesselman, Lily D. McNair, and Nancy Schniedewind (New York: McGraw, 2003), 123.

134 "Sara never had a sense of style," "dress for success . . .": TSR, 100.

134 "feels like Audrey Hepburn": TSR, 102.

134 "could've been Dashiell Hammett": TSR, 93.

135 as "class-driven" as London: TSR, 23.

135 "a hot-shot Jewish lady banker . . .": TSR, 24.

135 "capitalists like Nicholas Pym . . . Charing Cross Station": TSR, 8.

135 "primary color food": TSR, 40.

135 "Sara's help is on vacation": TSR, 52.

135 "fake Ungaro . . .": TSR, 43.

135 ". . . dreams of selling radio parts": TSR, 10.

135 "If Western culture is to survive . . . white European male": TSR, 40.

135 "The Concert of Europe," "hand in hand with European nationalism": TSR, 42.

135 "Lithuania has a culture . . .": TSR, 40.

136 "American Jewish girls . . .": TSR, 18.

136 "cannot be a just or loving god": TSR, 69.

136 "How AIDS Is Changing . . . Everything": Marcia Ann Gillespie, "HIV: The Global Crisis," *Ms.*, January—February 1991, 16.

136 "People like you and me . . .": TSR, 69.

136 "the only time I have a real sense . . .": TSR, 88.

136 The gay community . . . : Douglas Brinkley, "Politics and Policy in Washington," in Kallen, *The 1990s*, 15–26.

136 The Scarlet Pimpernel: wikipedia.org/wiki/The_Scarlet_Pimpernel.

136 "The second half of a woman's life . . .": Deena Metzger in Cathleen Rountree, *On Women Turning Forty: Coming into Our Fullness* (Freedom, CA: The Crossing Press, 1991), 162.

136 "Wasserstein's postmodern characters . . .": Robert F. Gross, "Generations of Nora: Self-Realization in the Comedies of Rachel Crothers and Wendy Wasserstein," in Barnett ed., *Wendy Wasserstein: A Casebook*, 13–35.

Chapter 5. *An American Daughter*

Quotations from Wendy Wasserstein, *An American Daughter* (San Diego: Harcourt Brace, 1999), abbreviated "AD."

139 "What happens to women, sometimes, I think is blatantly unfair": interview with author, Philip C. Kolin, *Speaking on Stage* (Tuscaloosa: University of Alabama Press, 1996).

139 one from the *New Yorker*: Sidney Blumenthal, "Letter from Washington—Adventures in Babysitting," *The New Yorker*, July 11, 1993, 32.

139 and one from the *American Lawyer*: Stuart Taylor, "Inside the Whirlwind," *The American Lawyer*, March 1993, 64–69..

139 *The New York Times* ran: Anna Quindlen, "Public and Private: The

Sins of Zoe Baird," *The New York Times*, January 20, 1993, and Ben Brantley, "In the Hostile Glare of Washington, the Media Define and Defy," *The New York Times*, April 14, 1997, C1, C14.

139 and the story made: Jill Smolowe, Margaret Carlson, Julie Johnson, and Elaine Shannon, "How It Happened," *Time*, February 1, 1993.

139 The *Chicago Sun-Times* headline: Mark N. Hornung, "Say it Ain't Zoe," *Chicago Sun-Times*, February 15, 1993.

140 "the physician to the nation": AD, 3.

140 "cold, capricious," if she had not been honest: Taylor, "Inside the Whirlwind," 63 and 69.

140 Clinton's affair: Nancy Gibbs, James Carney, John F. Dickerson, and Karen Tumulty, "The Clinton/Lewinsky Scandal," *Time*, February 22, 1999.

141 "Our task is to rise and continue": AD, 105.

141 "drawing-room comedy . . .": John Simon, "The Wizard of Odd," *New York,* April 28, 1997, 103.

141 "militant New York liberals," ". . . Charles Schumer's choice of domestic help," "it was still a man's world . . ." "Wasserstein's feelings about Monica . . .": Dan Sullivan, conversation with author, January 2009.

142 "'beyond meteoric' . . ." "superb networker," "gives good daughter," "liberal instincts and her practicality": Blumenthal, "Letter from Washington," 54, 55.

142 "Until men are fully equal inside the home . . .": Gloria Steinem, *Ms.*, September–October 1997, 83.

142 ". . . seventies having-it-all mythology": AD, 35.

142 "ingrained prejudices about women's roles . . .": Peter Marks, "An Outsider Goes Inside the Beltway," *The New York Times,* March 23, 1997, H5, H10.

142 "this protégé of men . . ." "feminists turned their backs . . . working women": Taylor, "Inside the Whirlwind," 70.

142 her babysitter had been an illegal alien . . . : Taylor, "Inside the Whirlwind," 61.

142 Lani Guinier . . . Madeleine Albright: Nancy Franklin, "The Time of Her Life," *The New Yorker*, April 14, 1997.

142 "There's a danger in that kind of thinking": Marks, "An Outsider Goes Inside the Beltway."

143 "Above all . . . frustrated middle class": Taylor, "Inside the Whirlwind," 69.

143 "I'm a middle-class guy . . ." most Washingtonians: Ibid., 67.

143 "A significant portion of the population . . .": Ibid., 59.

143 "selfish yuppie": Blumenthal, "Letter from Washington," 54.

143 a play about the liberal establishment: Marks, "An Outsider Goes Inside the Beltway," 10.

143 "the darkest chasms . . ." Russell Shorto, "All Political Ideas Are Local," *The New York Times*, October 2, 2005 56.

144 "Liberalism wagers . . .": Paul Starr, "Liberalism in the U.S.," *The New Republic*, March 2007.

144 "Look what happened to national health insurance": AD, 16.

144 "Even in big cities . . ." New York's mayoral race: Peter Beinart, "The Last of the Liberals," *Time*, November 10, 1997.

144 fifty-four percent of white women . . . : Sandy M. Fernández, "How Women Voted in 1994," *Ms.*, May–June 1996, 23.

144 "bad juggling of a working mother": AD, 86.

144 "because your heart is in the right place": *The Charlie Rose Show*, April 17, 1997.

144 "a blueprint for deconstructing liberalism," "Liberalism will live or die without you": AD, 40.

144 "the only academic . . . gets it": AD, 5.

144 "stuck in the past . . . right winger": AD, 21.

144 "embattled nomination . . .": AD, 53.

144 Charles Reich's best-selling: Charles Reich, *The Greening of America* (New York: Random House, 1970).

145 "There's some idea of America . . .": AD, 101.

145 "inconsistency of the left": AD, 46.

145 "Log Cabin Republican," Morrow loosely resembles Andrew Sullivan: Dan Sullivan, conversation with author.

145 Paul Krugman's: Paul Krugman, *The Conscience of a Liberal* (New York: W. W. Norton, 2009).

145 "the rise of a powerful centralized government . . .": Louise Mirrer, "Grant and Lee in War and Peace," New York Historical Society, www. nyhistory.org.

146 "Diversity is the succor . . .": AD, 8.

146 "The future vitality of this country . . .": AD, 46.

146 "How can you be adamant about . . .": AD, 34.

146 "female experience is political, not inevitable": Gloria Steinem, *Ms.*, September–October 1997, 82.

146 "American in all its branches . . .": AD, 99.

146 "prisoner of gender": AD, 5.

146 "brilliant record . . .": AD, 15.

146 "public health is good government": AD, 16.

146 "doctors are twice as likely . . .": AD, 82.

146–47 "still waiting for one gay man . . .": AD, 31.

147 "the jewel in the crown of the great society": AD, 27.

147–48 "Look after your mother . . ." Nelly's life was a disaster: AD, 103.

148 "Firm, not like a lady . . .": AD, 37.

148 "The best intentions . . .": AD, 49.

148 "My wife is a mother of two small children . . .": AD, 48.

148 "making her a little nutso": AD, 16.

148 "to create a fractured fairy tale . . .": Wasserstein, preface to AD, x.

148 "I've probably just set back the case . . .": AD, 53.

148 "shut the gate": AD, 97.

148 "a woman's life is all about boundaries," if Lyssa were a man . . . : AD, 53.

149 "should cease in the twentieth century like Soviet communism or the rotary dial": AD, 41.

149 Wasserstein's question: Ginia Bellafante, "It's All About Me," *Time*, June 29, 1998, 54–62.

149 In 1997: Betty Carter and Joan K. Peters, "Remaking Marriage and Family," *Ms.*, November–December 1996, 57, 59.

149 "I never meant for our lives . . .": AD, 96.

149 "play up Miss Porter's boarding school": AD, 65.

149 "knowing what people want . . ." AD, 66.

149 "feminine attire . . ." "Women respond to that": AD, 70.

149 "bake cookies," holding her husband's hand: AD, ix.

150 whiskey scandal: "A Hero Betrayed—The Presidency of Ulysses S. Grant," "The Whiskey Fraud Trials"—special dispatch to *The New York Times*, December 11, 1875.

150 "He made bad investments . . . imperfect like us all": AD, 86.

150 "ordinary Indiana housewife . . . canapés": AD, 45–61.

150 ". . . soccer mom's anti-Christ," "Dr. Icebox Shops": AD, 62.

150 ". . . Are you too perfect?": AD, 90.

150 "condescending and elitist . . . important humanitarian position": AD, 92.

151 "another political dynasty . . .": AD, 46.

151 "Simple people . . . official notice": AD, 66.

151 "My greatest privilege is my family": AD, 90.

151 "can put [her headband] on and take it off": AD, 53.

151 "'An American Snob' . . . Dunkin Donuts twins in Eugene . . . turns into a sandwich": AD, 54.

151 "You may be a privileged . . .": AD, 64.

151 Americans began leaving cities . . . : Eric Pooley, "Why Are Americans Fleeing Small Towns?" and Daniel S. Levy, "The Great Escape," *Time*, December 8, 1997.

152 "Someone in Alaska hates you!": AD, 71.

152 "Who are the good guys . . . ?" "I don't look at things in black and white": AD, 88.

152 Tippecanoe and Tyler too: wikipedia.org/wiki/Tippecanoe_and_Tyler_too.

152 "Americans will forgive . . .": AD, 65.

152 "I'll be here . . .": AD, 105.

152 "hung out to dry . . .": AD, 94.

152 "feminism means the right to choose . . .": Hillary Clinton to Jackie Judd, *ABC News*, March 26, 1992.

152 "repositioned by the media . . .": AD, 63.

152–53 "the women of America are furious with you . . .": AD, 64.

153 According to Marcia Gillespie: Marcia Gillespie, "How the Cookie Crumbles," *Ms.*, December 1996, 1.

153 "bright, complicated person . . .": AD, 102.

153 "see the U.S.A. in a Chevrolet," "any sense of adventure at all": AD, 45.

154 "Did you feel her horizons were limited?" "Many women in America feel . . ." "sacrificing for his career": AD, 90.

155 "American women should instead . . .": AD, 91.

155 all forms of social injustice: Gillespie, "How the Cookie Crumbles."

155 "soft-pedal": AD, 70.

155 "I'm a senator's daughter . . .": AD, 83.

155 "The question that Lyssa confronts . . .": Dan Sullivan in Marks, "An Outsider Goes Inside the Beltway."

155 "You never told me . . ." "You never asked": AD, 100.

155 "I'd give anything . . .": AD, 102.

155 "If there's any fault, it's mine": AD, 88.

156 "too good for public life": AD, 98

156 "There's nothing quite so satisfying . . .": AD, 92.

157 "There are plenty of not-nice people . . .": AD, 68.

157 "I forgot they were people . . .": AD, 78.

157 "a rapid rise of mean-spiritedness": Suzanne Pharr, "Taking the High Road,"*Ms.*, July–August 1996, 65–68.

157 "Do you hate us all because we're straight?": AD, 49.

157 "Is there anything people like you . . .": AD, 80.

157 "a persecuted minority . . . entitlement," "the brightest minds . . . happiness," "There won't be a national health insurance . . .": AD, 47.

157 "inconsistency of the left . . .": AD, 27.

158 "I really wanted that job . . .": AD, 93.

158 ". . . Doone & Burkey purse": AD, 100.

158 "I believe by denying . . .": AD, 76.

158 "tremendous reserves of strength . . .": AD, 46.

158 Eleanor Roosevelt: whitehouse.gov/about/first_ladies/eleanorroosevelt.

158 Florence Nightingale: wikipedia.org/wiki/Florence_Nightingale.

158 Amy Fisher: wikipedia.org/wiki/Amy_Fisher.

159 ". . . The Lyssa Hughes interview is a real get.": AD, 60.

159 "Where do you want to put her?" "bitterness," "envy," "baited": AD, 33.

159 "the one who can advance [Lyssa's] cause": AD, 81.

159 "bringing feminism into the twenty-first . . . ideology new": AD, 19.

159 "sweet women are trapped . . ." "sexism made simple," "disenfranchised her femininity": AD, 9.

159 "We're at a place now . . .": AD, 7.

159 "women's issues . . ." "exclusive on the fanatic . . .": AD, 82.

159 "show business, cosmetology, and aviation": AD, 4.

160 "to make heaps of money . . .": AD, 17.

160 "slightly hysterical," "overcommitted and determined . . ." "give up her own sleep": AD, 80.

160 "out of town lecturing . . .": AD, 38.

160 "You think a woman of my generation . . .": AD, Lincoln Center draft, 32.

160 "most women I know are booked . . .": AD, 9.

160 ". . . nanny disappeared with drug-dealing security guard": AD, 38.

160 "We have to give up the myths . . .": *Ms.*, 1997.

160 "frigid, overextended . . .": AD, 49.

160 soulless and unhappy: AD, 42.

160 ". . . have some fun, too": AD, 35.

160 ". . . to literally fight for one's principles": AD, 49.

160 ". . . a lot of heat . . . across America": AD, 61.

160 "a woman's life can have no boundaries": AD, 8.

160 "all about boundaries," neither "make life nor stop death": AD, 57.

161 "the career of a fifty-five-year-old man . . . fifteen-year-old girl: AD, 73.

161 "mega-doses . . . drugs": AD, 18.

161 "just grow up . . ." ". . . if I was a good girl and worked hard . . ." "all lives don't have to be about children": AD, 11.

161 "walking Crown Heights": AD, 34.

161 Lena Horne: wikipedia.org/wiki/Lena_Horne.

161 "So I had to make up for myself . . .": AD, 76.

162 "the sadness of a generation": Nancy Franklin, "The Time of Her Life," *The New Yorker*, April 14, 1997, 62.

Chapter 6. *Old Money*

Quotations from Wendy Wasserstein, *Old Money* (New York: Harcourt, 2002), abbreviated "OM."

165 "Cash has merged with class": Wendy Wasserstein, "Joining a Rich Tradition of Comedies About Money," *The New York Times*, December 3, 2000, 5.

165 "seated at a most fashionably attired table . . ." *The Age of Innocence*, "There was a bowl . . .": Wasserstein, preface to OM, vii–viii.

165 Coined by Mark Twain: Mark Twain and Charles Dudley Warner, *The Gilded Age* (New York: Harper & Brothers, 1901).

166 William Sumner: *What Social Classes Owe to Each Other* (New York: Harper & Brothers, 1883).

166 Clarence Darrow: notablebiographies.com/Co-Da/Darrow-Clarence.

166 "conspicuous consumption and conspicuous leisure": Thorstein Veblen, *The Theory of the Leisure Class* (London: MacMillan, 1912).

167 "The play of wealth . . ." "half merry, half desperate air": Lewis H. Lapham, introduction to Henry James, *New York Revisited* (New York: Franklin Square Press, 1994), 13–15.

167 "youth on the run . . .": James, *New York Revisited.*

167 "floating rounds of cocktails . . . yellow cocktail music": F. Scott Fitzgerald, *The Great Gatsby* (New York: Charles Scribner's Sons, 1925), 40.

167 Edith Wharton defined: Edith Wharton, *A Backward Glance* (New York: Curtis, 1933), 495.

167 In 1776, Adam Smith . . . : Valerie Paley, "New Money New York," in *Lincoln Center Theater Review*, Fall 2000, Issue 26, 10.

167 "Aristocracy in America . . ." death of John Jacob Astor: Eric Homberger, *Mrs. Astor's New York* (New Haven: Yale University Press), 2002.

167 "the Four Hundred," *The Four Million*: wikipedia.org/wiki/Ward_McAllister.

167 institutions like the Patriarchs . . .: Homberger, *Mrs. Astor's New York*, 2.

167 ". . . desperate to buy their way into society . . .": Wasserstein, preface to OM, viii–xi.

167 "From Henry Brevoort's . . . aristocracy," "All American society . . . fetes and receptions": Homberger, *Mrs. Astor's New York*, 1.

168 "During an earlier New York gilded age . . .": Wasserstein, preface to OM, viii.

168 "Talents, birth . . . are of little consideration . . .": John Adams, cited in Paley, "New Money New York."

168 ". . . society has merged with celebrity . . .": OM, 9.

169 "the huge American rattle of gold. . . yesterday's celebrity": James, *New York Revisited*, 11.

169 "staged costume balls . . ." ". . . vulgar splendor of the Waldorf . . .": Lapham, introduction to *New York Revisited*, 19.

170 "new gilded . . . producer was worth,": Wasserstein, preface to OM, viii.

170 "pinnacle of New Money society," "online panty manufacturer": OM, xv.

170 "arbiter of the new A-list": OM, 9.

171 *Old Money* belongs to a tradition . . . "the changes in values . . .": Wasserstein, preface to OM, ix.

171 "a museum of the digital revolution . . .": OM, 96.

171 "gauzelike quality . . .": OM, 3.

171 "but considered a renegade . . ." Lynch builds . . . Warburg's: Wasserstein, preface to OM, ix.

171 Warburg: wikipedia.org/wiki/Felix_M._Warburg.

171 ". . . creating a financial dynasty": OM, 74.

171 "new office buildings . . . place": James, *New York Revisited*, 13.

172 highest price ever paid . . . : Lapham, introduction to *New York Revisited*, 14.

172 "would never have been invited . . . can go in and out": OM, 34.

172 "the players . . .": OM, 4.

172 "Page Six of *The Chronicle* . . .": OM, 6.

172 "in the Home section": OM, 7.

172 "There's no glory . . .": OM, 58.

172 "Money insulates," "I'm putting my dibs . . ." "there's a waiting list": OM, 31.

173 "too white, too Republican": OM, 17.

173 "one of my friend's dad . . . housekeeper": OM, 33.

173 "master at high-risk arbitrage . . . just an hour," "you could lose it too . . . move numbers," "never abused . . . at least not directly": OM, 57.

173 "schvitzing in the garden": OM, 16.

173 "just did Vera [Wang's] . . . first on everyone's list": OM, 11.

173 "feng shui . . .": OM, 13.

173–74 "due for a comeback . . . Jane Fonda collected you," "dated and retro," "academics . . . what do they know?": OM, 29.

174 "what it's like to be them . . . no one can ever say no to you": OM, 85.

174 "Maybe the trick is not to care," "It's my entire life": OM, 86.

174 "Maybe all our lives . . ." "Yours most certainly is . . . 'a new gilded age'": OM, 8.

174 "Only someone who wasn't from this world . . .": OM, 10.

174 "Gotta be a little prickly to be at the head . . .": OM, 38.

174 "master at playing the world to his advantage": OM,33.

174 "Sid is showing up here tonight . . .": OM, 8.

174 "to get on the museum board": OM, 15.

174 "worked very hard to get you": OM, 24.

175 "Some people used to think . . .": OM, 98.

175 "Late nineteenth-century New York aristocracy . . .": Homberger, *Mrs. Astor's New York*, 3.

175 "I take our museum very seriously . . .": OM, 39.

175 "Dutch pirates": OM, 39.

175 "ticket to Breast Express . . .": OM, 35.

175 ". . . a way to pay for it": 37.

175 ". . .when you have perfect taste . . .": OM, 65.

175–76 ". . . you take it all much more seriously . . .": OM, 35.

176 "a distinguished New York family," "in a position to bring his name up . . .": OM, 67.

176 "Awards are all fakes": OM, 68.

176 ". . . this is a man without a trust fund": OM, 55.

176 ". . . a factual imitation . . .": Fitzgerald, *The Great Gatsby*, 5.

176 "You're hiding behind this party . . ." "What's the matter with these people? . . ." "Where have you gone, Jeffrey?": OM, 87.

176–77 "The man in front of you . . . happiness": OM, 88.

176 "In the equations of American failure and success . . .": Lapham, introduction to *New York Revisited*, 22.

177 "only losers have time . . .": OM, 95.

177 "It takes care of most things very nicely": OM, 88.

177 *The Rivals:* Richard Brinsley Sheridan (London: J. M. Dent, 1897).

178 "that update of *Citizen Kane* . . .": OM, 22.

178 "Kenny Branagh wants to do it . . . *Sense and Sensitivity*": OM, 20.

178 "Audrey Hepburn's Givenchy . . . you should too": OM, 31.

178 Puff Daddy: Sean John Combs, known by his stage names Puff Daddy, P. Diddy and now Diddy, is an American record producer, rapper, actor, men's fashion designer, entrepreneur, and dancer.

178 "I don't think Jews lived in these houses": OM, 17.

178 "My house was bought by a Jewish boy?": OM, 55.

178 "The hell with the people . . .": OM, 60.

178 J. P. Morgan, after all, did not lend money to Jews: David Gruben, *The Jewish Americans*, PBS documentary, 2009.

178 "how much Katzenberg is worth": OM, 17.

178 "under four," "not real money . . . couldn't afford this house," "I bet Bernstein's mother . . ." "Katzenberg still has to work for a living . . .": OM, 18.

179 ". . . we could never say out loud . . .": OM, 58.

179 ". . . cultivating a style, not a character": OM, 59.

179 ". . . I'm just a small businessman": OM, 8.

179 ". . . read for a purpose": OM, 6.

179 "distrust of the contemplative temperament . . .": Lapham, introduction to *New York Revisited*, 23.

179 "the road to liberation . . .": OM, 6.

179–80 "this house would have been the last place . . .": OM, 33.

180 ". . . between Cesar Chavez and Baron Rothschild": OM, 89.

180 "pioneered a fixed-income arbitrage bank . . .": OM, 4.

180 The American economy was thriving. . . : U.S. Economic History wikipedia.org/wiki/Economic_history_of_the_United_States.

180 "Beaux Arts painting . . .": OM, 4.

180 ". . . Wells Fargo Wagon . . ." "a bargain at five thousand a week," "It's the only way I've been able to work . . .": OM, 19.

180 "Money means I won't have to base my life . . .": OM, 79.

180 "What's the point of being rich . . .": OM, 19

180–81 "Since my dad left . . . terrified of everything": OM, 21.

181 "Seeds of Revolution: From Robber Barons to Emma Goldman": OM, 22.

181 Henry Clay Frick: wikipedia.org/wiki/Henry_Clay_Frick.

181 Goldman's writing: Emma Goldman, *Anarchism and Other Essays* (New York: Mother Earth, 1917).

181 "When you go into business . . . trusts were the best thing . . .": OM, 79.

181 "In every town . . . gave his entire fortune away": OM, 26.

181–82 "the sickest thing I've ever heard": OM, 54.

182 "I freed you of a legacy . . ." "You denied me a legacy," ". . . like the man who lives here now," "one of the most generous men in history," ". . . what cost you the least": OM, 81–82.

182 "the only place I felt safe": OM, 27.

182 ". . . arrested for dealing cocaine . . .": OM, 39.

182 ". . . I want the world to know I'm here": OM, 97.

182 Statistics show . . . personal achievement": wikipedia.org/wiki/Economic_history_of_the_United_States.

182 "People with real money owe it to society . . .": OM, 31.

182–83 "I can see the life my father has mapped out for me . . .": OM, 43.

183 "no one cares what your real name is": OM, 15.

183 kicked out of Italy . . . George Cohan to sing: OM, 16

183 "Can you tell me right now . . . who doesn't take advantage": OM, 80.

183 "No matter how regulated . . .": Alan Greenspan, wikipedia.org/wiki/Alan_Greenspan.

183 "The truth was . . . far superior": OM, 81.

183 "I have a recurrent dream": OM, 81.

183 "do whatever it is for yourself . . . never escaped": OM, 89.

183 "If you give up, you'll never know how strong you could be": OM, 69.

183 "It's not my place . . .": OM, 47.

183–84 "From now on . . . the century of American ingenuity": OM, 48.

184 "I've lived most of my life alone . . .": OM, 28.

184 "Don't waste your life alone": OM, 63 and 94.

184 "utopian Marxist Colony Club libertarian": OM, 75.

184 "My father wants to see his name . . .": OM, 44.

184 "I wish I could release you . . .": OM, 34.

184 "start a newspaper . . . lost in his shuffle": OM, 45.

184–85 "much too cynical," "much too forgiving," "a bitter man . . . beginnings, middles, and ends," "a big fan of chaos . . ." "Some are just better orchestrated," "life seemed to make utter and complete sense . . . to become one of them": OM, 45.

185 ". . . plans to make me important again," "the next wave, the cutting edge": OM, 61.

185 "She was interesting maybe fifteen years ago . . . that's just the truth": OM, 68.

185 "can't bear to be judged anymore": OM, 61.

185 "Until it all comes back again . . .": OM, 47.

185 "just a commodity . . . state of grace": Lapham, introduction to *New York Revisited*, 23.

Chapter 7. *Third*

Quotations from Wendy Wasserstein, *Third*, published in *American Theatre Magazine* (New York: Theater Communications Group, April 2006, 23, no. 4, abbreviated "T."

188 "look with fresh eyes . . . challenge the norms of the dominant culture": T, 1.

188 "revisionist view of King Lear": T, 1.

188 "the idea of making Goneril and Regan heroes is outrageous . . ." she behaves in this loving way with her own father: Director Dan Sullivan in conversation with the author.

188 *Girls Will Be Boys*: T, 13.

188 "the girlification of Cordelia": T, 1.

188–89 "In sports, the really powerful guys . . .": T, 11.

189 "some preppy, privileged wrestler," "walking red state": T, 18.

189 "fits right in with the power elite . . .": T, 12.

189 against labeling, "amazing collection of culturally and racially mixed students . . . has a wrestling program": Dan Sullivan in conversation with the author.

189 "You're the gender bender": T, 11.

189 "If Lear strips Cordelia of her dowry . . ." "Lear's wrath is the outcome . . .": T, 14.

189–90 "If I can't bang the president on the head . . ." "If we permit this kind of unethical behavior . . ." "It's about one kid with a good mind . . ." "Why waste your time on me . . . the war in Iraq": T, 18.

190 "weapons of mass destruction," "grave and gathering danger": T, 2.

190 Iraq War, "threatened democracy": wikipedia.org/wiki/Iraq_War.

190 "the House of Representatives passed . . .": T, 8.

190 In fact, in 2003 . . . almost 3,000 protests against the Iraq war. The 9/11 Commission . . . without factual evidence: wikipedia.org/wiki/Iraq_War.

190 "dangerously regressive climate": T, 19.

190 "It's unfair and I want to beat it": T, 16.

190 Patriot Act: The USA PATRIOT Act, commonly known as the Patriot Act, is a statute enacted by the United States Government that President George W. Bush signed into law on October 26, 2001. The contrived acronym stands for Uniting and Strengthening America by Providing Appropriate Tools Required to Intercept and Obstruct Terrorism Act of 2001 (Public Law Pub.L. 107-56). Opponents of the act feel it invades individual privacy.

191 ". . . that's how you lost this country": T, 37.

191 "Before Obama . . .": Dan Sullivan in conversation.

191 "The goddamn bastards took it from me": T, 7.

191 "He is interested in transacting deals . . ." : T, 12.

191 "a necessary evil . . .": Dan Sullivan in conversation.

192 "By championing freedom overseas . . .": Peter Beinart, *The Good Fight: Why Liberals–and Only Liberals–Can Win the War on Terror and Make America Great Again* (New York: Harper Collins, 2006), 1.

192 "I hate the times we're living in": T, 13.

192 "Most people feel pretty untethered . . .": T, 20.

192 "You decided he plagiarized . . .": T, 24.

192 "After 9/11 we are vulnerable": Dan Sullivan in conversation.

192 "no one with [his] verbal facility . . .": T, 20.

192 Groton School: www.groton.org.

192 "a living dead white man": T, 22.

192 "She said I plagiarized my paper . . . because I'm a wrestler": T, 23.

192 "You have a problem with me because . . .": T, 15.

192 "privileged, preppy, frat boy": T, 19.

192 "You categorized him and got it totally wrong . . .": T, 22.

194 "Liberalism cannot merely define itself against the right . . .": Beinart, *The Good Fight*, x.

194 "a bad risk . . . Goldman Sachs": T, 21.

194 "I've sort of had it with smart people . . .": T, 19.

194 "If it's money you're after . . .": T, 6.

194 "I want out of your world . . ." "because he's not a star": T, 24.

194 "a real person": T, 34.

194 "They're not supposed to ruin it for you . . .": T, 21.

194 "If you stole intellectual property . . .": T, 14.

194 "Maybe I'm the one who doesn't belong here . . ." "thought [she] could change the world": T, 31.

195 "Jameson is still holding the torch . . .": T, 15.

195 "When I first came here . . .": T, 18.

195 "Venus": www.frankieavalon.com and wikipedia.org/wiki/Venus_(Frankie_Avalon_song).

195 "liveliness of mind": T, 26.

195 "It's like wrestling . . ." T, 11.

195 "I keep thinking about a James Taylor song . . .": T, 29.

195–96 "At least you're protected . . ." "Woody, sometimes your protection can become your own confinement": T, 31.

196 "I always thought I was a regular guy . . ." "Stick with the hope": T, 32.

196 "You're the one who always had faith . . .": T, 28.

196 "a solid, good woman . . . without hating everything": T, 27.

196 "a reassessment of liberal values . . .": Dan Sullivan in conversation.

196 "soft on inflation . . .": Beinart, *The Good Fight*, 3.

197 "I know of no country . . .": Alexis de Tocqueville, *Democracy in America*, ed. Richard D. Heffner (New York: The New American Library, 1956), 12.

197 "Every citizen being assimilated to all the rest . . .": Ibid., 11.

Conclusion

199 "The theatre is an arena . . ." "lay preacher popularizing the pressing questions of his time," "The realistic playwright . . .": C. W. E. Bigsby, "Redefining the Centre: Politics, Race, Gender," *Modern American Drama 1945–1990* (Cambridge: Cambridge University Press: 1994), 339, 306, 270.

200 "There's some idea of America . . .": Wendy Wasserstein, *An American Daughter* (San Diego: Harcourt Brace, 1999), 101.

200 "I wish that on one of our birthdays . . . a moment or two": Wendy Wasserstein, *The Sisters Rosensweig* (New York: Harcourt Brace, 1993), 96.

200 "When you grow up Jewish . . .": Professor Ruth Prigozy in conversation with the author, 2009.

201 "Characters in feminist plays . . .": Helene Keyssar, *Feminist Theatre: An Introduction to Plays of Contemporary British and American Women* (London: Macmillan, 1984), 2.

201 "Gender is the defining issue of our social structure": Bill Clinton, television interview (2008 presidential campaign), CNN.

201 "The pressure is still on the woman": Jan Balakian, "Wendy Wasserstein," in *Speaking on Stage*, ed. Philip C. Kolin and Colby H. Kullman (Tuscaloosa: University of Mississippi Press, 1996).

201 Sara Rimer, "For Girls, It's Be Yourself, and Be Perfect, Too," *The New York Times*, April 1, 2007, A1.

201 Alison Solomon, Laurie Stone, Phyllis Jane Rose, "public images," "the private tensions . . .": Bigsby, "Redefining the Centre," 325.

202 "Why are successful men . . .": Balakian, "Wendy Wasserstein."

202 "No one calls men 'shrill' . . .": Cokie Roberts, National Public Radio, April 4, 2009.

202 "I truly believe that it's just like racism . . .": Jan Balakian, "Two Interviews with Wendy Wasserstein," *The Journal of American Drama and Theatre* 9, no. 2 (Spring 1997), 67.

202 "be at home, instead of in the Senate . . .": George Stephanopoulos, "Caroline Kennedy Withdraws to 'Put Family First,'" ABC News, January 22, 2009.

203 "I don't want to go home . . .": Wendy Wasserstein, "Aunt Florence's Bar Mitzvah," *Bachelor Girls* (New York: Vintage, 1991), 45.

203 "Women are capable . . .": Interview with Michelle Obama, *Sixty Minutes*, November 16, 2008.

203 "to help women transform their lives": Oprah Winfrey, "Oprah Talks to Michelle Obama," *O: The Oprah Magazine*, April 2009, 140.

203–4 "As somebody who believes in the individual voice . . .": Kathleen Betsko and Rachel Koenig, eds., "Wendy Wasserstein," in *Interviews with Contemporary Women Playwrights* (New York: Beech Tree Books, 1987) 431.

204 "I think the idea of finding moments . . .": Balakian, "Two Interviews with Wendy Wasserstein."

Index